Pedro Salinas and his Theater

Juan de la Cuesta
Hispanic Monographs

FOUNDING EDITOR
Tom Lathrop
University of Delaware

EDITOR
Alexander R. Selimov
University of Delaware

EDITORIAL BOARD
Samuel G. Armistead
University of California, Davis

Annette G. Cash
Georgia State University

Alan Deyermond
Queen Mary, University of London

Daniel Eisenberg
Excelsior College

John E. Keller
University of Kentucky

Steven D. Kirby
Eastern Michigan University

Joel Rini
University of Virginia

Donna M. Rogers
Middlebury College

Russell P. Sebold
University of Pennsylvania, Emeritus
Corresponding Member, Real Academia Española

Noël Valis
Yale University

Amy Williamsen
University of Arizona

The Poet as Hero:
Pedro Salinas and his Theater

by

SUSAN G. POLANSKY

Juan de la Cuesta
Newark, Delaware

Copyright © 2006 by Juan de la Cuesta—Hispanic Monographs
270 Indian Road
Newark, Delaware 19711
(302) 453-8695
Fax: (302) 453-8601
www.JuandelaCuesta.com

MANUFACTURED IN THE UNITED STATES OF AMERICA

ISBN: 1-58871-081-5

Table of Contents

ACKNOWLEDGMENTS 7
PREFACE 11
INTRODUCTION 15

Part I
The Genesis and Aims of Salinas's Theater 29

1 Salinas: Poet and Correspondent 31
      Salinas's Letters to Margarita 32
      Salinas's Letters to Jorge Guillén 39
      Salinas's Letters to Katherine Reding Whitmore 54

2 Salinas: Poet and Essayist 69
      Poets and their Vision of Reality in Salinas's Studies of
          Poets and Poetry 71
      Salinas's Studies of Jorge Manrique and Rubén Darío 77
      Salinas's Essays on Jorge Carrera Andrade
          and Federico García Lorca 83
      Modernity, Communication, and Theater:
          El defensor and *La responsabilidad del escritor* 85
      Spanish Playwrights and the Construction of Reality 94

3 Salinas: Poet and Émigré 101
      Exile as a Spanish Circumstance and a Defining Feature
          of Salinas's Generation 102
      Salinas's Literary Studies and the Theme of Exile 109
      Salinas's Separation from Spain 115

Part II
The Poet in the Theater 139

4	Poet and Plot: The "Fabula" of Confinement-to-Freedom ...	141
	"Reality in Fable Form": The *Fabula* of Confinement-to-Freedom	144
	Freedom and Felicitous Outcome	146
	Freedom and Tragic Outcome	152
	The Poet in the Plot	156
5	Poet and Plot: Two Variations	166
	A Nostalgic Transplanting: *El chantajista*	167
	An Anguished Prophecy: *Caín o una gloria científica*	187
6	Poet and Perception: The Poet as a Visionary	202
	Salinas's Views of the Poet's Capacity to See	203
	Viewer-Guiders and Guided Viewers	210
	Eyes, Windows, Mirrors, and the Scope of the Poet	219
	Sightedness and Blindness	230
7	Poet and Circumstance:	
	The Poet's Bridge between Tradition and Modernity	237
	Tradition, Modernity, and Cervantine Values	238
	The Poet's Bridge Completed: *La Estratoesfera*	245
	The Poet's Bridge Interrupted: *Judit y el tirano*	253
	The Poet's Bridge of Hope: *Los santos*	261
CONCLUSION		
	The Poet's Place	269
BIBLIOGRAPHY		281

Acknowledgments

THIS BOOK IS THE result of many years of research and attention to the works of Pedro Salinas, of many years of stimulating contact with a variety of individuals who have had a part in my work. I thank Robert L. Sheehan, Professor Emeritus of Boston College, for encouraging and guiding my study of Salinas during graduate school. I owe gratitude to Javier Herrero, director of a National Endowment for the Humanities Summer Seminar on Surrealism and Structuralism, and to the other seminar participants. The seminar advanced my research on Salinas and other members of his generation. I thank my colleagues Paz Macías and Mariana Achugar for their input regarding a number of the translations. *Mil gracias* to a most talented former student of mine, Jess Daniel Yarnell, who studied with me at Carnegie Mellon, and has subsequently, with a very keen eye, read and commented on the manuscript. The editors of Juan de la Cuesta—Hispanic Monographs have provided much appreciated guidance through the publication process. With much love I acknowledge my parents, Doris and Elliot Glunts, who have been extraordinary role models for me my entire life. I appreciate the contributions of my children Lisa and Alan through the years of writing this book, for their assistance with bibliography and their patience in bookstores and libraries. Above all, with deepest love I thank my husband Ron for his wisdom, enormous support, and encouragement.

For R*on*

Preface

MY INTEREST IN PEDRO Salinas's writings began when two inspiring teachers, Solita Salinas de Marichal, Salinas's daughter, and Edith Helman, close friend of the Salinas family, introduced me as an undergraduate to Spain's poets of the Generation of 1927. Salinas's poetry and essays initially captivated me and led eventually to exploration of his less well-known dramatic works. My study of his plays has come to focus on poet-protagonists who vivify communication with fellow characters. I investigate how Salinas, a poet living in exile, turns to theater to express nostalgia for his personal past, connection to literary tradition, and concern for the difficulties of modern life.

Attention to Salinas's own conception of the poet illuminates the evolution of his writing plays in exile. Salinas discusses the role of poet most explicitly in his essays, especially in *Mundo real y mundo poético* (*Real World and Poetic World*), *Reality and the Poet in Spanish Literature,* and *La responsabilidad del escritor* (*The Responsibility of the Writer*). According to Salinas, the poet, distant from the ordinary and mundane, thrives in a literary minority and voyages inward, while also possessing a feeling of community and endeavoring to connect with all society (*La responsabilidad del escritor* 179). Disagreement with the commonplace is the poet's first duty. The poet needs to affirm himself distinctively in order carry out his work (*La responsabilidad del escritor* 146).

Poets, for Salinas, extend beyond writers of poems to include authors exercising superior creative capacity in any genre (*La responsabilidad del escritor* 38). He deems the poet a visionary with exalted spiritual vision (*La responsabilidad del escritor* 182). Seeing more penetratingly than others, the poet transforms ordinary reality through apprehending it more completely and lovingly. The poet is a far-sighted wanderer constantly open to the possibilities of creative activity, a traveller seeking both social emancipation and solidarity (*La responsabilidad del escritor* 142, 179-82; *Mundo real y mundo poético* 32, 78). Boldly trying to share his or her perspective with others, the poet joins ordinary and extraordinary reality and builds a bridge between tradition and present circumstance.

Elaborating upon the poet's social function, Salinas has the visionary traveller acting as a protector, consoler, torch, expiatory victim, historian, judge, seer, civilizer of humanity, revealer, director of peoples, liberator, and clairvoyant magician (*La responsabilidad del escritor* 235). In these capacities the poet transfers the spiritual realm into the social realm, private space into public space. The poet's world is one of possibility, and "far from remaining pleasantly outside the world, he lives at its very center" (*Reality and the Poet* 4, 164).

Salinas envisions the genre of theater a prime setting for the poet-creator to exert social force. The poet-dramatist forges a unity with the audience by giving voice to what has been composed in solitude (*La responsabilidad del escritor* 81-82). Within the dramatic work, poet figures can be depicted reinvigorating conversational language and endowing it with special expressive power. By writing plays in which poetic characters are prominent, Salinas expands his voice as a poet. He creates key figures who act as poets endowed with "una pujanza que nos afecta de una manera muy diferente a como nos afectan las demás" (a forcefulness that affects us differently from how others affect us; *La responsabilidad del escritor* 218). Study of Salinas the poet correspondent and essayist in exile will show the urgency of his theater production. Study of his theater will highlight the relationship of the poet to the theater and the possibility of a social dimension for theatrical works in contemporary conditions. Although as a poet-playwright living outside Spain he finds staging his works frustratingly difficult, his theater affirms artistic freedom and responsibility.

Strictly only two lead characters in Salinas's plays are poets or writers of verse by profession. A few are authors, and among the others are a scientist, a shop owner, a model, a magician, a character in a book, a mother, a deity figure, and a fiancée. Yet all demonstrate exceptional creative abilities in their outlooks and dealings with others. A quest for emancipation guided by these key poet characters dominates each of the plays. In the genre of drama, the poet Salinas finds a structure through which to amplify his communicative voice and cast the poet into a role of liberator.

Until 1992, the most complete edition of the plays was *Teatro completo*, (Madrid: Aguilar, 1957), edited by Juan Marichal, which due to reasons of censorship, did not include one of his plays, *Los santos*. *Los santos* was first published in *Cuadernos Americanos* (México), 13, 3(1954): 265-91, and again in *Estreno*, 7(1981): 10-20, with introductory articles by Solita Salinas de Marichal and Francisco Ruiz Ramón. *Pedro Salinas Teatro completo* (Sevilla: Alfar), edited and introduced by Pilar Moraleda García, appeared in 1992. All references to the plays come from this complete compilation, and all translations of quoted Spanish excerpts are my own.

Introduction

...some people tell us that... poets know all the arts and all things human pertaining to virtue and vice, and all things divine... For the good poet, if he is to poetize things rightly, must... create with knowledge or else be unable to create. So we must consider whether these critics have not fallen in with such imitators and been deceived by them, so that looking upon their works they cannot perceive that these are three removes from reality, and easy to produce without knowledge of the truth. For it is phantoms, not realities, that they produce. Or is there something in their claim, and do good poets really know the things about which the multitude fancy they speak well?
PLATO, *Republic* X 598e-599a, Shorey trans.

BEST KNOWN AS A poet and senior member of Spain's Poetic Generation of 1927, Pedro Salinas (1891-1951) was described in the year of his death by contemporary Dámaso Alonso as perhaps the Spanish writer of most facets and most varied talents of the present moment ("quizá el literato español de más facetas y más aptitudes variadas del momento presente" Alonso, *Poetas* 197). In addition to nine volumes of poetry, seven volumes of essays and literary criticism that include seminal studies of the poetry of Rubén Darío and Jorge Manrique and *Reality and the Poet in Spanish Poetry*, four volumes of critical editions, several volumes of translations of Proust and Musset, and three volumes of narrative prose, Salinas authored fourteen plays. Jorge Guillén, poet, critic, and intimate friend of Salinas, divided Salinas's sixty years into thirty years of preparation and thirty years of production (*Reality and the Poet* ix; *Poesías completas* 11). The preparation that began in the Madrid of his infancy and youth was to engender in him a nostalgia for Spain that emerged in his later life and literary production. His activities as a student, teacher, writer, and lover of life and literature were closely linked to the turbulent artistic, historical, and political currents of the first half of the twentieth century. By the time of his premature death from cancer in 1951, Salinas's personal and professional pursuits had led him into a cosmopolitan life beyond his neighborhood and homeland. The Spanish Civil War and post World War II scene had forced him in 1936 into a fifteen-year exile from a Spain that remained near and dear to him.

Salinas confronted his exile—these final fifteen of the thirty years of his creative production—with enormous productive output. In addition to *Reality and the Poet in Spanish Poetry* (1940), he wrote numerous essays about the plight of the writer, language, and contemporary life which appeared in *El defensor* (*The Defender*) (1948) and posthumously in *La responsabilidad del escritor* (*The Responsibility of the Writer*) (1961). He published his studies of Jorge Manrique (1947) and Rubén Darío (1948), a novel, a collection of stories, composed four additional volumes of poetry, and wrote his dramatic works.

Fruit of his mature years, Salinas's dramatic works, though a less prominent part of his literary corpus, occupy a unique place in his artistic production. His composition of poetry spanned his entire lifetime—from his student days at the University of Madrid to the final months before his death on December 4, 1951. His earliest surviving poems were first published in Ramón Gómez de la Serna's literary review *Prometeo*, and his final poem, "Futuros," is dated September 28, 1951. Likewise, Salinas wrote and published critical and scholarly studies throughout his creative years. Somewhat different from his poetry and essays, Salinas's narrative prose represents the work of two distinct periods: his early beginnings as a writer and his final years. *Víspera del gozo* (*On the Eve of Joy*) (1926), a collection of prose sketches, appeared soon after his first volume of poetry, *Presagios* (*Portents*) (1924). The more complex narrative tales of *El desnudo impecable y otras narraciones* (*The Impeccable Nude and Other Narrations*) (1951) as well as his novel, *La bomba increíble* (*The Incredible Bomb*) (1950), were among the last works he was to publish. In contrast to his poetry, essays, and narrative works, Salinas composed his fourteen plays solely during the final part of his life, between 1936 and 1947, one prior to and the rest during his exile.

This book explores the significance of Salinas the poet's turn in exile to the genre of drama and addresses the following questions: How does Salinas come to write plays? What conditions of his exile and that of his generation contribute to his writing of plays? How does Salinas's conception of the role of the poet translate into his theater? How do his plays written in exile expand his poetic voice? Exploration of answers to these questions will indicate that through his theater, Salinas offers a challenge to the Platonic complaint that poets do not "do" anything, that they create "phantoms," that they are mere imitators whose production is not founded upon knowledge or experience. It will become clear that writing plays represents a significant development of the social dimension of Salinas's work, an expanded voice for his life in exile and his exploration of poetic expression, personal circumstance, and the modern world. Through his theater, Salinas projects the poet's voice with a special resonance and advances the role of the poet as an actor and a savior. Salinas the poet-playwright exemplifies the "good" poet who creates with "knowledge."

On one level, certain biographical and philosophical motivations lead the poet Salinas to extend his own preoccupation with reality beyond the more purely private and aesthetic realms of much of his poetry. As a playwright, Salinas builds a more elaborate structure for the dialogue and communicative activity of the poet. Through writing plays, he finds an outlet for his nostalgia for Spain and for Spanish as a living language, he amplifies his space as a poet in the modern world, and he pursues a reconciliation of traditional and modern values, a harmony between the human being and his or her circumstances. On a second level, that which transpires within the contexts of the dramatic works themselves, Salinas casts certain characters literally or figuratively as poets who redefine and recreate milieu and who guide heroically a redemptive action. Salinas's plays, dominated by the discourse and action of these guiding figures, may be viewed as modern yet universal morality plays that provide optimistic models for human interaction.

The interactions of Salinas's poet heroes with fellow characters exhibit a consistent pattern. His protagonists seek a spiritual and at times physical emancipation from limitations either self-imposed or determined by external forces. The constraints, arising from contemporary contexts, may be understood in universal terms. These characters spearhead a reorientation process and encourage others to embrace a new definition of self or an understanding and reshaping of circumstances. Those who follow their lead acquire a new view of self and situation in increasing affinity with the poet and the poet's world. Throughout Salinas's poetry, though there are approximations of a redemptive unification process as the poet seeks a meaningful union with his silent interlocutors, even in fulfillment, it is the solitude of the poet which reigns ultimately. The poet remains locked in contemplation of the ideal of creating that with which he seeks alliance. His thoughts draw him to his subjects and his subjects to him, but without the multiplicity of voices and actions he develops through writing plays. Through the genre of drama and his creation of poet heroes, Salinas expands his operating space as a poet.

At first glance, Salinas's characterization of the poet's relationship with reality in *Reality and the Poet in Spanish Poetry* might be considered to reflect the doubt of the Platonic inquiry. Salinas perhaps suggests the role of poet as a producer of phantoms when he calls the poet a maker of shadows:

> Poetry always operates on reality. The poet places himself before reality like a human body before light, in order to create something else, a shadow. The shadow is the result of the interposition of a body between light and some other substance. The poet adds shadows to the world, bright and luminous shadows, like new lights. All poetry operates on one reality for the sake of creating another. It cannot operate on a vacuum. So that the way a poet places himself, interposes himself between the radiant light of life and life itself will determine his peculiar way of being, his quality, that is, the form, the

personality of his shadow. Nothing is complete without its shadow. (*Reality and the Poet* 5)

Yet the poet creates shadows or new projections that are neither false realities nor removed from reality. The poet is not merely a redirector of light, but rather a source of light and a culminating force. This affirmative portrayal deems the poet a generator with connective power. The shadows produced by the poet join realities to make new realities, insights intertwined with mysteries and questions, luminous bridges linking with the surrounding world.

Relatedly, the influence of the Orteguian notion of "I am I and my circumstance" evident throughout Salinas's poetry evolves in his theater. In his dramatic works, Salinas finds opportunity to amplify expression of his powerful embrace of Spanish heritage and contemporaneousness, bound with a universal humanistic outlook. The poet-playwright Salinas through the perspectives of the leading characters of his plays builds a bridge between tradition and modernity. The connection gives him great comfort and inspiration in his state of separation from Spain and in his place facing the marvels and threats of the modern world. Juan Marichal describes Salinas's link with tradition, and particularly with his national heritage, as a kind of mission:

> Pero, sobre todo, Salinas en el exilio, mucho más que lo había sentido en España, vio la importancia de la tradición… Además, Salinas estimaba que él, fuera de España, tenía una función que podríamos llamar de expositor de todo lo que la literatura española (e hispánica, en general) había aportado a la cultura y la civilización modernas. ("Pedro Salinas y la ampliación del ensayo" 17)

> But, above all, Salinas in exile, much more than he had felt in Spain, saw the importance of tradition… Also, Salinas reckoned that he, outside of Spain, had a function that we could call exhibitor of all that Spanish literature (and Hispanic literature, in general) had contributed to modern culture and civilization.

Examination of Salinas's theater will highlight the key social function of the poet in the reconciliation of traditional and modern values and in the search for a harmony between the human being and his or her circumstances.

Modern critics have given less attention to his dramatic works than to his poetry. For the most part, they assess his theater largely in the light of his poetic production. A dominant perspective considers the dramatic works primarily an extension of his poetic work and a continuation of his concern with the theme of illusion versus reality (Cowes *Relación*; Hartfield-Méndez; Helman "Verdad y fantasía..." 207; Martínez Moreno 457-58; Moraleda *El teatro*; Rodríguez Richart; Torres Nebrera, ed. Pedro Salinas, *Teatro* 33-99). Cowes classifies realms of reality ("fantastic," literary, everyday, economic, artistic) and the *yo-tú* (I-you) relationships central to the transformations that the characters undergo. Hartfield-Méndez explores the I-you relationships with focus on Salinas's image of woman, epiphanic moments, time, and space. Helman emphasizes the importance of language in the shift from reality to fantasy. Martínez Moreno traces the search for an Eden-like reality. Moraleda's studies group the plays according to various phases or stages of reality and also examine specific plays in relation to geographical or literary influences ("Un pueblo andaluz," "Rasgos unamunianos"). Rodríguez Richart discusses two key themes that derive from Salinas's poetry: "los únicos dos," (two unique kindred spirits) who seek out each other, and "la víspera como gozo," (unfulfilled happiness) (420-21). Torres Nebrera, in his critical edition of four of the plays, traces Salinas's trajectory from poet to dramatist and groups the dramatic corpus into theater of discovery, rupture, and rebellion and confidence (33).

Recent research has provided information about the composition and chronology of the plays (Newman; Ruiz Ramón, "Contexto y cronología..."; Salinas de Marichal, "Tradición..."). Several studies have highlighted key aspects of the plays such as linguistic and structural elements (Materna, "Dialogue," "Ideology"), the use of irony (Ayuso), woman, the artist, and Giraudoux (Maurín), and Pirandellism (Newberry). Others have underlined the Salinian themes of love

(Escartín), self-authentication (Orringer), and modernity (Polansky, "Lorca and Salinas in New York"). The play *Los santos* has received the most individual study (Borrás; Cazorla; Cowes, "Realidad"; Crispin 153-55; Materna, "Ideology"; Ruiz Ramón, "Historia" 287-88; Salinas de Marichal, "Introducción"), and some articles have analyzed other specific works such as *El chantajista* (Gila; Polansky, "Mail and Blackmail"), *La fuente del arcángel* (Materna, "Dialogue"), and *Judit y el tirano* (Paco).

While the plays do exhibit features familiar in the poetry and may be said to represent the voice of the poet Salinas, their powerful social dimension—what Ruiz Ramón has appropriately deemed "teatro de salvación" (theater of salvation; *Historia* 282)—demonstrates a thrust importantly different from the poetry. Though many studies of Salinas's poetry have pointed to the significance of dialogue or to his preoccupations with modernity (Crispin 116-20; Debicki 113-17; Dehennin 194; Maurer "Salinas y 'las cosas'..." 137-50, "Sobre 'joven literatura'... 301-09; Soufas 63-101; Zubizarreta), less attention has been directed to these aspects in the dramatic works, where Salinas focuses more systematically upon human social interactions and circumstances to accent an aesthetic of redemption.

Borrás asserts correctly that the dramatic works of Salinas, like those of Rafael Alberti and Max Aub, help maintain the historical continuity of Spain's theater. Their theater of exile fills a gap in the evolution of Spanish theater between the poetic theater of Federico García Lorca and Alejandro Casona of the thirties and forties and Buero Vallejo's and Alfonso Sastre's realistic, social theater of the forties and fifties (Borrás 60). Salinas's theater, neither in the mold of the commercially successful, evasionist entertainment nor like the propagandistic theater of commitment or sharp social protest, blends aspects of both of these types that were popular during his time. His work is warm and humorous, but does not avoid issues that invite confrontation and painful consideration of change. His work is also serious, but not acerb or thesis ridden. His plays are rooted in the poet-turned-dramatist's adherence to a "tema vital," or vital, fundamental, essential, all-encompassing theme that illuminates how immersed he is as an intellectual in his cultural tradition as well as in his immediate circumstances as a citizen in the modern world and an exile from Spain. This vital theme upholds the quest of the poet and the poet's spiritual values that intertwine the play of self and circumstance, illusion and reality, tolerance and understanding, transformation and salvation.

Jorge Guillén, Salinas's life-long friend and fellow poet of the Generation of 1927, in two of the hundreds of letters they exchanged (dated December 20, 1948 and January 26, 1949), shares a memorable forecast for Salinas's theater offered by Hispanist Américo Castro. Castro suggests Salinas's theater might mark a culmination in his artistic production, a merging place for two key sides of Salinas's art, a harmonious union of the earth-bound, material, corporeal with the idealized, non-empirical, personal. Castro's words mark Salinas for a possible grandeur comparable with that of Lope de Vega (1562-1635), who invented a new kind of drama to develop his art. Castro hopes for Salinas to inject "las posibilidades célico-terrestres" (heavenly-earthly possibilities; PS/JG *Correspondencia* 482) into his theater, possibilities he does not see achievable solely through poetry. Through the theater, Salinas could blend the textures of empirical, immediate experience with poetic transcendence (PS/JG *Correspondencia* 482). Castro asserts:

> El arte de Salinas... tiene la gracia de abrazar ambas vertientes. Por eso tal vez tenga en el teatro la *forma* de suprema realización para él, en la cual pudiera reducir a unidad armónica las dos personas que bullen en él, y le inquietan la vida. Salinas se encuentra frente a un horizonte que fue el de Lope de Vega: ¿Cómo realizar la ambición de vida total que hungarea en el alma?.... Me parece que Salinas aspira a *realizarse* como pensador histórico y como creador poético a la vez... (PS/JG *Correspondencia* 473)

> The art of Salinas... has the charm of embracing both sides. Therefore perhaps there may be in the theater the *form* of supreme fulfillment for him, in which he may be able to reduce to a harmonious union the two persons that stir inside him. Salinas finds himself facing a horizon like that of Lope de Vega: How to realize the

ambition for a complete life that hungers in the soul?.... It seems to me that Salinas aspires *to fulfill himself* as a historical thinker and as a poetic creator at the same time...

Salinas's theater does not renovate the dramatic form in the way that Lope founded a Spanish national theater and a new art of creating drama, but Salinas the playwright achieves a vibrant amplification of his poetic voice through the medium of drama. With their artful orchestration of poetic and social sensibilities, his plays offer a powerful response to the impact of modernity and its certain specific dangers, and they resonate with the poet's desire for "vida total" 'total life'. Salinas the dramatist's characterizations of poet-like heroes, his attention to communication in the modern world, his embrace of tradition, and his charming blend of everyday circumstance with extraordinary elements reveal his evolution as a historical thinker and poetic creator. In a way, Castro's vision of poet's dramatic works bringing ultimate fulfillment is poignantly suggested if we consider accounts of the dramatist's elated reaction to the staging of *La fuente del arángel* (*The Fountain of the Archangel*), the only play he lived to see produced. Salinas's letters to Jorge Guillén and to his daughter Solita and her husband Juan overflow with his satisfaction over the reception of his work and his optimism about the communicative potential of the theater genre (PS/JG *Correspondencia* 558, *Cartas de viaje* 253). Yet lamentably, Salinas's death and the circumstances of his exile cut short this evolution.

Salinas considered his unstaged works incomplete and unfulfilled ("textos dramáticos previos"), and only very reluctantly, shortly before his death, acceded to requests to publish his plays in the hopes of facilitating their representation (Marichal, *Teatro completo* 12). This ultimately did not do very much to promote their production. Living in exile in an English-speaking environment, Salinas's outlets for staging his works were limited to two academic settings. *La fuente del arcángel* was performed by a theater group of Barnard College and directed by Laura de los Ríos on February 16 and 17, 1951 at Columbia University. *Judit y el tirano* (*Judith and the Tyrant*) was staged by a university theater group in Havana and directed by Luis Baralt on June 5, 1951. Salinas was too ill to attend this production. Since his death, a modest number of productions of a limited number of his plays have taken place in the U.S., Spain, Cuba, and Puerto Rico. In July and August of 1980, *Los santos* was staged at the Real Coliseo de Carlos III of the Escorial outside of Madrid. To conmemorate the centenary of his birth, a number of performances took place in Spain and Puerto Rico. In November of 1991, *Los santos* (*The Saints*) premiered in Murcia, Spain under the direction of César Oliva and then travelled to San Juan, Puerto Rico, where Oliva and César Bernard co-directed its production in December of 1991. On February 18, 1992, Pilar Massa staged a performance of *La Cabeza de Medusa* (*The Head of Medusa*) at the Círculo de Bellas Artes in Madrid. On July 9, 1992, *Judit y el tirano* opened at the Teatro Español in Madrid under the direction of Manuel Collado. For the most part, Salinas's theater has remained in the shadows, where coincidentally Salinas had placed the works of a few of his contemporaries before he himself turned to writing plays.

In two of his essays written in 1933, one on Unamuno the dramatist and one on Arniches, Salinas divides Spanish dramatic literature into two categories. He makes a distinction between plays by playwrights such as Benavente, the Alvarez Quintero brothers, and Arniches, which have been in the public spotlight, and plays that have remained in the shadows though their authors, for example, Unamuno, Valle-Inclán, and Azorín, have achieved great success with non-dramatic works. (Salinas, *Literatura española siglo XX* 69, 127). Little did Salinas know at that time, in appraising the positions of Unamuno, Valle-Inclán, and Azorín, how aptly he had described what was to be his own situation in Spanish dramatic literature. The total of his dramatic works—two three-act and twelve one-act plays—was published only after his death in 1951 and has not received the attention given to his poetry or essays. The present study aims to shed additional light on Salinas the poet dramatist and the role of his poet heroes and their dominant action.

This book, a validation of the theater of Salinas, embraces his "vida total" and centers on key interrelated dimensions of his life and art. The approach is by necessity highly intertextual. The first part of the study examines the genesis and aims of Salinas's theater by focusing on texts of different genres written by Salinas and other exiles of his generation, especially their correspondence and essays. Study of these autobiographical, biographical, and literary sources grounds Salinas's conception of the key role of the poet actors or guide figures in his dramatic production and clarifies the evolution of the social significance of the plays. These texts contextualize and inform the second part of the study that centers on the poet in the theater and takes a closer look at the dramatic works and the actions of Salinas's poet characters.

The three chapters of Part One trace the evolution of Salinas the dramatist through examination of Salinas the correspondent, the essayist, and the émigré. In Chapter One, a focus on Salinas the poet letter writer, through review of his voluminous correspondence (some of which has been made accessible only recently) and his well-respected body of essays provides fertile textual ground for appreciation of his engagement with the medium of drama. Biographical data and personal statements from Salinas's letters and essays show that the poet Salinas has an affinity for the theater from his boyhood and that this connection intensifies in the years of his exile from Spain, during which time the mature poet composes the main body of his dramatic works and also explicitly articulates a role for the poet and the theater. Salinas remained an avid letter writer throughout his life. His correspondences with fiancée and wife Margarita and friend Jorge Guillén contain explicit evidence of his attachment to theater and provide information about the history of the composition of his plays, the reasons for his turn to the theater, and his attempts to produce and publish his plays. In his letters to Margarita and Guillén and others, most notably to his clandestine beloved Katherine Reding Whitmore, and also in his essays, Salinas articulates his thoughts about the modern world, theater in general, the role of the poet, liberty, artistic freedom, and separation from Spain.

Chapter Two highlights Salinas the essayist to broaden perspective on the place and definition of his dramatic production. Salinas, a gifted essayist, analyzes the poet's navigation of exterior reality and inner psychic reality in the process of creation in his four major critical works on poets and their poetry: *Mundo real y mundo póetico, Reality and the Poet in Spanish Poetry, Jorge Manrique o tradición y originalidad,* and *La poesía de Rubén Darío.* The essays of *El defensor* and *La responsabilidad del escritor* evidence Salinas's special attention to the interrelationships between modern life, language, and theater, and offer insight into his approach to theater with its social dimension and his creation of poet characters who lead some form of redemptive action. His writings on Spanish playwrights and their construction of reality emphasize the values he places on the currents of orality, lyricism, humanity, and spirituality he finds in their works. His own theatrical works can be viewed in the light of his well-recognized and diverse essay production to consider the role of the poet and reality and the social, historical, and political functions of the genre of drama in combination with the significance of its lyrical and spiritual dimensions.

Chapter Three examines Salinas the poet émigré and the notion of exile as a Spanish circumstance. His existence in the United States separated from Spain leads to nostalgia for his homeland and its language as a living entity that finds outlet through the medium of dramatic dialogue. Contemporary scholarship concurs that the theater experience represents a means to broaden his powers of expression and that his turn to writing plays during the last fifteen years of his life grows out of his search for a more concrete, yet multifaceted representation of universal themes and viewpoints in a distinctly modern context (Baader 248-51; Crispin 148; Gullón 9; Helman "Verdad y fantasía…" 211; Maurín 1,3; Ruiz Ramón "Historia…" 315; Torres Nebrera 23-26; Zuleta 47). The single voice of his poetry, often engaged in dialogue and examination of various configurations of reality and their connections to the poet, gives way in his dramatic works to continued creative introspection, but through more complex and developed interrelationships between characters who communicate in the language of his Spanish homeland and who meet the challenges of being bound in circumstances exacerbated by the modern world. It will be shown that Salinas channels his bittersweet nostalgia, sorrow, and desperation with strong positive force into his theater. The experience of exile as rupture and redemption filters into the story lines of his plays. The exiled dramatist's preoccupation with separation, connection, restriction, and freedom vividly marks his dramatic works.

Grounded in the biographical and aesthetic positions of Salinas as evidenced through his letters and essays, the chapters of Part Two analyze the role of the poet in the theatrical works. From a number of angles, his poet figures function as key conductors. Chapter Four examines the structural coherence of the plots of the dramatic works and emphasizes the motivating force of the leading characters. Discernable across the corpus of fourteen plays is a fundamental story framework, a "fabula" of confinement-to-freedom. Two versions of the basic plot point to outcomes of felicitous or tragic nature. Examination of the components of Salinas's plot construction will locate the poet characters in the action and illustrate their pivotal role.

Chapter Five elaborates the two variations of the core story line with two exemplary plays. *El chantajista*, a nostalgic transplanting, and *Caín o una gloria científica*, an anguished prophecy, highlight the poet's directive force in confronting pressures of personal circumstance and modernity. Also, these examples resound with echoes of the life of Salinas the poet and support a view of his plays as autobiographical discourse. The circumstances of *El chantajista* and the budding romance between Lisardo and Lucila can be seen as a nostalgic reflection of Salinas's early correspondence with Margarita. The struggle of Abel and Clemente in *Caín o una gloria científica* communicates Salinas's poetic response in the 1940's to the threat of atomic destruction. These sentiments of distress resound in the compositions of *Todo más claro*, in his letters to Guillén, and late in the decade in his novel *La bomba increíble*.

Chapter Six studies Salinas's poet heroes in terms of their special capacity for seeing. The role of the poet as a visionary with spiritual and social force links with Salinas's own stance as a poet and with his reflections on perception found in his poetry, letters, and essays. Examination of prominent patterns of references to seeing in the dramatic works will highlight the communication between the poet guiders and guided viewers, the imagery of eyes, windows, and mirrors, and the representations of sightedness and blindness. This discourse of seeing will show that Salinas's poet visionaries possess the dual talent to see and to enable others to experience the material world and beyond.

Chapter Seven defines the function of the poet in bridging tradition and modernity. Salinas's vision of tradition as a liberating force is evident especially in his incorporation of spiritual perspectives that echo those of Cervantes as well as other traditional sources. Tradition plays a key part in the poet's overcoming the pressures of modern civilization and immediate circumstance. Salinas's leading characters bear notable resemblance to Cervantes's knight and can be viewed as descendents of Don Quixote in a contemporary world. Their behavior reflects definitions of poet and poetic action that Salinas sets forth in his correspondence and essays. Three plays with different outcomes exemplify poet's optimistic stance and preoccupation with ethical issues of justice and goodness in the process of a reconstruction of a milieu. In "*La Estratoesfera*," playwright Salinas in exile blends Spanish past and present through a lively group of characters with the quixotic poet Alvaro most prominent to construct a congenial Cervantine recreation that displays a romantic ideal fulfilled. In *Judit y el tirano*, Salinas recasts the biblical heroine, condemns tyranny in the modern world, and represents the interruption of the design of poet defender Judit. In *Los santos*, Salinas portrays the actions of saintly saviors and erects a strong bridge of hope for peace and fraternity by joining Christian symbolism with Cervantine threads of illusion and reality, tolerance, transformation, and salvation.

The conclusion of this work considers the place of Salinas the poet-playwright, the reception of his plays, and their future-oriented position at mid-century in the face of modernity with its promises and dangers. In this light, it also considers the unwritten dramatic works or ideas for theater that Salinas did not have the opportunity to develop. Tracing the genesis of the dramatic production of Pedro Salinas, examining his goals, and probing the social significance of his theater shapes a definition of the poet as actor and ultimately as dramatic hero.

PART I

The Genesis and Aims
of Salinas's Theater

1
Salinas: Poet and Correspondent

> ...en mí, al lado de una naturaleza contemplativa, interior, desprendida de las realidades, flotante sobre el tiempo y los hechos, hay otra naturaleza amante de la acción, de las realidades de crear material, de la vida práctica.
> Salinas, *Cartas a Katherine Whitmore* 201
>
> ...in me, beside a contemplative, interior nature, detached from realities, floating above time and deeds, there is another nature that loves action and the realities of creating material, of practical life.

IN HIS PASSIONATE ESSAY in defense of letter writing, Salinas exclaims "¡Gran invención, precioso hallazgo, la carta!" ("Great invention, precious discovery, the letter!"; *El defensor* 19). Indeed, Salinas's own letters, particularly those he writes to Margarita Bonmatí, Jorge Guillén, and Katherine Reding Whitmore, provide insight into his personality and preoccupations, his aesthetics and development as an artist, his attachment to the theater, and the evolution of his dramatic works. Though Salinas does not turn to writing plays in earnest until later in his life, his correspondence reveals that he was interested in drama from very early on. In letters to Margarita during their courtship (1912-1915) and decades later, and in correspondence with cherished friend Jorge Guillén (1923-1951), Salinas expresses his love of theater and discloses its early and crucial connections to his life and art. The correspondence with Margarita contains Salinas's nostalgic reflections on the importance of theater and his first reflections on the poet, poetic creation, and artistic freedom. The letters to Guillén further develop Salinas's conception of the role of the poet and his connection to contemporary events while providing us detail about the composition and chronology of his dramatic works. The letters to Katherine Reding Whitmore (1932-1947), a long-awaited collection accessible to readers since 1999, contain highly personalized definitions of the poet and his activity as well as indications of the poet's sentiments about the world situation and his exile. They also mention briefly the poet's ideas for theater that apparently never came to fruition. This chapter will focus on key passages from Salinas's prolific correspondence with Margarita, Jorge Guillén, and Katherine Reding Whitmore to trace the evolution of his play writing, to examine his clearly articulated thoughts about poetic activity and modern circumstance, and to provide basis for appreciation of the social dimension of his dramatic works and his construction of poet characters with leading roles.

SALINAS'S LETTERS TO MARGARITA
In Paris, separated from Spain and Margarita in 1915, Salinas writes of an early attempt at writing plays and makes mention of his love of theater together with the nostalgia for his boyhood years. In describing to Margarita how he attended a Sunday matinee, Salinas evokes powerful memories of this early and strong attraction to the theater:

> Margarita mía, hoy domingo, por la tarde he estado en el teatro. No sabes estas palabras 'teatro... domingo por la tarde...' el encanto que tienen para mí: es un encanto de mi infancia, un rosario de recuerdos de niñez: mis diez años reviven, pensando en aquella vida de niño triste y solitario que algunos domingos iba al teatro con sus tíos o sus abuelos. ¡Es toda una época de mi vida! (*Cartas de amor* 232)

> My Margarita, today, Sunday afternoon, I have been at the theater. You do not know the charm these words 'theater... Sunday afternoon'... have for me: it is a delight of my childhood, a string of memories of boyhood, thinking about that life of the sad and solitary boy who some Sundays would go to the theater with his aunts and

uncles or grandparents. It is a whole period of my life!

Salinas's boyhood theater excursions with relatives set in him such a powerful sense of theater as shared community that in later years he resists for some time going by himself to the theater. Attending alone initially seems too sad and unshared an experience, but eventually Salinas does go and feels a warm and pleasant nostalgia that he seeks to transmit to Margarita:

> ...y este recuerdo, Margarita mía, puro y sonriente, quiero ofrecértelo esta noche, recuerdo de cuando yo era niño rubio y silencioso y empezaba a soñar... (*Cartas de amor* 232)

> ...and this memory, my Margarita, pure and smiling, I want to offer to you tonight, a memory of when I was a young and silent child and began to dream...

Years later, this early recognition of the communal dimension of theater becomes an intense perception, manifested, for example, in Salinas's great reluctance to publish his dramatic works before they were performed and shared by spectators.

In September of 1915, Salinas writes with lack of confidence about an early attempt at writing plays. He mentions having completed a first act of a fantasy play that he is not sure about finishing, and describes the work as very unusual, and probably absurd and bad (Salinas de Marichal, "Tradición y modernidad..." 3). It is possible that this piece was entitled *La cama de matrimonio* (*The Marriage Bed*), because in a letter to Guillén dated April 11, 1930, Salinas indicates that he has been working on this, his first play (PS/JG *Correspondencia* 108). A manuscript of the work has not been found, and it is unclear that it was ever completed.

In October of 1915, describing cinema to Margarita, Salinas writes that though it communicates dramatic form, it is not yet drama. He refers to drama as the most complicated form of artistic production, one that joins together the individual and the social:

> Esto del teatro es lo más difícil de augurar de todo, pues como en ese arte lo individual y lo social se unen, es más complicado que otro cualquiera. (*Cartas de amor* 259)

> This business of theater is the most difficult of all to predict, since because in that art the individual and the social are united, it is more complicated than any other.

This is an idea upon which he will expound decades later in his essays.

In addition to these explicit references to theater, from the courtship letters to Margarita emerge early definitions by Salinas of the poet and of artistic freedom. In fact, in her introduction to *Pedro Salinas Cartas de amor a Margarita, 1912-1915*, Solita Marichal deems Salinas's vocation as a poet the central theme of the correspondence and asserts that the love letters at times seem more like short essays on the function of the poet and the meaning of poetry (27). These definitions are Salinas's earliest conceptualization of the poet as hero and his first articulation of the confinement-to-freedom theme that was to appear in his dramatic works. In 1914, from Madrid, Salinas defines for Margarita the distinction of the poet and the significance of the poet's work. The poet is a being set apart from those around him and one who faces a special challenge of self-expression with respect to the surrounding world:

> Tú supones que el poeta debe sentir una sensación de superioridad sobre los demás. Esto en cierto modo es exacto, no diré yo de superioridad, pero sí de distinción; lo primero que él nota no es que es superior a los demás hombres, sino que es distinto de ellos, de otra manera. Y al sentirse así, diferente, no sabe aún si es más o menos que ellos, y acaso durante toda la vida duda. Es la eterna lucha entre el pensamiento y la acción, lo externo y lo interior. (*Cartas de amor* 124)

You suppose that the poet should feel a sense of superiority over others. This is true in a certain way, I would say not of superiority, but yes, of distinction; the first thing he notices is not that he is superior to the rest of mankind, but that he is different from them, in another way. And feeling this way, different, he still does not know if he is more or less than they, and perhaps he doubts during his entire life. This is the eternal struggle between thought and action, between the external and the internal.

Here we see the young Salinas viewing the poet primarily as engaged in internal struggle because poetry is conceived to be thought rather than action.

According to Salinas, when the poet views his poetic writings, he can feel the noble pride of accomplishment, but cannot experience ultimate fulfillment in himself because the poet can never express all that he means to express. There is always some sense of dissatisfaction because of the thought that one is capable of more:

> Es decir, que el poeta debe sentirse contento por su obra hecha, pero no considerarla nunca completa, total, y por lo tanto no sentir el pleno orgullo de la vida realizada en la obra. (*Cartas de amor* 124)

> That is to say, the poet should feel content with his created work, but should never consider it complete, whole, and therefore does not feel the full pride of having life fulfilled in the work.

For Salinas, the poet is a producer of laudable work and a constant seeker. This view of the poet in the courtship letters reemerges and intensifies in his characterizations of the poet protagonists of his dramatic works, where these protagonists endeavor to find fulfillment, love, and freedom for themselves and others beyond their everyday spheres.

In 1913, in an early letter from Madrid to Margarita, Salinas's portrayal of the poet in search of love is a highly personalized outpouring of affection for his beloved. Though at this time he is composing less poetry, he nevertheless feels more like a poet because of the longing for her that he carries within. His desire for beauty and his love toward Margarita is what makes him more of a poet (*Cartas de amor* 65). The poet is filled with verses destined for his beloved, but even if they do not find expression in written form, her comprehension of the poetry of his soul will satisfy him. The ideal set by the Salinas is an intimate communication of kindred spirits:

> ...con que tú me comprendas me basta: no me importa la gloria. Margarita, dulce nombre, recibe toda la paz, toda la poesía, todo el amor de que mi alma está llena. (*Cartas de amor* 65)

> ...that you understand me is enough for me: fame is not important to me. Margarita, sweet name, receive all the peace, all the poetry, all the love that fills my soul.

In 1915 from Paris, toward the end of the courtship, Salinas again writes how his sense of fulfillment in his poetic vocation is tied to their relationship (*Cartas de amor* 224). His ambitions as a poet are now not literary pretensions or ambitions, but rather endeavors illuminated by his bond with Margarita. This intimate urging of a spiritual and amorous union with Margarita by poet Salinas finds strong voice in his creation of characters and situations in his dramatic works that depict these same longings for connection fueled by the enterprise of a poet. For example, Salinas's final dramatic work, *El chantajista*, illustrates well the poet's long-term identification with liberty, love, and redemptive union, and will later be shown to contain the most explicit of correspondences with the love letters to Margarita.

In addition to these first indications of Salinas's attaction to theater and his self-definition as a poet, passages from the courtship letters offer Salinas's earliest commentary on artistic freedom. From Paris in 1915, Salinas upholds as most sacred the freedom to express what is in one's soul. He criticizes the artificiality of adhering to techniques not truly one's own, not emanating from one's true interior voice:

> La libertad de expresar lo que se tiene en el alma, es la más sagrada de todas. Y esa libertad no se respeta si se encierra el arte en jaulas de preceptos y de reglamentos. (*Cartas de amor* 194)
>
> Freedom to express what the soul holds is the most sacred of all freedoms. And that freedom is not respected if art is enclosed in a cage of rules and precepts.

This vision later finds voice in his plays in the words and deeds of poet liberator characters he portrays as heroic in their attempts to fight confinement and oppression in everyday life and the modern world.

Years later, in 1936, after writing what is now considered his first play, *El director*, Salinas, in exile, expresses the irony and frustration of not having an audience for the work:

> ¡Pobre drama mío! En el momento en que me he puesto a escribir una clase de obra que necesita público, que se debe apoyar en lo colectivo, ese público posible y todas las posibilidades de llegar a él, se deshacen. (Bou, Soria Olmedo 90)
>
> Poor play of mine! At the moment I put myself to write a kind of work that needs an audience, that should be supported in a collective way, that audience and all possibilities of reaching it are ruined.

Here he presupposes the sense of community intrinsic to theater that he described during his boyhood years. This sentiment will intensify as he encounters similar difficulties with subsequent plays later in exile.

In 1937, Salinas communicates to Margarita his growing inclination for the dramatic medium. Salinas was finding that writing poetry did not allow him a certain kind of expression. Lyric poetry was not permitting him to create a realm in which to portray life-like characters in action. In January 1937, he writes, "Siento más que nunca, el fondo dramático de la vida humana, lo que podríamos llamar la materia dramática, vaga, eterna... ("I feel more than ever the dramatic foundation of human life, what we might call dramatic material, vague, eternal..."; Newman 212-13). He asserts that lyric poetry is separated from life and marginal to it while drama is down to earth and rooted in the reality of life:

> Pero lo que me tienta en el drama es la posibilidad de inventar criaturas vivas, ponerlas unas frente a otras, echarlas sobre los actos. Siento la atracción del teatro, pura, la afición a crear acto, encuentro, en suma, vida. Parece como si la poesía lírica estuviese más al margen de la vida, liberada de ella, independiente, como una nube que marca por su cuenta, sin tener que atenerse a más leyes que su rumbo libre. En cambio, el teatro está sujeto a la tierra, a la realidad. (Newman 213)
>
> But what attracts me in drama is the possibility of inventing living creatures, putting them face to face, and casting them into acts. I feel the attraction of theater, pure, the desire to create action, encounter, in short, life. It seems as if lyric poetry is at the margin of life, freed from it, independent, like a cloud that marks its own pace, without having to take into account any law other than its own free route. On the other hand, theater is tied to the land, to reality.

Of course he does not cease writing poetry or even decrease his output, since he writes four volumes while in exile. Nonetheless, expanding beyond lyric poety's celebration of freedom and love and its rather solipsistic expression of thought and feeling, Salinas moves in the dramatic works to place poet figures into greater confrontation with reality. Drama puts the poet concerned with freedom and love into contact with the constraints of interpersonal relations. The strong social dimension of drama forces the free-floating, cloud-like poet into more active engagement with the vital land of circumstance.

In the fall of 1947, in a letter to Margarita from Bogotá, Salinas writes of his reading of his play *La isla del tesoro* (*Treasure Island*) for two actors of a theater company there. Salinas appreciates their positive response, but is not overly confident about their mounting a production:

> Les gustó mucho; así lo dijeron, y creo que era la verdad. Pero de eso a la representación, hay distancia. Me aseguraron los dos que les parece muy teatral, muy bien dialogada, etc. (*Cartas de viaje* 207)

> They liked it very much, so they said, and I believe that was true. But from that to performance, there is a distance. They both assured me that they think it's very theatrical, very well dialogued, etc.

On this same trip, Salinas writes to Margarita and to daughter Solita and son-in-law Juan Marichal of getting "una panzada de teatro" ("a bellyful of theater"; *Cartas de viaje* 211) and of attending an enjoyable variety of productions in the Colombian capital. This continuing enthusiasm for the stage echoes the sentiments from his earliest letters to Margarita during their courtship.

SALINAS'S LETTERS TO JORGE GUILLÉN

Like his letters to Margarita, Salinas's letters to Guillén reveal clearly his attraction to the medium of drama. To Guillén he discloses his enjoyment in writing and also his serious reflection upon personal and public events contemporaneous with his writing. The delight in composing plays partly explains his turn to theater as also does his social awareness and his sense of the significance of theater.

These letters also clarify the chronology of the composition of the plays. It appears that *El director*, the first play that Salinas finished, is the only one completed prior to his emigration (PS/JG *Correspondencia* 169). He composed his other thirteen plays in exile, and principally in Puerto Rico, between 1943 and 1946. The following chronology has been established based on the letters: *El director* (*The Director*), January 1936; *El parecido* (*The Resemblance*), between December 1942 and August 1943; *Ella y sus fuentes* (*She and Her Sources*), before November 1943; *La Bella Durmiente* (*Sleeping Beauty*), November 1943; *La isla del tesoro* (*Treasure*

Island), January 1944; *La Cabeza de Medusa* (*The Head of Medusa*), before February 1945; *Sobre seguro* (*The Insurance Envelope*), before February 1945; *Caín o una gloria científica* (*Caín or the Glory of Science*), before February 1945; *Judit y el tirano* (*Judith and the Tyrant*), May 1945; "*La Estratoesfera*" *Vinos y cervezas* (*The Stratosphere. Wines and Beers*), May 1945; *La fuente del Arcángel* (*The Fountain of the Archangel*), January 1946; *Los santos* (*The Saints*), between May and December 1946; *El precio* (*The Price*), before June 1947; *El chantajista* (*The Blackmailer*), June 1947 (Ruiz Ramón "*Contexto...*" 197-98).

Although it is after leaving Spain that Salinas turns in earnest to writing plays, letters prior to his exile mark his early attempts and reflect experiences that connect to the creation of his plays. In April of 1930, he writes with enthusiasm of his first, apparently never completed, project for the theater, a three-act play entitled *La cama de matrimonio* (*The Marriage Bed*) (PS/JG *Correspondencia* 108). Two months later, in June of 1930, he laments his incapacity to work on the play and other writings, not only for lack of time, but also from an absence of desire or pleasure (PS/JG *Correspondencia* 114). With words that echo some years later in his plays, vivid indications of Salinas's despondence during this period both over the death of the Spanish writer Gabriel Miró and the political climate of Spain and Madrid at that moment precede the confession of his inability to write. His reaction to the suicide of Miró prefigures the torment, fragmentation, and quest for identification with the suffering and image of another being that he was to depict in a number of his plays of tragic outcome, especially both three-act plays, *El director* and *Judit y el tirano*, and also *Caín o una gloria científica*. Salinas writes to Guillén:

> ...Mi manía, ahora agudiza, de parecerme a Miró. Claro es que no en sus cualidades mejores sino en su humor, en sus modos, en sus defectos. De parecerme a él en el tipo, también. Viendo los retratos publicados con ocasión de la muerte, me asaltaban los parecidos. Y los parecidos con la muerte. Traía yo ya una mala temporada de preocupaciones y disgustos, importantes y mínimos. Y ahora

condensa en torno de mi estado de ánimo una atmósfera de acabamiento, de inestabilidad, de desesperanza. Estoy muy decaído. Pienso en cosas absurdas. Dejar todo lo de Madrid, irme a cualquier parte con mi mujer y mis hijos, a esperar. A esperar lo de Miró. En fin ya conoces tú mi obsesión, ese terrible punto céntrico, ese foco de atracción en mi vida espiritual... (PS/JG *Correspondencia* 112-13)

...My mania, now acute, of resembling Miró. Of course not in his best qualities but in his humor, his manners, and his defects. To resemble him in build, also. Seeing the portraits of him on the occasion of his death, the similarities assaulted me. And the similarities to death. I was suffering a bad time of worries and upsets, important and insignificant. And now condensing around my state of being is an atmosphere of death, instability, hopelessness. I am so down. I think about absurd things. To leave what is happening in Madrid, to leave with my wife and children, to wait. To await what happened to Miró. In short, you already know my obsession, that horrible focal point, that focus of attention in my spiritual life...

Salinas is disgusted with the Spanish political scene in 1930, the final year of the dictatorship of Primo de Rivera. He writes:

...esto de la política es uno de los elementos de perturbación y de incoherencia que es menester rechazar para que la vida espiritual no sea caos completo... es que la política que España impone es de tan baja y zafia condición que arrastra detrás de su ejercicio todas las virtudes espirituales (PS/JG *Correspondencia* 114)

...this matter of politics is one of the elements of disturbance and incoherence necessary to reject so that spiritual life not be complete chaos... it's that the politics Spain imposes is of such low and uncouth condition that it drags behind its exercise all spiritual virtues.

In letters the following year, in January and April of 1931, he contemptuously defines engagement in politics as asphyxiating and characteristic of those of low spriritual caliber. He strongly condemns the descent of the intelligentsia, José Ortega y Gasset, José Bergamín and others, into simpleminded posturing. He observes:

> ...lo que me subleva es la pretensión de reducir la vida, nada menos que la vida, a esa actividad política, con desdén del resto (el *resto* mío es lo político), y lo que es más grave, con la afirmación imperial e imperiosa de su ejercicio so pena de señoritismo o frivolidad. Yo no digo que la política no sea a veces sacrificio, abnegación. Pero otras muchas es pereza, facilidad, abandono a lo más tópico y vulgar de todo. (PS/JG *Correspondencia* 135)

> ...what infuriates me is the pretension to reduce life, nothing less than life, to that political activity, with its disdain for everything else (my *everything else* is what is political), and what is more serious, with the imperial and imperious affirmation of its practice on penalty of exaggerated gentility and frivolity. I am not saying that politics is not sometimes sacrifice, abnegation. But many other times it is laziness, docility, and giving in to the most current and vulgar of all.

While odious conflicts and the weak moral fiber of those competing for power leave him unable to write for a time and wishing to withdraw, eventually this frustration finds a positive outlet in his theater. In his three most political plays, *Judit y el tirano*, *Caín o una gloria científica*, and *Los santos*, Salinas will counter mundane engagement in politics with elevation of ordinary reality through a broader vision of a better humanity free from ideologies.

In January of 1936, Salinas indicates that he has completed *El director* during eight days spent in Alicante, but has not been able to rework it (PS/JG *Correspondencia* 169). Six years later, at the beginning of 1942, from Baltimore he writes to Guillén of a play already completed in his mind, but not yet written (PS/JG *Correspondencia* 271). This is *El parecido*, which Guillén praises in a letter of August 16, 1943, and which he encourages Salinas to complete quickly (PS/JG *Correspondencia* 308). Apparently after conceiving *El parecido* in Baltimore, he completes it in San Juan. Writing from San Juan in 1943, Salinas indicates to Guillén his completion of *La Bella Durmiente*. Salinas's years in the Spanish-speaking environment of Puerto Rico fuel his creativity and generate a great variety of output. A letter of November 6, 1943, reveals that his theater is evolving along with his contemplative poetry inspired by the Sea of San Juan, his essays about Spanish literature, his criticism of the Spanish political situation, and the emergence of his more socially conscious poetry, in particular the poem "Cero" ("Zero"), about the impending doom of world destruction. About a year later, in a letter dated January 12, 1944, to Guillén, Salinas writes that he has finished his poem "Cero," that he is continuing work on other poetry, and has composed a first version of his play *La isla del tesoro*, although still toying with a title change to *Reserva absoluta* (*Absolute Confidence*). Salinas expresses effusive delight in writing plays:

> Tengo ya otra de esas piececitas pensada, y si no fuera por las clases ya estaría puesto en ella. Me divierte una enormidad esto de escribir teatro. ¡Suponiendo que sea teatro, lo que resulta! (PS/JG *Correspondencia* 320)

> I have now another of those little pieces in mind, and if it weren't for classes, I would already be set to it. This writing of theater gives me enormous enjoyment. Supposing that what results is theater!

The following year, in February of 1945, Salinas lists for Guillén seven completed little pieces: *Ella y sus fuentes, El parecido, La Bella Durmiente, La isla del tesoro, La Cabeza de Medusa, Sobre seguro,* and *Caín o una gloria científica*. He indicates that only very few people are aware of his plays, and shares that he longs for an opportunity to do readings. Guillén responds enthusiastically and suggests that Salinas try to get them staged and also send material to actress Margarita Xirgu (PS/JG *Correspondencia* 346-47).

World events continue to incite fervor in Salinas's letters of 1945, which brings the conclusion of World War II. Criticizing Truman's Victory Day speech as too matter-of-fact, dispassionate and sanctimonious, Salinas is jubilant over the fall of the Nazis, and cries ardently for freedom:

> ¡Cómo quisiera estar hoy en París o en Londres! De seguro que allí, no obstante haber sufrido horriblemente, no ponen ese freno protestante a la alegría. Claro que el porvenir está lleno de sombras, pero eso es razón para gozar un día de claridad, y en él darse fuerza. ¿Sabes lo que echo de menos? Un grito, que desde niño me conmovía extrañamente, hoy *demodé*, ridículo: ¡Viva la libertad! (PS/JG *Correspondencia* 351)

> How would I love to be in Paris or London today! Surely there, notwithstanding having suffered horribly, they are not putting that Protestant brake on happiness. Of course the future is full of shadows, but that is reason for enjoying one day of light, and taking strength from it. Do you know what I miss? A shout, that since I was a boy touched me to the core, though today *outmoded*, ridiculous: Long live freedom!

At the conclusion of this letter, Salinas mentions two more plays: *Judit y el dictador*, later titled *Judit y el tirano*, which he terms "dramita" or a little play that he has a tremendous time writing, and *"La Estratoesfera" Vinos y cervezas*, a one-act play that has given him a chance to paint the local color of his native Madrid. He writes how he has longed to read this dramatic work as well as his others to Guillén, and for the first time, Salinas expresses that he considers his plays unpublished until they are read (PS/JG *Correspondencia* 352-53). This letter juxtaposes Salinas's enthusiasm about the liberation with his need for an outlet for dramatic expression.

Guillén continues to encourage Salinas to publish the plays and points out that five or ten more years of exile could impede the staging of the works. After Guillén reads the plays, he is all the more encouraging and lauds them as a new, important addition to dramatic poetry. Yet he cautions that *Judit...*, susceptible to misunderstanding by a certain politically conscious public, might not be the play to stage first (PS/JG *Correspondencia* 398).

The correspondence through the forties between Salinas and Guillén repeatedly addresses the threat of the atomic bomb. Tormented by the possibility of nuclear holocaust, Salinas writes *Caín o una gloria científica* some six months before the bombing of Hiroshima. At this time he is also writing some of his most socially conscious poetry. He points to *Caín...* and also to his longest poem, a mournful meditation on the bomb entitled "Cero," completed by January of 1944, the final composition of his volume *Todo más claro (All Things Made Clearer)*, to share with Guillén his horror of man's creation of such an instrument of destruction. In August of 1945, Salinas expresses regret that he has not published *Caín...* earlier to be a prophecy of the catastrophic event (PS/JG *Correspondencia* 357). His continuing fears about possibilities of the bomb's future effects lead to the writing of his novel *La bomba increíble* in 1950 (PS/JG *Correspondencia* 523). His plays, like this novel, combine reality and fantasy.

The next mention of a completed play, *La fuente del arcángel*, situated in a town of Andalusia, appears in a brief line at the end in a letter dated January 28, 1946. From Puerto Rico in May of 1946, Salinas refers to this work by its early title, *La fuente del ángel*, and also mentions *Los santos*:

> ...voy a ver si escribo una piececita sobre un episodio—inventado, claro— de la guerra de España, que se llamaría *Los santos*. No sé si te dije que tenía otra comediella nueva, *La fuente del ángel*, que no he leído a nadie. ¡Figúrate cómo voy a llegar a los Estados Unidos, cargado de inéditos, y ansioso de lectores— quie ro decir de vuestra audiencia! (PS/JG *Correspondencia* 389)

> ...I am going to see about writing a little piece about an episode—invented, of course—about the war in Spain, that would be called *The Saints*. I don't know if I told you that I had another little comedy, *The Fountain of the Angel*, which I have not read to anyone. Imagine how I will arrive in the States, laden with unpublished works, and eager for readers—I mean your audience!

The clear Spanish settings and linguistic features of both of these works reflect Salinas's enduring need to connect with the Spanish milieu.

In the late forties, Salinas continues to be troubled by conflicts between the United States and Russia, the doctrinaire outpourings of the Vatican, and the continuing manifestations of intolerance and threats to freedom (PS/JG *Correspondencia* 484). The letters after his return to Baltimore from Puerto Rico reveal his growing preoccupation with publishing and staging his plays as well as continuing concerns about the post war climate worldwide and in Spain. On October 26, 1946, after his return from Puerto Rico, Salinas writes of Américo Castro's praise of his theater and the positive reception of his readings of three of his "actos" or 'one-act plays' at Princeton. In a letter to Castro before leaving Puerto Rico, Salinas offers bitter reflection on his theater:

> Va a resultar que soy un dramaturgo senil porque a estas horas me veo con una obra en tres actos y cuatro en un acto. Naturalmente sin vislumbre de representación posible. Aquí no hay teatro. La gente se nutre de la bazofía peliculera. Y no me gusta publicarlos en libros. (*Cartas de viaje* 181)

> It will turn out that I am a senile playwright because at this time I see myself with one three-act work and four with one act. Naturally without the slightest possibility of staging. Here there is no theater. The people feed on the swill of cinema. And I do not want to publish them in books.

Salinas asserts to Guillén that he will not permit his plays to premiere in

Spain as long as the rule of U.S. interests under the power of Franco persists there (PS/JG *Correspondencia* 405). On June 16, 1947, Salinas writes to Guillén of the completion of his final short dramatic work, *El chantajista o la invención de Romeo* (*The Blackmailer or the Invention of Romeo*), subsequently titled *El chantajista* (PS/JG *Correspondencia* 421). On September 14, 1947, he writes of a possible production of *La isla del tesoro* in Bogota (PS/JG *Correspondencia* 425). A few months later, on January 3, 1948, Salinas refers to a possible staging of *El chantajista* at Harvard. Though expressing some reservation about the play's not very Spanish title, *Chantaje* (*Blackmail*), Salinas explains that it gives a true sense of the work, and he writes that the play will be easy to produce because of its limited cast of two characters (PS/JG *Correspondencia* 434).

In the same letter, Salinas responds to Guillén's letter from Paris, where the latter has been exploring with Marcelle Auclair the translation and publication of Salinas's plays. Salinas hesitates, explaining his preference for direct staging, his aversion to seeing a play in French instead of first in its original Spanish, and his big reservation about their first choice of *Los santos* and its possible politization:

> ...pero me temo que en el motivo de la preferencia pueda entrar lo que tanto nos repugna a ti y a mí, la explotación del tema de la guerra de España para el público llamado de izquierdistas, el confusionismo cultivado hoy día por los comunistas con poetas, por lo demás tan auténticos como Federico, Neruda y Alberti, y con otros tan secundarios como ese tu homónimo Nicolás Guillén, que ahora acaba de dar la vuelta al ruedo de las Américas, patrocinado por los comunistoides de esos países. (PS/JG *Correspondencia* 433)

> ...but I fear that into the motive for the preference may enter what is so repugnant to you and me, the exploitation of the theme of Spain's war for the leftist audience, the great confusion cultivated nowadays of communists with poets, otherwise so authentic such as Federico, Neruda and Alberti, and with others so secondary like your namesake Nicolás Guillén, who now has just travelled all over

the Americas, supported by the despicable communists of those countries.

Salinas is adamant that the social dimension of his work, of supreme importance to him, should not be undermined by propagandistic agendas.

A noteworthy digression in the same letter of January 3, 1948, provides a complementary view of Salinas's social concerns and his emphatic focus on individual fellow humans experiencing so-called modern progress. Sharing an anecdote about the difficulty of finding a doctor to make a house call and getting early attention before needing serious treatment, Salinas lashes out against the "American way of living," especially in cities, where one will find real medical attention only after a serious event and only then in a hospital:

> El caso, bien mirado es un cruce típico de esa racionalización monstruosa y ese seudocientifismo modernos, combinado con la pérdida de todo interés por la persona, por el prójimo, que se sustituye por el interés en la *comunidad*, en lo *social*, o cualquiera de esos ídolos de nuestros días. En el fondo es egoísta, cómodo y antihumano. (PS/JG *Correspondencia* 434)

> The case, properly considered, is a typical crossing of that modern monstrous rationalization with pseudoscience, combined with the loss of all interest in the person, in one's fellow human being, which is substituted by interest in the *community*, in the *social*, or whichever of those idols of our times. Deep down it is selfish, smug, and antihuman.

In the modern settings he establishes for his dramatic works, whether the world of insurance, advertising, government, or science, for example, Salinas underscores the consequences of social forces on the humanity of individuals.

Three months later, in July of 1948, inspired by his reading and

teaching French works at Duke University Summer School, Salinas quotes Bernanos to expound on his vision of modernity:

> "Un monde gagné por la Technique est perdu pour la Liberté... Le progrès n'est plus dans l'homme, il est dans la technique, dans le perfectionnement des méthodes capables de permettre une utilisation chaque jour plus efficace du matériel humaine." Esa expresión del *material humano*, gemelo de la americana *man power*, es horripilante.... Y lo mejor, y más serio me parece esto: "Nous n'assistons pas à la fin naturelle d'une grande civilisation humaine, mais à la naissance d'une civilisation inhumane que no sauraits'établir que grâce à une vaste, à une universelle stérilisation des hautes valeurs de la vie." (PS/JG *Correspondencia* 449)

> "A world won by Techique is lost to Freedom... Progress does not lie in man, it lies in technique, in perfecting methods capable of permitting utilization of man power more effective each day." That expression of *human material*, twin of American *man power*, is horrifying. And what is better, and what seems graver to me is this: "We are not attending the birth of a great human civilization, but rather the birth of an inhumane civilization that will know how to establish itself only through an enormous, universal sterilization of life's highest values."

A number of Salinas's plays dramatize these powers of modern society to jeopardize what is genuinely human and kill freedom itself. Significantly and most forcefully, for example, in *Sobre seguro, La Bella Durmiente, Judit y el tirano,* and *Caín..,* he is prophetic in his depiction of the dehumanization of individuals by certain modern institutions and their operations.

While Guillén gives additional indications that Marcelle Auclair will translate *Judit...* and *Los santos* and perhaps have the latter staged along with Lorca's *Así que pasen cinco años,* Salinas is receiving less encouraging input from Dámaso Alonso (PS/JG *Correspondencia* 437, 441, 443). Alonso judges the works original, but likely difficult to stage. He cites high costs for actors and the complications of mounting three different sets for the performance of three single act works in one evening's performance (PS/JG *Correspondencia* 443). This leaves Salinas less than enthusiastic about travelling to South America to find a stage for his works.

Six months later, in a letter dated December 15, 1948, Salinas recounts details of another conversation with Alonso about the aims of his theater. Salinas disagrees with Alonso's opinion that there be only one theater with a single audience, the common people, with whom a dramatist should seek to connect honestly. Salinas sees a differentiation of theater audiences as he does readers of poetry and novels, and expresses hope that in attempting to write for no group exclusively, he might reach audiences on a variety of grounds (PS/JG *Correspondencia* 471). With his works still not published or staged, Salinas writes with some frustration in May and November of 1950 of putting some of the stories he is writing in his "cajón del teatro" or theater drawer with his plays and of a failed attempt to publish his works with Editorial Sudamericana (PS/JG *Correspondencia* 529, 546). But in a letter dated October 3, 1950, Salinas makes reference somewhat optimistically to the translations of two of his works being done by John Otto Scrimger and encourages Guillén to remain on the lookout for possible theater companies to present his works (PS/JG *Correspondencia* 542). Their subsequent correspondence during this final year of Salinas's life describes plans for possible productions of a number of his plays, for the staging of his play *Judit y el tirano* and the actual production of *La fuente del arcángel* at Columbia University, N.Y., February 16, 1951. In a letter dated February 24, 1951, Guillén describes his attendance at a successful reading of *Judit y el tirano* in Mexico and indicates the plans developing for production of the work (PS/JG *Correspondencia* 555-56). *La fuente...* is the only one of his plays Salinas lives to see performed. Salinas's illness prevents him from attending the premiere of *Judit y el tirano* in Cuba in May of 1951.

On January 1, 1951, Salinas writes that he has attended the first phase of rehearsals for *La fuente del arcángel* and that it is too early to judge the outcome (PS/JG *Correspondencia* 552). His theater, his writing, and his family are clearly crucial consolation to him in the face of an escalating cold war and the perils he sees facing humanity. The poet playwright's social consciousness and need to give voice to the consequences of quest for salvation are clear in the concluding words of his letter:

> Dejemos este día limpio de toda monstruosa ceguedad suicida en que se complace la humanidad, con los diversos pretextos y en diversas latitudes, y que nos va a hacer vivir en vilo Dios sabe cuánto tiempo.... Lo que nadie dice es que habría que buscar con tanto empeño, con tanta actividad y con tanta energía como se pone en preparar la guerra, caminos de paz, incansablemente, y con los sacrificios necesarios de lo menor, que es todo, en comparación con lo mayor, que es la vida y la dignidad de la humanidad, que sucumbirán en una guerra, sin salvación posible. (PS/JG *Correspondencia* 552-53)

> Let's leave this day free from all the monstrous, suicidal blindness in which humanity takes pleasure, with all the diverse pretexts and diverse latitudes, that we will be made to live suspended in God knows how long.... What no one is saying is that it is imperative to seek, tirelessly, ways of peace, with as much persistence, activity and energy that is put into war, and with the necessary sacrifices of the least kind, which is everything, in comparison with the greatest kind, which is the life and dignity of humanity, that will succumb in a war, with no possible salvation.

Guillén continues to praise Salinas's work and its significance as an antidote to the pain of political stresses (PS/JG *Correspondencia* 554). Though there are times when circumstances leave Salinas unable to write or doubtful about his work, his literary productivity in exile signals his vigorous approach to seeking personal peace and sharing with others dynamic vision with a poetic outlook.

On February 20, 1951, the week after attending the performances of

La fuente del arcángel at Columbia, Salinas emphasizes the uniqueness of the theater as a living medium with a vastly different impact from that of poetry:

> Es curiosísimo el efecto de ver el propio teatro: no es que lo sintiera ajeno, no; pero sí como distante, con mucha perspectiva, ya desprendida de mí, viviendo por su camino. No se parece nada al leer poesías, ni al oírlas leer. (PS/JG *Correspondencia* 558)

> The effect of seeing one's own theater is so strange: it is not that I felt it alien, no, but yes rather distant, with much perspective, now detached from me and living on its own path. It does not resemble at all either reading poems or hearing them read.

The performance of *La fuente del arcángel* generates Salinas's confidence as a playwright and leads him to regret that his works have not reached the stage sooner. He is awakened to the enormous influence a dramatist can wield over audiences by enveloping them in the depth and authenticity of the communications of the actors on stage:

> Por lo pronto, he visto una cosa. Mi teatro no es pura ilusión de mi deseo de hacer teatro; se tiene, en las tablas, logra lo esencial, sujetar la atención de las gentes, llevarlas por el camino que uno quiere, durante cincuenta minutos. Los personajes no suenan a muñecos o a recitadores de vaniloquios, con un fondo pintado. Ya es algo; he cobrado cierta confianza en mi capacidad de escribir teatro. Pero esto se refiere, sólo a esta obra. ¿Y las demás? ¿Se sostendrán, también, como ésta? Ahora tengo más ganas que nunca verlas. Y ahora me doy cuenta del daño que me ha hecho en no poderlas ver antes: quizá eso hubiera decidido un rumbo de lo que escribo, en un sentido o en otro. (PS/JG *Correspondencia* 559)

> Suddenly, I saw something. My theater is not solely an illusion of my desire to make theater; it stands, on stage, it achieves the essential,

> to hold the attention of the people, to carry them on the path one wants, for fifty minutes. The characters do not sound like puppets or reciters of empty dialogues, against a painted backdrop. Now it is something; I have acquired a certain confidence in my ability to write drama. But this refers only to this work. And the rest? Will they sustain themselves, also, like this one? Now I have the desire more than ever to see them. And now I realize the harm that not being able to see them before has done to me: perhaps that would have determined a direction for my writing, in one sense or another.

Salinas also writes to Solita and Juan Marichal about the performance and emphasizes to them as well the communicative power and social dimensions of the experience and his eagerness to test the reception of some of his plays (*Cartas de viaje* 253).

This university production of *La fuente del arcángel* has an audience of students, professors, and associates, a middle class group, not all Spanish-speaking, but does not represent a highly diverse audience. Nevertheless, Salinas reemphasizes the waste of resources on vapid productions for the masses and advocates theater with substance aimed at a wide public (PS/JG *Correspondencia* 559). Guillén's supports Salinas's view of theater as nonpropagandistic, appropriate to a wide public and as an exploration to promote probing of motivations and heightening of understanding. Simply put, "No se escribe *para*... Se escribe *porque*..." (One does not write *for*... One writes *because*...; (PS/JG *Correspondencia* 562).

To celebrate the success of his friend, Dámaso Alonso, who sat beside Salinas at the premiere of *La fuente del arcángel*, adopts the definition by Salinas of the poet and the creation of a poetic world, an ideal realm awaiting the entrance of others. Signaling the crucial role of the poet as activator of change and architect of the bridge between a concrete reality and a new, ideal space, this earliest of assessments of Salinas's theater also notes the poet's entry into a social and moral realm, and praises the talent of the poet in the theater:

Esta perfecta transmisión, este dificilísimo, peligrosísimo paso insensible desde la realidad de un pueblo español hasta una atmósfera irreal en que todos los valores han cambiado, en que cosas y personajes han cobrado nueva significación, no habría sido posible sin el poeta, claro.... sin el técnico tampoco, porque Salinas —parece— ha llevado la rienda con la sabiduría de un experimentado hombre de teatro. (Alonso 201)

This perfect transmission, this very difficult, very dangerous, imperceptible step from the reality of a Spanish town to an unreal atmosphere in which all values have changed, in which things and characters have acquired new meaning, would not have been possible without the poet, of course.... nor without the technician either, because Salinas —it seems— has been in control with the knowledge of an experienced man of theater.

Definitions of the poet as essential catalyst and agent of liberating change appear in many of Salinas's essays and become a leit-motif of his dramatic works and an integral element of their plot structure. The poet protagonists of Salinas's plays offer to fellow characters the possibility of an uplifting transformation to transcend the conventionality and restrictions of everyday existence.

The rich correspondence between Salinas and Guillén illustrates well Salinas's sense of place as an evolving poet-playwright in exile. The letters show him to be keenly aware of the modern scene and its impact on his personal circumstance as a citizen of the world and a writer. Communicating to Guillén his frustrations, criticisms, and ideals in response to the experiences of life in the Twentieth Century, Salinas points to the social dimension of his work and suggests a heroic role for the poet, a key feature of his dramatic works.

Salinas's Letters to Katherine Reding Whitmore

This body of 354 letters, particularly significant for its information about the inception and composition of Salinas's most famous love poetry and

the relationship between him and his secret beloved, contains brief mention of plays in process or idea form, characterization of the role of poet and poetry, and indications of the poet's sentiments about world events and exile. During the summer of 1932, Salinas and Katherine meet in Madrid and soon begin a passionate affair. An intense, at times more than daily correspondence continues between 1932 and 1934 after Katherine returns to Smith College in September of 1932. She returns to Spain for the 1934-1935 academic year, during which time Margarita learns of the affair and attempts suicide. Although Katherine then tries to end the relationship, it continues due to circumstances of the Spanish Civil War and Salinas's exile to the United States in 1936. Katherine lives in Mexico during the 1937-1938 academic year. In 1939, she marries Brewer Whitmore, a Smith College professor. The affair ends and letters become much more sporadic after 1936 (*Cartas a KW* 14). While the letters occupy much more the private space of Pedro and Katherine than what Salinas calls his external or exterior life, Salinas's attention to both realms can be linked to his theater. His obsession with the intimate reality of himself and Katherine, his intensely personal definitions of the poet, poetry, and freedom, and his sentiments about circumstances outside their closed world echo in his dramatic production.

Salinas mentions his theater twice in the course of his correspondence with Katherine. In December of 1932, he writes of an upcoming four day holiday in Alicante, where he would bring along notes for poetry and his "drama medio hecho" ("half completed play"; *Cartas a KW* 122). This may have been the never found *La cama de matrimonio* (*The Marriage Bed*), mentioned to Guillén in 1930 and also referred to in a letter to Margarita in 1915 (PS/JG *Correspondencia* 108, Salinas de Marichal, "Tradición y modernidad..." 3) or perhaps his first play, *El director*, completed in 1936. The second allusion appears in a letter dated July 21, 1941, written from Berkeley, a few days after Salinas attends a production of the Ice Follies. Entranced by the skaters, Salinas is disappointed by the trivialization of the themes staged, common imitations of operetta or vaudeville (*Cartas a KW* 366). He playfully proposes a tragedy on ice in which he will explore the souls of the

skaters:

> ... bellísimo el patinar. ¡O seres nuevos! Qué liberación de la pesadez, de la gravedad. Es otro mundo, que el *pisado*. Ni mujeres ni hombres. Raza nueva. Tampoco ángeles o sílfides... se me empezó a ocurrir una obra nueva, creo. Un drama para patinadores... Un *Hamlet* para patines, ésa es mi idea. Porque no hay duda de que seres que se mueven en patines tienen pasiones y almas distintas. Voy a explorar las almas patinadoras, a escribir el primer drama sobre el hielo. (*Cartas a KW* 366)

> ...very beautiful skating. Oh new beings! What freedom from weight, from gravity. It is a world different from the treaded one. Neither women nor men. A new race. Nor angels or sylphs... A new work began to occur to me, I think. A play for skaters.... A *Hamlet* for skates, that is my idea. Because there is no doubt that beings that move on skates have different passions and souls. I will explore skater souls, and will write the first play on ice.

This play did not appear, nor do notes for this project appear among his collected papers.

Repeatedly, Salinas writes to Katherine that loving and being loved by her transports him to a higher, transcendent space. These sentiments will echo in the dialogues and situations of his plays as poet characters seek to elevate others out of ordinary or constricting circumstances. Conceiving his exalted postion in terms of a variety of lofty signs such as birds, wings, flight, and clouds, Salinas emphasizes that existence in this high domain is intrinsic to his self-definition as a poet and to the meaning of poetry for him. Passages from the letters of late 1932 and 1933, during the first months after Katherine's departure from Spain, are especially explicit outpourings of the poet's sense of soaring and salvation. In December of 1932, the poet writes that he has ascended to a place above earthly ground, to a kind of airscape of promise and happiness:

Tú eres mi *anti-tierra*. La elevadora, la que me lleva suspendido, como en alas, por encima del suelo descarnado, óleo, del paisaje, y me das la impresión de que yo no pertenezco a *esto*—frío, pasado, gris—sino a *aquello*—fe, porvenir, alegría (*Cartas a KW* 109)

You are my *anti-ground*. The elevator, that which carries me suspended, as if on wings, above the bare ground, an oil, a landscape, and you give me the impression that I do not belong to *this*—cold, past, gray—but to *that*—faith, future, happiness.

In a letter of January of 1933, he conveys his sense of transcendence in this occupation of a higher realm, a place of refuge that comes to define his being:

Tengo la impresión de trasponer, de traspasar, de haber salvado una resistencia del mundo, ¿comprendes? De haber atravesado una capa, una zona más del mundo. .... Te repito que tu amor me ha ascendido, me ha elevado. ¿De qué? No es de algo, a algo. No es con un fin. Es puramente de ser. Mi ser es más alto, ahora. Todo más alto. Y se ha intensificado todo en esa altura. (*Cartas a KW* 137)

I have the impression of changing place, crossing over, of having endured a resistance of the world, do you understand? Of having passed through a layer, another zone of the world. .... I repeat to you that your love has uplifted me, has elevated me. From what? It is not from something or to something. It is not with an end. It is purely of being. My being is higher now. Everything higher. And everything has intensified in that height.

A few weeks later, in February of 1933, Salinas describes himself and his poetry more elaborately in terms of his sense of elevation. Lamenting the veracity in Ralph Waldo Emerson's statement "It takes a great deal of elevation of thought to produce a very little elevation of life," he marvels at how naturally and effortlessly Katherine's love has transported him a to place of ascendence (*Cartas a KW* 154). He has always felt set apart from others in his "afán de elevación" 'urge for elevation', and he struggles with tensions between acceptance of the commonplace and aspiration to higher spiritual reality:

> Me han gustado siempre todas las cosas *ascencionales, upwards,* las torres, los surtidores, los árboles altos y puntiagudos, el cántico, la flecha. Todo lo que no se resigna a un nivel, lo que rompe el módulo medio, como El Greco. Pero hay otra ley de la gravedad no ya física, sino espiritual. La que no me deja ir hacia arriba, elevarnos, la que nos recuerda a cada momento nuestro *carácter* de ser *común*, igual que todos, ordinarios, de serie. Nos resignamos a ella en la mayoría de los momentos de la vida al comprarnos zapatos *ready-made*, al ser ciudadanos obedientes del Estado, etc. Pero no hay alma noble y viva que no haya soñado en la excepción a la ley de la gravedad, en la *elevación*. Eso ha sido uno de mis tormentos en mi vida. Te confieso, Katherine, que desde niño he sido *un disconforme con el nivel*. (*Cartas a KW* 154-55)

> I have always liked all *rising* things, *upwards,* towers, fountains, sharp-pointed trees, the canticle, the arrow. Everything that does not resign itself to one level, that which breaks the common medium, like El Greco. But there is another law of gravity not now physical, but spiritual. That which does not allow me to move upward, to elevate ourselves, reminding us at every moment of our *character* of being *ordinary*, the same as everybody else, ordinary, standard. We resign ourselves to this in the majority of moments in life when we buy *ready-made* shoes, when we are obedient citizens of the State, etc. But there is not a noble and alive soul that has not dreamed of an exception to the law of gravity, who has not dreamed of *elevation*. That has been one of the torments of my life. I confess to you, Katherine, that since I was a child I have been *at odds with the standard*.

Though Salinas is still conscious of the conditions limiting their contact, he experiences that Katherine's love has made possible an easy leap out of the ordinary. He indicates the poet's role to produce, in crucial combination with the inspiration of his beloved, the vehicle for their transcendence to a higher realm. Salinas's comparison of his previous poetry to his new creation suggests the increasing driving force of the poet and prefigures a definition for the poet characters of Salinas's plays, whom he casts as navigators of everyday reality toward redemptive spiritual unity with others:

...Mi poesía antes, jugaba a aceptar y no aceptar el nivel, a escaparse a ratos y a conformarse otros con las cosas de la tierra como son. Había *distracciones, dudas*. Pero el libro nuestro, Katherine, es el gran *salto* hacia arriba, en la *unidad* absoluta, de atmósfera, de nivel, es mi poesía *en elevación*, en tu amor.) Vivimos ahora, Katherine, como podemos, transaccionalmente, provisionalmente, separados, ausentes. Pero en otra *zona*, Katherine, de la vida. Muchos ratos, muchas horas, seguimos viviendo en el nivel de todos, donde antes, sí, porque es preciso, pero en el alma llevamos la conciencia y la alegría de nuestro poder de elevación, de los momentos maravillosos, *de que es posible, de que existe la vida en elevacion*, de que los dos nos la damos, nos la hemos dado y daremos. (*Cartas a KW* 155-56)

...My poetry before, played with accepting and not accepting the standard, escaping at times and conforming at others to things on earth as they are. There were *distractions, doubts*. But this book of ours, Katherine, is the great *leap* toward above, in absolute *unity*, from the atmosphere, from the standard, it is my poetry *in elevation*, in your love.) We live now, Katherine, as we can, transactionally, provisionally, separated, absent. But in another *zone*, Katherine, of life. Many times, many hours, we continue living on the level of others, like before, yes, because it is necessary, but in our souls we carry the consciousness and happiness of our power of elevation, of the marvellous moments *of what is possible, of what exists in life in elevation*, of what the two of us give of ourselves to it, what we have given of ourselves to it, and what we will give.

In March of 1933, Salinas sends to Katherine the book *The Beauty of Flight* by Manfred Curry, published in 1932. The fantasies he entertains based on the book's aerial photographs and cloud images show his early fascination with modern invention, as well as the poet's notion of a higher reality entwined with a sense of freedom and redemption. He writes that when he thinks about Katherine, when he liberates his fantasies for these representations, he liberates himself and he saves himself (*Cartas a KW* 185-86). Salinas understands poetic activity and the feeling of emancipation to grasp life in the broadest way. Emancipation means a sense of totality, of an enormous, all-encompassing unity. In many of the letters, Salinas sends to Katherine first versions of the poems that were to become part of his trilogy of love poems. After the publication of the first volume of love poetry, *La voz a ti debida* (*My Voice Owed to You*), and the grand critical acclaim it receives, Salinas's expression of delight in occupying a high place reveals that poetic creation carries into every dimension of his existence. Propelled by the love of Katherine, Salinas encounters a profound oneness:

> Por ti he sentido lo que hay de eternidad, de inmortal. De salvado ya, en mi vida, y lo que hay de fugaz, de arriesgado, de perecedero. Todo lo *revisado*, a tu luz. Mis sentimientos y afectos familiares, mis amigos, mi profesión, y sobre todo yo, yo me he *revisado*, me he examinado, como nunca. (*Cartas a KW* 260)

> Because of you I have felt what there is of eternity, of immortality. Of now saved, in my life, and of what is fleeting, dared, and perishable. All *reexamined*, in your light. My feelings and my family affections, my friends, my profession, and above all, myself, I have *reexamined* myself, I have examined myself, as never before.

The work of the poet, a comprehensive examination of self and circumstance, is an aspiring toward height also in that it constantly incites him to be ever better and more. Katherine encourages him in precisely the same way that poetry does to be his best self and to be more (*Cartas a KW* 259). The making over of self, the transcendence of time, and the sense of wonder in everyday life are elements that resurface in the characterizations and circumstances of the poet characters of his theater, for example in the veil of illusion placed on Claribel by Florindo in *La fuente del arcángel*, the crossing of conventional temporal restrictions by Julia Riscal and Desiderio Merlín in *Ella y sus fuentes*, and Marú's idealization of the journal and hotel room in *La isla del tesoro*.

Salinas's quest for a higher, transcendent, redemptive space derives in significant measure from his reaction to tragic contemporary events. Another view by him of the poet's place appears in a comparison of his perspective on existence with that of his poet friend Guillén. In a letter dated February 26, 1939, Salinas mourns the loss of Lorca and Antonio Machado and the terrible post civil war circumstances in Spain and France. Salinas marvels at Guillén's ability to withstand being dragged down spiritually and creatively, to keep his work aloof in a positive sense, untainted by present evil and baseness. To Salinas, Guillén, at times seemingly egotistical, distracted, or inhuman, remains intensely focused on his goal of creating "la poesía perfecta y sin sombra" ("pure poetry without shadow"; *Cartas a KW* 341). By contrast, of himself, Salinas writes:

> Y yo me siento, a su lado, tristemente humano, *demasiado humano*, demasiado entregado al sufrir, a la preocupación, a la tragedia. Da gusto, me lo da a mí, sentirle distinto y *superior*. (*Cartas a KW* 340)

> And I feel, next to him, sadly human, *too human*, too given over to suffering, worry, tragedy. It gives pleasure, it pleases me, to feel him different and *superior*.

Guillén is able to build with poetry a well-insulated dwelling in a spiritually superior realm. While Salinas gives voice to this same ideal, he reveals vividly in the letters to Katherine how he feels jeopardizing forces. Intertwined with his insights into the definition of poet, his private reality, and his aspirations are his attitudes toward external pressures, modern events and his experience in exile, topics that would accent the social dimension of his dramatic works.

In the context of the affair with Katherine, he struggles with the dichotomy between yearning and fulfillment, desired reality and attained reality. He views these realms to be tragically separated, and feels that the soul needs to know if what does not exist can exist (*Cartas a KW* 190). The role he ascribes to Katherine in their relationship, that of "ángel tutelar" or guiding angel, foreshadows characterizations of visionary poet characters in his plays.

In February of 1933, a few years before leaving Spain, Salinas writes about the challenges of his employment. Frustrated with having to struggle with three government bureaucracies in the founding of the Universidad Internacional in Santander, Salinas describes himself as a man of action caught in between doing what he is doing and what he does not like to do:

> Me encuentro enredado en un *maremagnum* de obligaciones, de deberes, de responsabilidades, y todas ellas me pesan, me sujetan, sobre todo me dan una gran tristeza. (*Cartas a KW* 176)

> I find myself tangled in a *great sea* of obligations, duties, responsibilities, and all weigh on me, tie me down, and above all give me a great sadness.

Recognizing himself to be the author of his own discontent, he acknowledges that it is he who has taken on the burdens of work. He also describes his dual nature, constantly endeavoring to balance action and contemplation, to reconcile his introspective side with his desire to act in the outside world:

>...al lado de una naturaleza contemplativa, interior, desprendida de las realidades, flotante sobre el tiempo y los hechos, hay otra naturaleza amante de la acción, de las realidades de crear material, de la vida práctica. .... Me gusta *hacer*. Y no por ambición, ni por dinero, por el simple gusto de hacer. Lo grave es que por esta terrible ambivalencia de mi ser, lo activo y lo contemplativo, lo real y lo tras-real, no se combinan bien; se miran como enemigos, sufren la una de la otra, se hacen reproches, luchan en mí, me desgarran. (*Cartas a KW* 201)

>...beside a contemplative, interior nature, detached from realities, floating above time and deeds, there is another nature that loves action and the realities of creating material, of practical life. .... I like *to do*. And not out of ambition, or for money, but for the simple pleasure of doing. The serious thing is that because of this terrible ambivalence in my being, the active and the contemplative, the real and the trans-real, do not combine well; they look at each other like enemies, the one suffers from the other, they reproach each other, they struggle inside me, they tear me apart.

Salinas sees himself a poet and a man of action. Through the years up to his departure from Spain, while his daily work at times serves as his shield and protection from other personal and worldly pressures, he indicates that this world does not allow him to live fully (*Cartas a KW* 240). He emphasizes the notion of life as potential and possibility (*Cartas a KW* 242).

After his arrival in the United States, though the letters become much less frequent given his proximity to Katherine and the eventual end of their affair, Salinas shares many thoughts about existence in the contemporary world. As a poet living in the modern era, Salinas advocates the reestablishment of wonder in everyday life. A memorable letter, unique in that he writes it in English to Katherine, captures clearly Salinas's ideal of encountering marvel in the conventions of modernity, of redefining today's commonplace as fulfillment of yesterday's dream.

With this outlook, the poet remembers the past, alludes to the interplay of tradition and modernity, and laments what contemporary beings have neglected:

> Nevertheless, my theory is that we, modern people, are too inclined to overlook the magic power, the miracolous (sic) reality of many things, that we use as prosaic tools in our ordinary, ever-day (sic) life, just because custom and habit have caused us to loose (sic) our powers of comprehension and appreciation of these wonders. We take for granted too many things, we fail to realize that lots of things around us go far beyond many of the dreams and illusions of a human mind a century ago, that they are really *working-dreams*. (*Cartas a KW* 289)

Lack of wonder can be associated with the complacency of those without a sense of purpose in modern life. Salinas criticizes those people occupied with superficial diversions, who do not give themselves wholeheartedly to anything, whether a dream, a hobby, an individual, or a social ideal (*Cartas a KW* 305). The individual should convert his or her purpose, which is often accompanied by conflict, into a positive sign and a source of inner strength, something Salinas claims to do with his and Katherine's relationship. A concrete exposition of this perspective appears in a letter dated October 27, 1938. Here Salinas rationalizes a failed plan for him and Katherine to meet in New York and finds compensatory delight in three letters he has received from her:

> Así me gustaría que tomáramos siempre las cosas de nuestra vida: aprovechando cada aparente contrariedad o fracaso, como ahora, para convertirlo en un motivo de inteligencia y amor más. (*Cartas a KW* 326)

> In this way I would always like us to accept things in our life: taking advantage of every misfortune and failure, like now, to convert it into one more reason for understanding and love.

This optimistic search for redemption, apparent in the outlook of the poet figures of his plays, also colors many of his comments on world events and his condition of exile.

In his blunt criticism of the wars and world leaders, Salinas the pacifist and humanist stands positively on principles of liberty and humanity. He projects hope while he abhors fascism, condemns the cruelties of the Nazis, the roles of Chamberlain and Mussolini, the abuses of Franco, the treatment of Spanish Civil War refugees by the French on the border of Spain. In the midst of the Spanish Civil War, in a letter dated September 17, 1938 from Wellesley, Salinas makes a distinction between himself and Guillén to underscore his hopeful perspective on Spain. Salinas knows that Guillén also feels profoundly the tragic turns of world events. Admiring his friend's capacity to reach inward and perservere undistracted, he finds Guillén's apparent invulnerablity remarkable but believes him to be profoundly pessimistic about his fellow Spaniards. Salinas is disgusted by the war and repudiates the activities of the French, the English and the Germans, but digs faithfully for some core of humanity in his country (*Cartas a KW* 318). At the same time, Salinas shares Guillén's fundamental confidence in life and mankind, and includes in the letter Guillén's poem "Los amigos," a reflection on the beauty of friendship and the spiritual freedom of those that enjoy it. The poem was published in Guillén's *Cántico* en 1945. Salinas's words about the poem echo in the creation of the poet characters of his plays, who represent a select minority with a special orientation toward spiritual emancipation. Salinas writes to Katherine that the only solution for those who do not decide on open political struggle is to live in a minority, with a group of friends, in the profound sense of the word, human and free, and at leisure to communicate the treasures of the spirit, in order to face the masses vilefied by the Hitlers, Mussolinis or even the Chamberlains of this world (*Cartas a KW* 319-20).

A few weeks later, he lashes out against the Nazis with a view toward future, survival, and redemption:

> Yo creo que mientras exista una Alemania nazi el mundo está deshonrado, y el primer deber de todos es hacerla desaparecer. No sólo por dignidad, sino por espíritu de conservación, porque de otro modo ella nos hará desaparecer a nosotros. (*Cartas a KW* 325)

> I believe that as long as a Nazi Germany exists the world is dishonored, and the first duty of everyone is to make it disappear. Not only for the sake of dignity, but also for a spirit of survival, because if not Germany will make us disappear.

As his fears grow, so does his outrage over the crimes perpetrated against humanity. In the fall of 1939, with sarcasm he refers to fatality numbers to show war to be a safer state than peace, and to the irony of the survival of Czechoslovakia, unaided by England, and the devastation in Poland, aided by England (*Cartas a KW* 350-51). In 1941, he writes that the war is the punishment of humankind for the grand stupidity of world leaders (*Cartas a KW* 366). Grounded in Spanish tradition, in Unamuno and Cervantes, the poet expresses an enlightened comprehension of the dangerous absurdity and narrowmindedness from which he seeks deliverance:

> ¡Qué razón tenía Unamuno al decir que el enemigo nato de Don Quijote no era el bueno y pobre Sancho, sino el bachiller Sansón Carrasco, representante de los intelectuales, los sensatos, los prudentes, los cobardes, los Chamberlaines de siempre! (*Cartas a KW* 336).

> How right Unamuno was when he said that the arch enemy of Don Quixote was not the good and poor Sancho, but rather the bachelor Sanson Carrasco, respresentative of the intellectuals, the sensible, the prudent, the cowards, the ever present Chamberlains!

In the same letter, he alludes to a delicate situation related to offending the people at Wellesley if he were to publish biting views of political allies. Salinas opts for keeping a local peace and again expresses to Katherine the challenges of the poet who seeks to balance practical reason and spirit.

Both in matters of the world at large and in his intimate relationship with Katherine, Salinas the poet correspondent urges freedom of thought and expression and sees dramatic potential. Enric Bou, in his preface to the letters to Katherine, relates Salinas's quest for ideal reality to a tendency on Salinas's part to theatricalize existence and to imagine circumstances in which they find supreme happiness together (*Cartas a KW* 34). Propelled by love, and communicating to Katherine his struggle living a dual life, Salinas describes the poet's creative ideal:

> Suplir, reemplazar la forma que no veo, el ser que no tengo, por la forma ideal que pienso, por el ser ideal que quiero. (*Cartas a KW* 63)

> To substitiute, to replace the form I do not see, the being I do not have, with the ideal form I am thinking, with the ideal being I want.

Also, Salinas offers a vague augury of his writing plays, and he identifies his life with theater:

> Ahora bien, Katherine, algo sí se puede decir, aunque ya lo sepas: tú, yo, lo nuestro, lo mío, lo tuyo, han sido los temas de esos asuntos de dramas y comedias sin fin que he tejido en la cama. Mi mujer también, Katherine, ha entrado en lo nuestro. (*Cartas a KW* 239)

> Well now, Katherine, yes, something can be said, though you may already know it: you, I, what is ours, mine, yours, have been the themes of those plots for endless dramas and plays that I have woven while in bed. My wife, also, Katherine, has entered into what is ours.

In an affectionate and sweeping passage to Katherine, Salinas's self description summarizes the poet's overwhelming, productive capacity and points to how he would cast the poet characters of his plays:

> Recapitulo las cosas de mi vida, mis esperanzas, mis ilusiones, lo poco hecho y lo mucho por hacer, y me acometen al mismo tiempo un gran amor a la vida, a cumplirme en ella, y un gran temor a no vivir más. (*Cartas a KW* 238-39)

> I sum up the things of my life, my hopes, my illusions, the little done and the great amount to do, and at the same time I am overcome by a great love of life, to fulfill myself in it, and a great fear of not living more.

The poet is driven by optimism, love, and a compulsion to realize life's dreams. These are the same forces that move the poet characters of his dramatic works.

Attention to Salinas the correspondent has exposed views of Salinas the playwright and revealed a complex portrait of Salinas the poet, the man, young man courting Margarita, long time friend of fellow poet Guillén, lover of Katherine, pacificist in a world of conflict, Spaniard in the United States. These complexities are reflected in his dramatic works, which bear evidence of the poet's dream to transcend ordinary reality and harmonize the multiple dimensions of existence. Examination of Salinas the essayist and émigré will amplify the definition of the poet, his relationship with modern circumstance, and his connections to the theater, with highlight on its social significance.

2
Salinas: Poet and Essayist

> El hombre es uno y, además, uno de tantos y uno de muchos, y es el poeta el que ha de llevar adelante con insigne dificultad este dual destino.
> Salinas, *La responsabilidad del escritor* 142
>
> Man is one, and, in addition, one of so very many, and it is the poet who must carry forward with notable difficulty this dual destiny.

SALINAS CALLS HIMSELF "THE defender" in his role as an essayist. He is critical of commonplaces of his day, and defends humanism emphatically (Guillén *Reality...* xx). Guillén consequently speaks of Salinas's tendency toward a profound sense of unity with his fellow men. Salinas's portrayal in his dramatic works of poet characters in quests for harmonious, emancipatory alliances reflects his assimilation of a broad spectrum of intellectual and artistic currents flowing especially from Spanish and European sources. In his numerous essays devoted to Hispanic literature and aspects of modern life and communication, Salinas demonstrates explicitly a firm grounding in his native tradition while he searches for its universal nature. Not plagued by a narrow nationalism, yet deeply rooted in Spanish cultural tradition, he seeks to illuminate the unity and the totality of an artistic process or production. In "Pedro Salinas y los valores de la literatura hispánica" ("Pedro Salinas and the Values of Hispanic Literature"), the introductory essay to Salinas's collection *Ensayos de literatura hispánica (Del Cantar de Mío Cid a García Lorca),* Juan Marichal emphasizes Salinas's constant preoccupation not only with visions of human values through the ages, but also with how these representations inform the contemporary orientation toward existence:

> Funciones inseparables que llevan al escritor español, para poder estimar adecuadamente su patrimonio literario y para saber enlazarlo con las necesidades vitales contemporáneas, a trascender los límites de su cultura nacional y a absorber el espíritu de nuestro tiempo. (*Ensayos* 10)

> Inseparable functions that lead the Spanish writer to be able to appreciate adequately his literary heritage and to know how to link it with vital contemporary necessities, to transcend the limits of his national culture and to absorb the spirit of our time.

Salinas's essays show a rich appreciation of contemporary and classical Spanish writers and provide keen insight into the processes of literary creation and aspects of modernity. Critical studies of Salinas's essays have probed especially the relationship between his poetics and his poetry (Crispin 33ff; Costa Viva; Debicki, "Estudios..."; Dehennin, Díez de Revenga, Feal Deibe, Juan Marichal, Scarano, Zubizarreta) and traced his affinities with Ortega y Gassett (Devlin, Harvard, Silver, Soufas), the Generation of 98 (Pozuelo Yvancos), Unamuno and Eliot (Sotelo Vázquez), and classical and Spanish traditions (Escartín Gual). They have also investigated his evolution as a critic and explored to some extent his views of modernity and the responsibilities of the poet as they appear in his literary production (Ciplijauskaité; Debicki, "La obra crítica..."; Di Pinto; Rodríguez Monegal, Rotger Salas).

A look at Salinas's essays, with a focus on his conception of the powers and responsibilities of the poet and the relationships between the poet, modern life, language, and theater, will illuminate Salinas's own theater. In his key critical studies of poets and their output, *Mundo real y mundo póetico* (*Real World and Poetic World*), *Reality and the Poet in Spanish Poetry, Jorge Manrique o tradición y originalidad* (*Jorge Manrique or Tradition and Originality*), and *La poesía de Rubén Darío* (*The Poetry of Rubén Darío*), Salinas underscores the interplay of exterior reality and inner psychic reality in the process of creation and he defines repeatedly the special capacity of the poet as a visionary. In the essays of *El defensor* (*The Defender*) and *La responsabilidad del escritor* (*The Responsibility of the Writer*), Salinas again sets forth the unique powers of the poet and emphasizes special links between modernity, modes of expression, and the medium of drama. His essays on twentieth century Spanish literary production and the theater of a number of his contemporaries stress the value he places on spiritual and lyrical elements and reveal his views about the social, historical, and political functions of the genre of drama. With the exception of Salinas's early lecture *Mundo real y mundo poético*, his essays are contemporaneous with his theater, and the topics to which he pays close attention clearly make their way into his dramaturgy. Salinas the essayist articulates well his thoughts on three broad and interconnected themes: poets and their vision; modernity, communication and the theater; and Spanish playwrights and the construction of reality. Salinas the dramatist gives additional voice to these themes in his dramatic works. A review of Salinas's key studies will mark connections to his theater and provide grounding for examination of his plays.

POETS AND THEIR VISION OF REALITY
IN SALINAS'S STUDIES OF POETS AND POETRY

Mundo real y mundo portico and *Reality and the Poet in Spanish Literature*

Salinas's lecture *Mundo real y mundo poético*, first delivered in 1930 in Madrid and other cities in Spain and in 1933 in Barcelona, and first published in a critical edition by Christopher Maurer in 1996, prefigures his *Reality and the Poet in Spanish Literature* and offers one of his earliest formal reflections on the role of the poet and on the poetic and real worlds the poet bridges in order to create a new reality. Amidst the fluidity of Salinas's notions of "poetic world" and "real world" appears a definition of the poet as a transporter of others out of their concrete, everyday spheres into strange territory, into a new and mysterious system of relationships. With a refined irony, Salinas employs negative terminology to characterize the disquieting activity of poet. He writes that poets are suspicious beings, that first and foremost a poet is a vagrant, unreliable and distracted, in a perpetual state of openness and change and therefore disposed to the possibilities of creative activity:

> Un poeta ante todo es un vago. Así debe ser. El estado de vacancia, de vagancia, de estar vacante y vagante, es decir a la disposición entera y total de la fuerza poética, es indispensable para el gran poeta. (*Mundo real*... 32).

> The poet above all is a vagrant. He must be so. The state of vacancy, of vagrancy, of being unoccupied and wandering, that is to say, at the full and total disposition of poetic power, is indispensable for the great poet.

The poet, untrustworthy and dangerous, can be like a traitor who enters surreptitiously the domain of others, interrupts the complacency of those comfortable with their immediate reality, and kidnaps or tempts them to leave the familiar behind (*Mundo real*...38-39). Salinas carries this definition into the dramatic works with an emphasis on redemption facilitated by the poet. Obvious examples of poet characters engaged in such activity are conspirator Judit of *Judit y el tirano* who hides in the chambers of the tyrant and navigates his transformation, and the startling Alvaro of *"La Estratoesfera"* who lifts Felipa out of a disturbing past.

Salinas demonstrates a keen consciousness about the world of the twentieth century and the extraordinary potential into which the poet can tap in contemporary times. In the discussion of the relationship between the psychic world of the poet and what Salinas calls the real or exterior world, there are indications of the poet's preoccupation with the social dimension and with the drama and mystery of existence to be probed by the poet. Realities in the modern world are multidimensional and complex, and poetry can be discovered everywhere:

> La realidad de hoy es multilateral. Se desarrolla en profundidades insospechadas. No es ya la cara de las cosas, es lo mismo la cara que

el revés. La realidad de un objeto se ve hoy, es cierto en su superficie, pero además se escudriña en su composición química. Y no es ya lo real, lo evidente, lo claro, lo resuelto, todo lo contrario. La realidad de hoy está henchida de misterio y de dramatismo. La realidad de hoy es angustiosamente problemática. (*Mundo real...* 72)

The reality of today is many sided. It develops into unsuspected profundities. It is no longer the face of things, the face is the same thing as its reverse. The reality of an object is seen today, it is certain on its surface, but in addition it is scrutinized in its chemical composition. And it is no longer the real thing, evident, clear, resolved, but quite the contrary. The reality of today is bulging with mystery and dramaticism. The reality of today is distressingly problematic.

Salinas's first play, *El director*, echoes the words of his early treatise. He demonstrates this preoccupation with exploring the enigmatic faces of reality through his creation of a divinity figure with dual countenances who tries to enlighten the typist and ultimately leads her toward a painful discovery about his identity:

Pero créame usted, hija mía, todo, todo necesita su revés, lo tiene, lo lleva, no puede vivir sin él, aunque lo ignore o le pese. (*Teatro completo* 354)

But believe me, my child, everything, everything needs its reverse, it has it, it carries it, it cannot live without it, even though it may ignore it or regret it.

The essay asserts that unlike the poetry of poets of the past like Garcilaso de la Vega or Fray Luis de León who could escape external, worldly forces completely, the poetry of today must face the real world in all its complexity. Both impressive and oppressive, the inventions of modernity impact the poet. The poet must manage to dwell in both ordinary and poetic reality. When imagination and creative spirit—what Salinas calls the poetic world— come into contact with the real world, the modern poet must find a way to navigate the two realms in dynamic tension:

> ...aunque el poeta ande por las calles entre escaparates, en las imperiales de los tranvías, con su cédula personal en el bolsillo, es siempre un pasajero, está de paso. Y en cuanto se aparte la mirada un momento, se verá que ya no está a nuestro lado, que la policía o los ángeles lo arrebataron a su destino, a su órbita, a girar en el mundo distinto, a estar en las nubes. (*Mundo real*... 78)

> ...although the poet may travel on streets past shop windows, in the upper decks of streetcars, with identity card in his pocket, he is always a traveller, he is passing through. And as soon as one looks away for a moment, one will see he is no longer at our side, that the police or the angels carried him off to his destiny, to his orbit, to turn in a different world, to be in the clouds.

The appearance and disappearance of poet characters such as Melisa and Julia in Salinas's plays *El precio* and *Ella y sus fuentes* dramatize Salinas's conception of the poet's travels through real and poetic worlds. For a brief time they visit and transform the existence of others, but soon return to the realms they inhabit beyond everyday reality.

Teacher-poet Salinas expanded in *Reality and the Poet in Spanish Poetry* (1940) the treatment of Spanish poets he had begun in *Mundo real y mundo poético*. In this book, the published version of the lectures he had delivered at Johns Hopkins University in 1937, he developed how in different epochs poets forged a new relationship between poetry and reality. The poet's purpose is to create a new reality within an old reality of an already made world of "things, society, beings, all of life from a blade of grass to a moral doctrine elaborated over centuries (*Reality and the Poet* 3)." Salinas identifies six different attitudes and their exemplary models in his analysis of the connection between the inner spiritual world of the poet and the material world surrounding him: 1) the reproduction of reality by the anonymous composers of *The Poem of the Cid* and the medieval ballad of Alora, 2) the acceptance of reality by Jorge Manrique and Calderón de la Barca, 3) the idealization of reality by Garcilaso de la Vega, 4) the escape from reality by Fray Luis de León and San Juan de la Cruz, 5) the exaltation of reality by Luis de Góngora, and 6) the revolt against reality by romantic poet José de Espronceda. In each case, Salinas studies the special creative process by which the poet perceives reality, absorbs it, and produces something new. Salinas considers the six perspectives to be different and beautiful solutions to "that insuperable problem of the two worlds, the poetic and the real (*Reality and the Poet* 164)." For Salinas, the work of the poet is very serious, and to stress the social dimension of poetic action, he writes that the poet, "far from remaining outside the world, ... lives at its very center (*Reality and the Poet* 164)."

In a sense, through the characters of his fourteen plays, Salinas creates a kaleidoscope of the poetic perspectives he has identified in a historical trajectory in *Reality and the Poet*. Melisa of *El precio*, who has stepped into life off the pages of a book, suggests Salinas's first category of reproduction of reality. A living escapee of the poetic imagination of Jáuregui, she is a pure fusion of poetry and reality. In *El director*, the divinity figure projects Salinas's second category, acceptance of reality, with its fleeting qualities, deceptions, and dream-like adventures that end in the typist's forced confrontation with the nature of the Director. The scientist Abel Levya of *Caín o una gloria científica*, a kind of inverted Renaissance spirit, reflects the third perspective Salinas identifies in poet Garcilaso: the idealization of reality. Salinas writes that "Garcilaso sacrificed without hesitancy the invisible man, his secret, inner person to the visible man, the man of the world and duty (*Reality and the Poet* 74)." For the sake of the perfection and goodness of nature, Abel sacrifices the visible man who will be forced to destroy mankind. In *Los santos* appears a manifestation of the fourth attitude, escape from reality. Through the supernatural saint images, Salinas constructs a kind of mystical escape from the everyday reality weighing on their counterparts, the prisoners awaiting death. Salinas's fifth perspective, the exaltation of reality, is seen in Marú of *La isla del tesoro* and Florindo of *La fuente del arcángel*. Marú undertakes the exaltation of material reality by converting a hotel into a treasure island, and Florindo does so by transforming Claribel into a Byzantine empress who in turn connects with a complex deity icon. Salinas's sixth category, revolt against reality, appears in *Judit y el tirano* and *Sobre seguro*. Here poet characters lead this revolt, but different from the romantic stance that Salinas discusses in the work of Espronceda, the death and strong opposition to external pressures do not suggest total despair. This revolt against reality and the other attitudes from *Reality and the Poet*. seen in the plays point to two comprehensive factors that figure into the perspective of the poet-dramatist: a fundamental optimism and the recognition of the need for sacrifice.

A fundamental optimism defines the poet-playwright's attitude toward reality. Whether the characters seem to reproduce, accept, idealize, escape, exalt, or revolt against reality in Salinas's dramatizations of the quest for liberation and salvation, the transformations that take place enhance appreciation of the nature of the poet by fellow characters. These characters increase their affinity with the poet and the poet's world and acquire a new view of self and situation. Whether the plays conclude with happy or unhappy outcome, the call of the poet is energizing. Even in the face of overwhelming forces of circumstance, Salinas upholds the potential of the poetic voice. This optimism, however, hardly means that the transformation is easy. Another essential aspect of the poet's attitude toward reality is the poet's embrace of the necessity of sacrifice. While Salinas continuously lauds the spiritual effort of the poet, he recognizes that the poet may have to yield to unrelenting pressures in the process of salvation and liberation. The poet thus stands a hero because success may come dear.

In the conclusion to his discussion of the poetic attitude of revolt against reality in *Reality and the Poet,* Salinas links this romantic position with the plight of modern man:

> Modern man, this new man, is man divided, in the highest degree.

And he will continue to live desperately in a world which is his because he is born into it, but which is not his, since he cannot adapt to what he feels within him. The two worlds are not only different but even hostile. The real world destroys the poetic world and denies it all possibility of expression. And only the grandeur that poetry still retains at this stage of the human spirit is the grandeur of the complaint, the desperate cry, the magnificent revolt of the poetic world, of human illusion, against the real world. (*Reality and the Poet* 163-64)

Salinas's plays move beyond the response of romantic complaint to dramatize the plight of the poet facing modern reality. The poet often bemoans situations in the exterior world, but the laments do not represent the poet's total disenchantment. Moreover, the poet meets the challenge to bring together disparate worlds via affirming action and liberating sacrifice.

SALINAS'S STUDIES OF JORGE MANRIQUE AND RUBÉN DARÍO
In his two other book-length works on poets and their poetry, *Jorge Manrique o tradición y originalidad* (1947), and *La poesía de Rubén Darío* (1948), and in many of his shorter studies on poets appearing in the two collections *Ensayos de literatura hispánica (Del Cantar de Mío Cid a García Lorca)* and *Literatura española siglo XX*, Salinas continues to seek the essence that defines each poet and the totality of each's work. This "tema vital," or fundamental theme, captures the vision of the poet and binds together the poet's internal reality with external circumstance. Salinas underlines how through this blending emerges an extraordinary creation, a transformation of external reality through the lens of the poet.

In his book on Manrique, for example, after examining the medieval traditions of love, death, fortune, and rejection of worldliness that filter into the poet's compositions, Salinas uncovers the poet's exceptional capacity to harmonize this constellation of themes into a humanized, heart-felt elegy with the theme of mortality its axis. From philosophical contemplation of the inescapability of death and the brevity of life to a concrete placement of the deceased in his time and his comparison with other great figures of history, the poet delivers the deceased into a deeply personal space. Surrounded by wife, children, brothers, and servants, Don Rodrigo gives his soul to the Almighty, and dies in deep, serene peace. Salinas both appreciates the erudition and foundation in tradition underlying the construction of the elegy and applauds the simplicity and realism of the poet's intensely personal song of his father's demise. Salinas's identification with the humanity of the poem, as well as his praise of the melding of literary and cultural heritage, historical, social, and personal circumstance and an essential lyricism and optimism, resounds through the poet voices of his own dramatic works. In his work on Manrique, Salinas writes that tradition is the poet's natural habitat and a force that enables a full freedom to move ahead (*Jorge Manrique o Tradición y originalidad* 115). Chapter Seven of the present study makes this perspective the springboard to examine in Salinas's dramatic works the poet's bridging of tradition and modernity and to show how the roots of tradition are interwoven with the poet's creative outlook on surrounding circumstances.

Salinas's study of Rubén Darío's navigation of inner and external domains centers on the modernist poet's singular expression of the erotic, and also finds in Darío's work two important subthemes: his social concerns and his attention to art, poetry, and the poet. It is clear that the influence of Rubén Darío upon Salinas is profound. Noting this influence in Salinas's poetry, Feal Deibe writes after receiving this initial modernist injection, Salinas soon finds his own voice in a poetry with an intimate and colloquial tone, often based on the elements of everyday life (*Poesía y narrativa*...300). Scarano indicates that Salinas has imbibed the influence of Rubén Darío in that he demonstrates explicitly a consciousness about his aesthetics and writes often about his art and artistic production, and especially about the role of the poet and poetry (97, 99). What Salinas the essayist has chosen to highlight in the work of Rubén Darío points directly to the key converging elements in his own work: the role of love, social consciousness, and preoccupation with the function of poetry and the definition of the poet. While Salinas touches Darío's biographical and conceptual bases in his discussion of the impact of these vital themes, he holds primary the poet's creative process, the profound, ineffable course that leads to production:

> El tema no es aquello que el artista quiere reflexivamente, lo que se propone hacer en su obra; es lo que hace, es lo que se suma al propósito, en el proceso de su ejecución. Es lo puesto—por inexplicable agencia—sobre lo propuesto. (*La poesía de Rubén Darío* 50)

> The theme is not that which the artist wants reflexively, what he proposes to do in his work; it is what he does, it is what is joined to the purpose, in the process of its fulfillment. It is what is placed—through inexplicable agency—upon what is proposed.

This emphasis on the poet's doing underlines the role of poet in action, the poet as maker, the position Salinas constructs for the poet characters of his dramatic works.

As in his work on Manrique, Salinas analyzes the poet's powerful fusion of tradition and modernity, this time showing his own affinities with the currents of symbolism and modernism. Salinas sees Darío's use of mythology as a means to extend the imagery of love beyond more immediate or material forms to a limitless world of metaphor, "un mundo de traslación" (*La poesía de Rubén Darío* 86). For Salinas, Darío's creative passage through a wealth of amorous adventures and sensibilities in the realms of deities and imaginary figures captures best the representation of desire (*La poesía de Rubén Darío* 89). With echoes of the modernist exotic, Salinas's weaving of the themes of love and desire with mythological figures, is apparent, for example, in his plays *La fuente del arcángel* and *La Cabeza de Medusa*.

Widening the orbit of the vital theme of love, Salinas explores two significant subthemes of Darío that link importantly with Salinas's own theater: social poetry and poetry about the function of poetry and the definition of the poet. Salinas describes social poetry as derived from the poet's sense of belonging to an organized community or society, where his acts always appear in relation to other people (*La poesía de Rubén Darío* 215). Differentiating historical, national, political, and humanitarian modes of social poetry, he points to temporal, spacial, and conceptual dimensions that delineate the first three modes, and to the broader scope of the humanitarian mode:

> ...el caso de que el sentimiento de comunidad sea vivido por el poeta, sin limitación alguna; no por referencia a tal o cual sector de la sociedad de los hombres, sino a toda ella, a los hombres del universo. Es el modo humanitario. (*La poesía de Rubén Darío* 216)

> ...the case of the feeling of community that is lived by the poet, without any limitation; nor by reference to this or that sector of society of people, but rather to all society, to the people of the universe. It is the humanitarian mode.

Salinas's analysis of Darío's social poetry traces the poet's steps beyond the limits of the first three categories: of historical poetry, with its projection toward a collective past, of national poetry, oriented toward particular homelands and territories, and of political poetry, with particular credos. His summary characterization of Darío's work in the broadest terms of the humanitian mode serves well as a label for his own dramatic works:

> Generosidad humana, amor desbordado a todos los prójimos, libertad para la creación de las obras del hombre, disfrute de ellas en común, imperio de la fraternidad, esos son los materiales con que Rubén Darío labraba en su imaginación y a su deseo la ciudad futura. Y ese ideal universal de amor y paz es el que no deja de sonar de poema en poema, como la nota más imaculada de su lírica social, que así viene a ganar un hermosísimo aspecto de monumental unidad. (*La poesía de Rubén Darío* 252)

Human generosity, unbound love for all one's fellow beings, freedom for the creation of the works of man, the shared enjoyment of these works, the empire of brotherhood, those are the materials with which Ruben Darío forged the city of the future, in his imagination and to his desire. And that universal ideal of love and peace is what does not cease to sound from poem to poem, like the most immaculate note of his social poetry, which thus will come to attain a most beautiful appearance of monumental unity.

In his examination of Darío's second subtheme of art, poetry, and the poet, Salinas focuses on tensions inherent to a poet's self-definition and process of creation. In pursuit of sincerity, of authentic expression of self as a man and a poet, the poet stands in an equivocal position, caught between everyday existence and search for the ideal, a position similar to that occupied by poet characters of Salinas's plays. The poet is at once a blind dreamer and a visionary capable of extraordinary spiritual depth. Salinas notes a rebellion against Nineteenth Century positivist tendencies in Darío's quest via art for salvation from the bitterness and pain of life:

> Es así el Arte, no por propósito didáctico ni sumisión a ninguna doctrina moral, sino por efecto de su inmanente pureza, de su inmaculada perfección, el gran enemigo y develador de los vicios, el campeón del bien. (*La poesía de Rubén Darío* 264).

> Thus is Art, not by didactic purpose nor by submission to any moral doctrine, but by the effect of its inherent purity, of its immaculate perfection, great enemy and unveiler of vices, champion of the good.

Cognizant of the accompanying disorientation, solitude, and suffering, as well as the possible glory in artistic making, the poet maintains strong faith in the process of creation.

Salinas appreciates in Darío's definition of the poet the fusion of disparate French influences. On the one hand, Darío shares Victor Hugo's conception of the poet's role in society as a dreamer, a prophet with divine inspiration, with a mission oriented toward a wide world, toward multitudes on the outside (*La poesía de Rubén Darío* 272-73). On the other hand, Darío reflects the more exclusive, elitist orientation of "l'art pour l'art" (art for art's sake), where the poet is removed from base publics, and is dedicated to artifice, to the perfection of the artistic product for its own sake (*La poesía de Rubén Darío* 273-74). Ultimately, the poet is a hero in sweeping terms. With the widest possible social mandate, the poet is a hero on a mission for all times and places:

> Personaje de todas las tierras, y los tiempos, volando con las dos alas de la Armonía y la Eternidad. (*La poesía de Rubén Darío* 276)

> Figure of all lands, and times, flying with the two wings of Harmony and Eternity.

Yet perceived as detached from social spheres in the modern sense, the poet is also like a mythological, superhuman hero on divinely inspired creative flight:

> La poesía es fuerza elemental, energía puesta en un hombre, pero que le eleva al través de la empresa mítica, la doma del caballo inmortal, a momentánea categoría de semidios, que hiende el azur simbólico, el cielo del arte, yendo cada vez más lejos en su vuelo. (*La poesía de Rubén Darío* 276-77)

> Poetry is elemental force, energy placed in a man, but that elevates him to cross the mythical enterprise, the taming of the inmortal horse, to the momentary category of demigod, who makes his way through the symbolic blue, the sky of art, going ever farther away in his flight.

To conclude the book, Salinas draws together the vital themes of Darío's work by emphasizing the joining in Darío's soul of erotic desire, peace, and eternity (*La poesía de Rubén Darío* 286). The poet protagonists of Salinas's dramatic works intertwine quests for love, peace, and transcendence as depicted in the analysis of Darío.

SALINAS'S ESSAYS ON JORGE CARRERA ANDRADE AND FEDERICO GARCÍA LORCA

In addition to his longer studies, *Mundo real y mundo póetico*, *Reality and the Poet in Spanish Poetry*, *Jorge Manrique o tradición y originalidad*, and *La poesía de Rubén Darío*, many of Salinas's shorter essays devote attention to how particular poets apprehend reality with exceptional vision and how they relate to the social circumstance. Two salient examples are his studies of Jorge Carrera Andrade and Federico García Lorca. What he finds central to the works of these writers resonates in his own theater in his portrayals of the main characters and their relationships to surroundings.

"Registro de Jorge Carrera Andrade" ("Jorge Carrera Andrade's Register") is one of Salinas's most explicit treatises on the poetics of seeing. Here he links the faculties of sight and metaphor-making with the function of the poet and the poet's relationship with the surrounding world. Poets must be hunters who journey, seek, and apprehend with their eyes:

> La función del poeta habrá de ser la caza de cosas, de objetos, pertenecientes a esa enorme fauna de la presencia que puebla la corteza del mundo y del tiempo.... Ojos viajeros, que den ardorosas batidas por todos los rincones de nuestra selva terrenal, en busca de las cosas. (*Ensayos de la literatura hispánica* 360)

> The function of the poet must be the hunting of things, of objects, belonging to that enormous fauna of the presence that inhabits the earth's surface and time.... Travelling eyes, that should comb ardently throughout the reaches of our earthly jungle, in search of things.

Salinas affirms that poetry is "largo incesante viajar de la vista" (a long,

incessant travelling of sight), and lauds the popular refrain "Vivir para ver" (Living to see) (*Ensayos de la literatura hispánica* 360). He then develops a brief discussion of the truth claim of poetry, and drawing from French symbolist tradition, Salinas refers to Mallarmé's distinctions between seeing or concrete observation and imagining or envisioning. Salinas claims that Carrera Andrade does not know how to see because he knows how to envision, and deems the poet a master of the metaphor for this capacity to see beyond basic materiality (*Ensayos de la literatura hispánica* 362):

> La metáfora empieza donde "el ojo" termina de ver y la imaginación comienza a visionar. (*Ensayos de la literatura hispánica* 362)
>
> The metaphor begins where "the eye" stops seeing and the imagination begins to envision.

Salinas connects the metaphor of the window in the poetry of Carrera Andrade with the power of sight. A conduit from the interior to the exterior and vice versa, a window, like a poet endowed with special vision, serves to illuminate and ventilate, a kind of eye with magical powers to frame views of natural beauty and delineate fragments of the world. Playwright Salinas communicates these same conceptions in his plays through an extensive construction of references to seeing, subject of Chapter Six of the present study.

In "García Lorca y la cultura de la muerte" ("García Lorca and the Culture of Death"), repeating his definition of the work of a poet as an intent to conceptualize humankind, life, and the world, Salinas finds García Lorca's vision of existence to be grounded in the theme of death (*Ensayos de la literatura hispánica* 371). Salinas sees in Lorca's consciousness of death a profound grasp and affirmation of life. Salinas's explanation in this essay of his own view of the culture of death sheds light on his theater. According to Salinas, humans lack true understanding of themselves if they do not integrate the presence of death into life. An existence in which the notion of death is suppressed lacks the

profundity and essence which give life its intensity and dramatic tone:

> Lo que yo entiendo por la cultura de la muerte es una concepción del hombre y su existencia terrenal en que la conciencia de la muerte actúa como signo positivo, es estímulo, acicate al vivir y a la accion y permite entender el sentido total y pleno de la vida. Dentro de semejante concepción, el ser humano se afirmaría no solo en los actos de su vida, sino en el acto de su muerte. (*Ensayos de la literatura hispánica* 375)

> What I understand by the culture of death is a conception of man and his earthly existence in which death functions as a positive sign; it is a stimulus, a spur to living and action and it permits understanding the whole and full sense of life. Within such a conception, the human being would affirm himself not only in the acts of his life, but also in the act of his death.

Chapter Four of the present study will show that Salinas's plays may be classified into two principal categories based on their happy or tragic outcomes. In both variations, Salinas confirms the poet's mission, and even in the most tragic conclusions, death appears in the context of an optimistic affirmation of the poet's enterprise in the modern world.

MODERNITY, COMMUNICATION, AND THEATER:
EL DEFENSOR AND *LA RESPONSABILIDAD DEL ESCRITOR*
In the essays of *El defensor* and *La responsabilidad del escritor*, while Salinas repeats views from his studies on poets and their vision of reality by continuing to define the select position of the poet, he places more emphasis on the social function of the poet. Three key essays, "La gran cabeza de turco o la minoría literaria," ("The Great Head of the Turk or the Literary Minority") "Aprecio y defensa del lenguaje" ("In Appreciation and Defense of Language"), and "Los poderes del escritor o las ilusiones perdidas" ("The Powers of the Writer or Lost Illusions"), highlight Salinas's mission for the poet seer and his perspective on the

interrelationships between modern life, language, and the theater. The first two essays were published originally in *El defensor* as "Defensa de la minoría literaria" and "Defensa del lenguaje" and later published in *La responsabilidad del escritor* as "La gran cabeza de turco o la minoría literaria" and "Aprecio y defensa del lenguaje." In "La gran cabeza...," Salinas offers a vivid characterization of the poet as a visionary:

> ...el poeta, el creador *latu sensu*, es equiparado, según tradicional paralelo, con el vidente, ve más largo que los demás, que los prójimos que viven a su lado, en sus años. La distintiva del poeta es estar dotado de una penetración de visión, de una vista espiritual superior. (*La responsabilidad del escritor* 181-82)

> ...the poet, creator in a broad sense, is compared, according to traditional parallel, with the seer; he sees farther than the rest, than those that live at his side, in his time. The distinguishing characteristic of the poet is the being endowed with penetrating vision, with a superior spiritual vision.

Salinas amplifies the term "poet" to include authors of literary works in any genre, whether in verse or prose, in which there is evidence of superior creative capacity. In Salinas's sense, poets, better than all others, can express how they feel: their joys, their sorrows, their aspirations, their souls (*La responsabilidad del escritor* 38). Experiencing profoundly both individual existence and social circumstance, poets struggle to reconcile these two realms that shape identity, to carry forward "este dual destino" (this dual destiny) of human beings who are both one and one among so very many (*La responsabilidad del escritor* 142).

The poet strives to thrive in a literary minority, which Salinas defends as a climate of emancipation, "una atmósfera de libertad" (an atmosphere of freedom; *La responsabilidad del escritor* 179). Salinas's conception of the poet echoes the Orteguian notion of a select minority, set apart from the masses, superior to the majority in that the poet sees his or her possibilities as a unique being. Dedicatedly distant from the commonplace, the poet is a visionary who struggles with individuation and connection, a voyager who travels inward but also moves to become part of a society whose axis is outside the self. Salinas communicates this select status and orientation through the key actors of his dramatic works. Transcending the ordinary, his poet characters endeavor to open the eyes of others to new perspectives.

The poet, according to Salinas, performs the functions of "protector, consolador, antorcha, víctima expiatoria, historiador, tribuno, vidente, civilizador de la humanidad, revelador, conductor de pueblos, liberador, vidente mago" (protector, consoler, torch, expiatory victim, historian, judge, seer, civilizer of humanity, revealer, director of peoples, liberator, and clairvoyant magician; *La responsabilidad del escritor* 235). This expansion by Salinas of Victor Hugo's definition of the poet as "pasteur, juge, prophète, apôtre" (pastor, judge, prophet, apostle) not only describes the poet Hugo but sustains valid application to Salinas himself as well as to the poet characters of Salinas's dramatic works (*La responsabilidad del escritor* 234). It is in these roles that the poet achieves the transformation of some private realm into a public space, that is, the movement of the spiritual into the social, the objectification of something interior. A poet is recognized as such by the unique effect of his words and works (*La responsabilidad del escritor* 218). The spiritual power of the poet, as it translates into one of the above-mentioned roles, thus ideally carries important social force. Salinas places hope in this potential of the poet, and he calls attention to obstacles on the path of meeting modern circumstance.

In his key essay on language, *Aprecio y defensa del lenguaje*, Salinas laments that there is a proclivity in all times, and especially in the modern period, toward shallowness in communication. The way of life that has resulted from the many technological advances of the twentieth century has, paradoxically, stunted linguistic development and has contributed to erosion of the individual's power over language and action. For example, the shortening of time for particular tasks and for travel has become an end in itself. Salinas is unable to see how this acceleration of time, this "psychosis of haste," as he calls it, is at all beneficial to the development of language, which, like any spiritual creation, defies submission to a mechanical timetable (*La responsabilidad del escritor* 62). Salinas also attacks the way in which contemporary society values things above all for their practicality or material worth and that language use has come to reflect this mercenary idolatry. He describes the language of advertising, with its effective twists and turns, its distortions of literary language's metaphors, combined with technical terms and everyday language—all to seduce the consumer. Salinas points out that this indicates that language suffers from no diminution of resources, but that there is great poverty in its end results when all energies are directed toward ultra-efficient consumption. Salinas beckons the poet and the theater to reverse this negative evolution, and in his own plays, most notably *La Bella Durmiente* and *Sobre seguro*, set in the worlds of advertising and insurance, he engages poet figures in struggle with these forces.

The communal, linguistic, and visual dimensions of the theater provide important ground for the poet-creator to operate as a model of social force, to break from solitude, and to inspire others to ascend to consciousness and contemplation of their lives and destinies in spiritual union with him and others:

> El creador individual, el poeta, siente que está cumpliendo su destino en aquel preciso momento de la representación, a través de sus prójimos. Lo escrito en retirada soledad, entonces versos o frases mudas, ahora en alas de la espléndida voz, llena el ámbito de la sala y se divide en tantas realidades psíquicas como seres escuchan... Prodigio es ver la unidad humana del artista multiplicándose instantáneamente ante sus ojos... Sin dejar de ser cada cual lo que es, al contrario, siéndolo más intensamente, todos son uno. Se logra la unanimidad, unidad de las almas. (*La responsabilidad del escritor* 83)

> The individual creator, the poet, feels he is fulfilling his destiny in that precise moment of the performance, through his fellow men. What was written in retired solitude, then mute lines and phrases,

now on the wings of splendid voice, fills the limits of the room and divides into as many psychic realities as beings who are listening... It is a marvel to see the human oneness of the artist multiplying itself instantaneously before his own eyes... Without anyone abandoning who he is, on the contrary, being that more intensely, all are one. A unanimity, a unity of spirits is achieved.

This ideal conception of the function of the theater, of language and dialogue, and the role of the poet appears woven into the design of Salinas's dramatic works, where the poet emerges as key savior within a theater defined as the most effective medium through which to communicate both social virtues and the refinement of conversational language. Justifying Salinas's choice of the title *La responsabilidad del escritor* for this volume, Marichal cites the phrase Salinas uses to locate the difficult place of the poet and the poet's connection to social forces:

Quizá no sea simplificar en demasía mantener que la preocupación central de Salinas en muchos de sus ensayos generales fue delimitar con claridad 'las obligaciones y las responsabilidades del poeta cogido entre la espada y la pared'. (*La responsabilidad del escritor* 11)

Perhaps it may not be simplifying too much to maintain that the central concern of Salinas in many of his general essays was to delineate with clarity the 'obligations and responsibilities of the poet caught in difficult straights.'

Salinas makes the rehabilitation of theater an important part of his policy-remedy for combating the degeneration of peoples' modes of communication and the death of creative capacities connected with it. For Salinas, the ultimate aim of the theater is for individuals to gain full control of their means of expression and thus contribute significantly to the spiritual resources of their society. Salinas believes that education in language usage such as that undertaken in the theater should aspire to the integration of the spontaneity and vitality of the spoken word with the precision of the written word. Dramatic works are peculiarly appropriate for achieving this blending because they are carefully crafted literary productions that imitate conversations:

> El gran dramaturgo usa en su obra el vocabulario mismo de nuestra vida práctica diaria. ¿Pero por qué extraño acontecer esas mismas palabras nos afectan ahora como si vinieran desde arriba, desde una lengua más significante que la nuestra? (*La responsabilidad del escritor* 81)

> The great dramatist uses in his work the very vocabulary of our practical daily lives. But how strange that these same words now affect us as if they had come from above, from a language more significant than our own?

The public can experience through a dramatic work the transformation of the words of everyday life into more highly expressive, more illuminating communication:

> ...llega un instante en que esa misma palabra traspasa su significación ordinaria, entra en una especie de nueva atmósfera, que le reviste de nuevas claridades, y el espectador ya se le representa como otra, henchida de una fuerza reveladora que nunca la conoció. (*La responsabilidad del escritor* 81-82)

> ...a moment arrives in which that same word transcends its ordinary meaning and enters a kind of new atmosphere, that cloaks it in new clarities, and now the spectator sees it as something different, filled with a revealing force that he did not know before.

Theater, in the elevated sense to which Salinas refers, can be the agent of the poet's reinvigoration of ordinary language. By remaining close in its dialogue to everyday conversational style, while infusing this speech with unaccustomed expressive power, theater can utilize all the vitality of living language:

> Recoge el teatro en un solo haz todas las fuerzas expresivas del lenguaje, es su apoteosis. (*La responsabilidad del escritor* 81)

> Theater gathers together in a single stroke all the expressive forces of language; it is its apotheosis.

Salinas dramatizes through his theater the double-edged power of words—their power to deceive and mislead, and thereby to undermine human relationships, and their power to enlighten and to bring about communication in its most positive, life-improving form. A witness to the many tragedies of the twentieth century, Salinas fervently hoped for contemporary man to recover the positive power of words. Doing so, people would not so readily allow themselves to be deceived and trapped into undertaking unfortunate action. In his defense of language, he states this overriding purpose, a purpose that lends structure to his theater and points to its social function:

> Ojalá sea cierto que las gentes han descubierto ya, ¡y a qué costo!, que con las palabras, oídas sin discernimiento, comprendidas a medias, vistas sólo por un lado, se les atrae a la muerte, como atrae al pájaro, por el diestro manejo del espejuelo, el contemporáneo se decidiría, ya de una vez, a cobrar plena conciencia de su idioma a conocerle en sus fondos y delicadezas, para, de ese modo, prevenirse contra todos los embaucadores de mayor o menor cuantía que deseen prevalecerse de su inconciencia idiomática para empujarle a la acción errónea. (*La responsabilidad del escritor* 18)

> Would that it be true that peoples have now discovered—and at what cost!—that words heard without discernment, half understood, seen only from one side, lure them toward death, as the bird is lured through the dextrous handling of a looking glass; that the contemporary person would decide, now once and for all, to gain full con-

sciousness of his language and know its origins and subtleties, in order, thus, to take precautions against the impostors of greater or lesser account who may desire to take advantage of their linguistic incompetence and push them toward erroneous action.

For Salinas, dialogue is the paradigmatic form of language that best enables the individual to go deeper into the self and also reach out toward others. Dialogue can be a metaphor for intellectual life, and the best means of transmission of one's inner life toward comprehension, both by the self and by others. Salinas notably incorporated dialogue into his poetry, a topic probed by Zubizarreta in *Pedro Salinas: El diálogo creador* (241-84). The genre of theater affords a significant development of this power of the dialogue form so valued by Salinas. The inner discourse flows into the more open and natural current of conversation in the drama. The formerly silent thoughts are sounded so that they might approach the ideal that Salinas has set for language: communication and community (*La responsabilidad del escritor* 32). In Salinas's theater, the theme of linkage of individuals becomes charged with multidimensional social significance as characters unite in word and deed and find salvation in their joint pursuit of an extraordinary reality beyond the restrictions of their immediate circumstances. Salinas identifies poet-creator characters as key generators and conduits of the redemptive action.

Ever endeavoring to attain spiritual emancipation of the broader circles circumscribing his or her inner circle and of his or her own circle, the poet is the protagonist of a self-society, liberation-confinement dialectic. The majority reacts to the exceptionality of poets with a kind of resistance or restraint against their emancipatory movement. Salinas proposes that poets can find space inside the radius of the minority, that is, the gifted few, where originality and difference are permitted to flourish, and possibilities for freedom of expression exist. Salinas believes that the minority should transmit its superior, more far-reaching vision to the majority that sees too narrowly. It might save the majority from its "caprichos de actualismo," (whims of contemporaneousness), that is to say, its overpreoccupation with the trivialities of the here and now; the majority's inadequate perspective could be replaced with nobler, more eternal truths (*La responsabilidad del escritor* 183). Poetic liberation, in its most potent and ideal form permeates the collective atmosphere. Emanating from the interior of the creator, it distracts, attracts, and envelops others.

The social arena of Salinas's theater, then, is firmly founded upon the poet's internal artistic and ethical imperative ("su propio 'imperativo interno' artístico y ético"; Maurer, "Sobre 'Joven literatura'...." 308). In other words, Salinas's theater derives from his powerful affirmation of artistic freedom and responsibility. Moreover, this indicates his rejection of trivial *arte social* and ordinary politics. In a lecture about theater he delivered at the University of Madrid, before the appearance of his own dramatic works, Salinas had clearly differentiated between what he considered petty politics and that which aimed at a genuine cultural reformation of society:

> Todo el mundo (arguye) debe 'hacer política, pero política en su sentido más amplio, política de educación, política de capacitación, no política estricta de carácter administrativo, ni política de personas...' (Maurer, "Sobre 'Joven literatura'...." 308)
>
> Everyone (he argues) should 'make politics, but politics in the broadest sense, politics of education, politics of training, not strict politics of bureaucratic character, nor politics of persons...'

His theater forcefully attests to this broad social perspective. In his work as a dramatist and through the voices of his lead characters, Salinas dramatizes the poet's coming to terms with his or her surroundings and the resulting whole-spirited engagement in a process of renovation and deliverance.

SPANISH PLAYWRIGHTS AND THE CONSTRUCTION OF REALITY

Broad social, historical, and political functions of the genre of drama along with its lyrical and spiritual dimensions receive emphasis also in his essays on modern Spanish literature and the theater of his contemporaries. These writings offer additional perspective on the place and definition of Salinas's dramatic production, as his theatrical works can be held up to values he recognizes in his general appraisals of Spanish authors. The currents of orality, lyricism, humanity, and spirituality he highlights in his essays clearly flow through his plays as well.

In "La vida literaria en España" ("Literary Life in Spain"), a version of a speech delivered to the Boston Authors' Club, Salinas attends to the social dimensions of literary production and underlines the significance of national context in defining the character of literature. He asserts that literature represents distinct values and characteristics associated with the people of a country. Salinas then defines Spanish literature in terms of its potent oral character. In a sweeping generalization, he deems Spain a country of talkers, "un país sobre todo oral" (a country above all oral; *Ensayos de literatura hispánica* 292). He considers this orality fundamental for Spanish literature and underscores the value Spanish authors place on the spoken word as a vivid expression of living people. He mentions the popularity of *tertulias*, social gatherings or literary circles, where Spanish authors meet for discussions that later find their way into written form. Lauding the accessibility of Spanish authors and the open-spirited, familiar nature of their literary milieu, he claims that many of their literary creations, and not just theatrical works, read as conversations translated into writing (*Ensayos de literatura hispánica* 298-99).

Salinas reproduces this warmly human conviviality in his plays. Characters speak openly and vivaciously in everyday language, sometimes with colorful local Spanish dialect, for example that of Madrid in *"La Estratoesfera,"* of Castille in *Los santos*, and of Andalusia *La fuente del arcángel*. Conversational exchanges dominate in his theatrical compositions, and some believe that his preoccupation with verbal communication leads to a downplaying of other essential aspects of the dramatic medium. Ruiz Ramón has written, "Generalmente, la pieza teatral de Salinas está construida desde el diálogo y no desde la acción, estando ésta confiada al dinamismo y a la tensión de la palabra" (Generally, the dramatic piece by Salinas is constructed from the dialogue and not from the action, the latter being entrusted to the dynamism and tension of the word; Ruiz Ramón, *Historia del teatro español Siglo XX* 284). Scenic effects and other theatrical elements stand secondary to the expressive force of the dramatic dialogue. In Salinas's plays, this key oral component possesses a literary and lyrical quality, a mark he considered emblematic of modern Spanish literature.

For Salinas, lyricism is the distinguishing sign of Spain's literature of the twentieth century, the penetrating characteristic attributable even to Generation of 98 writers such as Unamuno and Ortega who were more famous for their prose works (*Literatura española siglo XX* 34; *Ensayos de literatura hispánica* 282-83). Salinas sees great diversity in the lyrical bearings of his contemporaries. Some incline toward Spanish poetic tradition and the inheritance of popular balladry of the *Romancero* or of Golden Age poets such as Lope de Vega and Góngora. Some exhibit the European vanguardist influences of the futurists, dadaists, surrealists, or others. Many combine both tendencies and experiment with a variety of genres. In Salinas's view, this defining feature signals common ground between Spain's generationist and modernist currents (*Ensayos de literatura hispánica* 277). Lyricism, *la nota capital del arte nuevo* (the keynote of the new art), marks not only the renewed flourishing of poetry of Salinas's time but also permeates other genres (*Ensayos de literatura hispánica* 282):

> Ese lirismo básico, esencial (lirismo no de la letra, sino del espíritu), se manifiesta en variadas formas, a veces en las menos esperadas, y él es el que vierte sobre novela, ensayo, teatro, esa ardiente tonalidad poética que percibimos en la mayoría de las obras importantes de nuestros días. (*Literatura española siglo XX* 34-35)

> That basic, essential lyricism, (lyricism not of the word, but of the spirit), manifests itself in varied forms, at times in the least expected, and it is what flows into the novel, essay, theater, that ardent poetic

tonality that we perceive in the majority of the important works of our days.

Salinas underscores the force of this tendency by surveying lyricism and the theater of the twentieth century. He mentions López Alarcón, Marquina, Villaespesa, Valle-Inclán, and the Machado brothers to trace a trajectory culminating in the theater of Lorca, "sin duda el más puro teatro poético de nuestro tiempo" (without a doubt the purest poetic theater of our time; *Literatura española siglo XX* 41).

Salinas praises the coherence and poetic vitality of Lorca's work and sees in it a blurring of the boundaries between theater and poetry. In both genres, Salinas points to Lorca's probing of the spirituality and mysteries of humanity through the fusion of historical and literary currents and popular Andalusian culture. In his essay "Dramatismo y teatro de Federico García Lorca" ("Dramaticism and Theater of Federico García Lorca"), Salinas contends that Lorca turned to the genre of theater because he needed more complex artistic resources and wider expressive means to develop what he was already communicating through his poetry, namely, the dramatic fatality of earthy existence (*Literatura española siglo XX* 193).

In important measure, Salinas's observations about Lorca hold true for his own creative production. Salinas's works fuse traditions from myth, literature, and history with popular and everyday culture. Unlike Lorca, familiar, conversational dialogue and not the stylistic and linguistic devices of his poetry predominate in his plays, but the thematic cohesiveness of his poetry and theater is discernable in his exploration of spheres of reality and the interplay of reality and illusion, his concentration on *yo-tú* (I-you) relationships, and the search for a redemptive fulfillment. Salinas's turn to the genre of drama, like that of Lorca, provides an avenue for the expansion of the themes of his poetry. Salinas's need for the new medium, though, derives especially from his condition of exile, his search for an outlet for his nostalgia for Spain, and from his concern with upholding the positive promise of humanity in the face of the pressures of modernity. Entering the artistic and social realm of theater, Salinas sounds with an amplified lyrical voice his faith in human potential.

While Salinas recognizes the financial motives of some professional writers who turned to theater and he criticizes the quality of Spanish theater in the context of the difficult economic and political times (*Ensayos de literatura hispánica* 298), he affirms the lofty spiritual and human elements bound in the social purpose of theater and he praises exemplary models. One successful case was the dramatic production of Carlos Arniches. In his essay "Del género chico a la tragedia grotesca: Carlos Arniches" ("From the Genre of Short Farses to Grotesque Tragedy: Carlos Arniches"), to introduce his appreciation of the work of Arniches, Salinas contemplates the unifying power of theater in its ideal form. Theatrical works deserving of success, according to Salinas, bridge the distance between artist and audience. To a public that holds on to customs and tradition to defend the past, the creator of the dramatic work puts forth a system of values—artistic, human, and spiritual—that are ahead of their time and look toward the future. The consummate dramatic work propels author and spectators toward mutual understanding (*Literatura española siglo XX* 126-27). Salinas praises the ability of Arniches to bridge comedy and tragedy, address serious topics in a comic vein, and thereby engage his public.

Salinas's short plays, though less farsical and slice-of-life-like than those of Arniches, possess some of the flavor of the latter's *sainetes* (one-act comic pieces). Salinas blends serious and comic themes. He plays with dialects, everyday customs, and commonplaces. At the same time that he employs contemporary society as a model for his art, he fuses an orientation toward the future with elements from traditions that would be familiar to his audience. Less like Arniches and more like Giraudoux and Cocteau, contemporary French writers he admires who inject magic and fantasy into the things of ordinary life, Salinas explores reality and appearances and uncovers the marvels hidden in everyday items, for example, the hats in *La Cabeza de Medusa*, the hotel room and diary of *La isla del tesoro*, the ashtray of *El parecido*, and the money in *Sobre seguro*.

Another significant difference between his plays and those of

Arniches was their public reception. In his essay "Unamuno, autor dramático" ("Unamuno, Dramatic Author"), dated January 1933, Salinas divides Spanish dramatic literature into two categories. He makes a distinction between plays by playwrights such as Benavente, the Alvarez Quintero brothers, and Arniches that have been in the public spotlight, and plays that remain in the shadows though their authors, for example, Unamuno, Valle-Inclán, and Azorín, have achieved great success with non-dramatic works. Salinas writes:

> Hay en la literatura dramática española dos zonas de producción netamente distintas: la zona de luz y la zona de sombra. De luz pública, se entiende. Dramaturgos como Benavente, los hermanos Alvarez Quintero, Arniches, etc., por una perfecta adecuación, quizá lograda a fuerza de costumbre, entre sus obras y el público más extenso, viven plenamente en la primera de esas zonas. Pero otro grupo de escritores, en ningún caso menos valiosos que ellos, y que en otros géneros de acción artística logran la cima de la difusión y el éxito posible..., se mueven sin embargo, en cuanto a su labor dramática se refiere, en una zona de sombra; y sus obras de teatro salen rara y difícilmente de ella para asomarse a la única publicidad cabal para una obra dramática: la representación. Así Unamuno, Valle-Inclán y Azorín. (*Literatura española siglo XX* 69)

> There are two clearly distinct spheres of production in Spanish dramatic literature: the sphere of light and the sphere of shadow. By sphere of light, public light is understood. Playwrights such as Benavente, the Alvarez Quintero brothers, Arniches, etc., because of a perfect suitability of their works for the broader public, perhaps achieved through force of tradition, live fully in the first of these spheres. But another group of writers, in no case less worthy than they, and who in other genres of artistic activity achieve the height of circulation and possible success..., move, nevertheless, as far as their dramatic work is concerned, in the shadows; and their theatrical works emerge from the shadows rarely and with difficulty

to achieve the only consummate publicity for a dramatic work: performance. So it was with Unamuno, Valle-Inclán and Azorín.

Salinas repeats the categorization a few months later in his essay on Arniches (*Literatura española siglo XX* 127-28). Ironically, he has described his own situation in the "zone of shadows" even before he writes his first play. Attention in the next chapter to his condition as an exile will address further the topic of fulfillment of the communal function of his dramatic works.

Some thirty years after Juan Marichal wrote "Pedro Salinas and the Values of Hispanic Literature" to introduce Salinas's collection of essays on Spanish literature, he again published an assessment of Salinas the essayist. Placing him solidly between the contemplative, introspective posture of Unamuno and the didactic, expository style of Ortega y Gassett, Marichal aptly calls Salinas an essayist deeply steeped in Spanish tradition and profoundly affected by exile, who expertly tempered the anguish and problems associated with the Spanish condition (Marichal, *Pedro Salinas y la ampliación del ensayo* 19). Marichal observes that the prose of Salinas's letters and essays is often indistinguishable (Marichal, *Pedro Salinas y la ampliación del ensayo* 22). Both are conversational and reflective, communicative and contemplative. In a way akin to his letter-writing process, Salinas composed many of his essays as speeches to deliver to a specific audience. Without heavy, pedantic analysis or dark criticism, Salinas's writings on poets, poetry, poetics, the medium of drama, modernity, and communication reveal his keen sensibility to the many facets of the individual spirit, artistic creation, personal actions and interactions. In their dramatizations of human social circumstance and visions of a redemptive reality, his plays also exhibit prominently these identifying marks of his essays. It is no accident the poets, traditions, and contemporary topics Salinas analyzes in his essays come to bear on his own dramatic works. Clearly conscious of the responsibilities of the poet, Salinas expresses through his drama a fundamental confidence in the process of creation, he explores the significance of forging connections, and he looks ahead with optimism at possibilities of social amelioration. Salinas's essays and letters, in addition to providing insight into the history of the dramatic works, the role of the poet, and his conception of artistic freedom, illuminate his personal and political perspectives as an artist in exile and shed light on the place of the poet in his plays.

3
Salinas: Poet and Émigré

> Sobre mi alma llevo, de todo esto, la parte que me toca; como hombre que soy, como europeo que me siento, como americano de vivienda, como español que nací y me afirmo.
> Salinas, Preface, *Todo más claro*, *Poesías completas* 595
>
> Upon my soul I carry, from all this, the part that touches me; as the man I am, as the European I feel myself to be, as American by residence, as the Spaniard I was born and affirm myself.

THE SITUATION OF SALINAS the poet émigré fundamentally shapes Salinas the playwright. To be sure, living outside of Spain increases his nostalgia for things Spanish, his longing for a linkage with Spanish as a living language, and his inclination to write plays. His condition of exile is a profoundly Spanish experience and a key characteristic of his generation. Salinas the poet émigré occupies a complex position with a number of significant dimensions. While exile for Salinas means rupture from his native Spain, this sense of separation engenders a broader relationship with humankind, provokes his contemplation of existence in the modern world, and motivates his pursuit of connection and redemption. Salinas combats his circumstance by turning to the theater as an antidote for his condition of exile. To link Salinas the poet with his theater, this chapter will first consider the state of exile as a Spanish circumstance and a defining feature of Salinas's generation. Then examination of Salinas's incorporation of the topic of exile into his works on El Cid, Don Quixote, and Meléndez Valdés will show his strong sense of the theme of exile in

Spanish literature and his identification with the complexities of struggle to adapt and continue by those who are disconnected. Finally, a look at the evolution of Salinas's separation from Spain will highlight his conception of displacement as an integral part of the modern human condition and as an inspiration for the preoccupation with linkage and salvation seen in his dramatic corpus.

EXILE AS A SPANISH CIRCUMSTANCE
AND A DEFINING FEATURE OF SALINAS'S GENERATION

Political turmoil in Spain during the first half of the Twentieth Century provoked the exile of thousands of intellectuals. Many men and women left Spain in the wake of turn-of-the-century events associated with the war of 1898 and Spain's loss of imperial stature. In the decades to follow, prior to, during, and after the Spanish Civil War, thousands more fled from Spain. The members of the Generation of 1927 were politically liberal and many participated actively in Spanish Republican causes. There has been some debate about the membership in this group. Most widely accepted is the list of ten names that includes Salinas (1891-1951), Jorge Guillén (1893-1984), Gerardo Diego (1896-1987), Dámaso Alonso (1898-1990), Federico García Lorca (1898-1936), Vicente Aleixandre (1898-1984), Emilio Prados (1899-1962), Rafael Alberti (1902-1999), Luis Cernuda (1902-1963), and Manuel Altolaguirre (1905-1999), although other male and female poets have received attention as part of this generation as well: Juan José Domenchina (1898-1960) (Gaos 140; Lama 425); Fernando Villalón (1881-1930), Juan Larrea (1895-1980), José María Hinojosa (1904-1936) (Lama 399, 413, 433); Concha Méndez (1898-1986), Rosa Chacel (1898-1994), Ernestina de Champourcín (1905-1999), Josefina de la Torre (1907-2002), and Carmen Conde (1907-1996) (Miró 5). The murder of García Lorca in 1936 in the early months of the Spanish Civil War rocked the generation. Except for Aleixandre and Alonso, most of these writers left Spain when Republican defeat was imminent, or when the Civil War ended in 1939. Like thousands of Republican Spaniards, Salinas lived for many years away from his homeland and died in exile, though his situation was somewhat different from a number of his contemporaries in that initial circumstances apart from politics led him out of Spain in the early months of the Civil War. He left Spain in the summer of 1936 to accept a position as a visiting professor at Wellesley College and later chose not to return to Spain.

Numerous studies have explored the complexities of the historical, social, and spiritual forces that led to the Generation of 1927's experiences of repression, expatriation, displacement, separation, loss, absence, memory, nostalgia, desire for reconnection, return, and renewal (Abellán, Alonso, Andújar, Ayala, Bellver, Berenguer, Berroa, Bou, Campos, Ciplijauskaité, Durán, Feal, González, Ilie, Lama, Lida, Lloréns, Magnini, Juan Marichal, Miras, Monleón, Morón Arroyo, Naharro-Calderón, Oliva, Newman, Pérez-Stanfield, Pope, Ramoneda, Rivera, Rubio, Ruiz Ramón, Solita Salinas de Marichal, Ugarte, Williams, Zueras Torrens). A common view is that after some period of disorientation, most of the displaced poets recovered their voices, sometimes with expression similar to that prior to exile, sometimes with a new accent. For example, Luis Cernuda, Rafael Alberti, and María Teresa León spend time in Europe, and then, like Jorge Guillén, Emilio Prados, Manuel Altolaguirre, and Salinas, continue to write prolifically in the Americas. Some critics have pointed to the Generation's progression in exile beyond aesthetic preoccupations toward an intensification of concerns with human, ethical, and social problems. Summarizations such as those by Ramoneda and Lama are representative of this perspective:

> En todos se intensifica el proceso de rehumanización que se había desarrollado a lo largo de los años treinta y se mantiene el compromiso entre la estética y la ética. Más grave y preocupada, su voz tiende a reflejar los problemas humanos y sociales del tiempo histórico que ahora les toca vivir. (Ramoneda 61)

> In all of them the process of rehumanization that had evolved through the thirties intensifies and a compromise between aesthetics and ethics is maintained. More serious and concerned, their voices tend to reflect the human and social problems of the historical time

that now it is their turn to live.

Todos ellos testimoniaron en sus versos la queja, el dolor o la nostalgia. En general, su poesía deja de ser estetizante y da cabida a los problemas humanos y sociales. (Lama 60)

All of them gave testimony in their verses to complaint, pain or nostalgia. In general, their poetry ceases to project solely aesthetic sensibilities and makes room for human and social problems.

The tensions and challenges of the adaptation process were profound and in some senses peculiarly Spanish. Pérez Minik and Borrás assert that Spanish exiles differed uniquely from other exiles of other ages because transformation of their thoughts derived less from the impact of the host cultures than from their tapping deeply into their own roots (Pérez Minik 494, Borrás 60). Ayala links some of the generation's contemplations of Spain and "lo español" (the Spanish experience) or "la 'esencia' española" (the Spanish essence) with the focus of the Generation of 98 on the Spanish problem (Ayala 46-47). Monleón notes extreme cultural attachments to the memory of Spain and the disappointed hopes of those expecting a quick return home (Monleón 9). Ugarte, citing Lloréns, writes of "exilic loss of balance as a characteristic of Spanish literature from the Cid, through the Romantics cast into exile by Ferdinand VII, to Unamuno, as well as the Generation of 1927 poets" (Ugarte 99, Lloréns 11-30). Ilie explores fundamental spiritual, psychological, intellectual, and ethical characteristics of exile. Whether exile entails a geographical expatriation or an inner exile such as that experienced by writers who do not leave their native country, he upholds the premise that literature is the voice of a culture speaking with itself. He analyzes in depth the particularities of the exile from Franco's Spain and points to numerous dimensions of living uprooted. On the negative side, he mentions the pain of feeling out of place and the defenselessness against being surrounded by all things foreign that would break down one's native cultural sensibilities, and in a more positive vein, the triumphs of transplantation and the exercise of intellectual freedom (Ilie 19-24). Like Campos and Lida, he views the political exile of 1939 as a huge, recurring wave in a country with a history of painful and extended political expulsions and separations from the homeland across centuries (Ilie 23, Campos 11, Lida 107). Solita Salinas de Marichal identifies both cohesiveness and multiplicity in the Spanishness of the exiles who at the same time identify closely with the humanitarian principles of the Second Republic and hold highly personalized images of homeland and Spanish tradition (Salinas de Marichal, "España..." 94-95). Ramoneda also sees unity and diversity in his characterization of the uniqueness of the generation:

> Debe advertirse también que, a diferencia de lo que ocurrió con otros emigrados europeos desde finales del siglo pasado, ninguno de estos poetas se integró plenamente en sus nuevas patrias. La evocación melancólica y serena de tierra lejana, los denuestos y las imprecaciones contra los vencedores, la aceptación dolorosa y resignada de un difícil cambio político, el recuerdo emocionado de los amigos perdidos, el ansia de regreso, están presentes, en mayor o menor medida, en la obra de todos. (Ramoneda 62)

> It should be pointed out also that unlike what happened with other European émigrés since the end of last century, none of these poets assimilated fully into their new homelands. The melancholic and serene evocation of distant land, the insults and imprecations against the victors, the painful and resigned acceptance of a difficult political change, the emotional remembrance of lost friends, the yearning for return, are present, to a greater or lesser extent, in the work of all.

These poets exhibit in their creative expression a broad spectrum of mentalities of exile. Alberti, Altolaguirre, and Prados notably link exile with feelings of expatriation, expulsion, and political persecution. Sometimes exile connects with a search for freedom and salvation, or with nostalgia for the homeland. This is the dominant tone in Alberti's

"Por encima del mar, desde la orilla americana del Atlántico" ("On the Sea, From the American Shore of the Atlantic"), Altolaguirre's "Es la tierra de nadie" ("It is No Man's Land"), Prado's "Cuando era primavera en España" ("When It was Spring in Spain"), and also in Guillén's "Despertar español" ("To Awaken Spanish"). In Cernuda and Lorca, exile often surfaces as a sense of separation from loved ones, be it the homeland or some other entity. For them, exile is often associated with alienation, isolation, or death, such as in Cernuda's "Impresión del destierro" ("Impression of Exile"). Sometimes it appears dominated by a perspective on the coldness of urban and modern life, for example, in the poetry of Lorca's *Poeta en Nueva York* (*Poet in New York*), in some of the compositions of Salinas's *Todo más claro* (*All Things Made Clearer*), and Guillén's *Clamor* (*Clamor*). In Guillén's poem "El descaminado" ("Misrouted One") and Cernuda's "Peregrino" ("Wanderer"), exile can be seen as a voyage of discovery. For all exile is connected with a consciousness of one's solitude and of the passage of time.

Salinas himself captures the division, unity, pain, and hope of his generation in his response to Eleanor Turnbull when she asks him to write a few words for her anthology of poets:

> Sí, miss Turnbull (sic). A todos los conozco, a unos más, a otros menos. Separados estamos; un viento malo y sucio nos dispersó por el mundo. Quién en la Argentina, Alberti; uno en Inglaterra, Cernuda; otros en los Estados Unidos, en Méjico; solo tres, Gerardo, Vicente y Dámaso, en aquel suelo de España. Sí, le agradezco a usted mucho que me dé motivo para reunirnos todos, en el suelo provisional, el recuerdo, como antes, como mañana, en nuestra España limpia." (*Ensayos de literatura hispánica*, "Nueve o diez poetas," 342)

> Yes, Miss Turnbull. I know them all, some more, some less. We are separated; an evil and vile wind scattered us through the world. Who in Argentina, Alberti; one in England, Cernuda; others in the United States, in Mexico; only three, Gerardo, Vicente and Dámaso, on that soil of Spain. Yes, I thank you very much for giving me a

reason for us to gather together, on provisional ground, our memory, like before, like tomorrow in our pure Spain.

Salinas's portraits of his friends ring with his own nostalgia for Spain and bring to life the sounds, sights, and colors of their lives and works. He revisits the magic little space of Morena Villa in Madrid's Residencia de Estudiantes. He locates Alberti in Puerto de Santa María, Burgos, Santander, Cádiz, and next to the sea. He traces steps on the paths where his friend Guillén would follow him, to the Sorbonne, Seville, Cambridge, and Boston. He imagines Prados in solitude, in a Holy Week procession in Seville, then in Mexico, and later absent from a shop in Malaga. Salinas connects his student Cernuda with his days of teaching in Seville, and he revisits through a recollection of the serious, simple house of Cernuda the poet's fragile transparency. He places Altolaguirre in Andalusia and beyond: Málaga, Madrid, París, Londres, el salto, la Habana, y ahora, quién sabe donde! (Malaga, Madrid, Paris, London, the jump, Havana, and now, who knows where!; *Ensayos de literatura hispánica*, "Nueve o diez poetas," 353). At the end of this sketch he taps at the roots of his colleague's Andalusian soul:

> Así en una Andalucía secreta de su alma, de la que no se ha movido jamás, en un jardinillo andaluz donde está él solo, la poesía brota y brota, mientras él camina por el mundo en una imprenta de ruedas... (*Ensayos de literatura hispánica*, "Nueve o diez poetas" 354)

> So in a secret Andalusia of his soul, from which he has never moved, in a little Andalusian garden where he is alone, poetry sprouts and sprouts, while he travels through the world on a printing press with wheels...

Salinas's bittersweet musings about the magnetism of García Lorca also take him back to Andalusia to describe the poet's inner vibrations and to paint a picture of the poet's exterior world:

¿Cuántos ruiseñores de la Alhambra, cuántas viejas de la Vega, cuántos garzones del Albaicín, cuántos duendes de ninguna parte, no le cantaban, le reían, le suspiraban, le lloraban a Federico dentro, en su muchipersona? ¿Cuántos seres no se le habían juntado, se le habían ido a vivir allí en él, atraídos por su gracia, y en su interior los llevaba? (*Ensayos de literatura hispánica*, "Nueve o diez poetas" 345)

How many nightingales of the Alhambra, how many old women of La Vega, how many youths of the Albaicin, how many magic spirits from nowhere did not sing, laugh, sigh, cry to Federico, inside his exuberant person? How many beings had not joined together and gone to live there in him, attracted by his grace, and inside himself he carried them?

At the conclusion of the piece, Salinas mentions Dámaso Alonso, who has remained in Spain, to underline Alonso's absence from the collection. His words about Alonso, like all the preceding highly personal reminiscences, project Salinas's nostalgia, as well a sense of separation from homeland, a soul searching, a desire for connection and community, and an optimistic view of the endeavor of the poet:

—y sin embargo se le siente junto a todos, que más me ha dado que pensar de los lejanos, en España, tengo que poner aquí su nombre, por acto de justicia del corazón: Dámaso Alonso, al que no se escapará de la poesía que apenas quiere escribir, y que le acecha a todas horas, hasta que triunfe. (*Ensayos de literatura hispánica*, "Nueve o diez poetas" 357)

—and nevertheless he is felt together with all the others, that has brought me to think more about the distant ones, in Spain, I have to put his name here, by an act of justice of the heart: Damaso Alonso, who will not escape from the poetry that he hardly wants to write, and that stalks him at all hours, until it triumphs.

SALINAS'S LITERARY STUDIES AND THE THEME OF EXILE
Salinas foregrounds the theme of exile and Spain not only in this semi-autobiographical recollection of his friends but also in his more elaborate literary studies well grounded in history and biography. His explorations of the exile of the Cid and Don Quixote relate the predicaments and actions of these figures in specific literary and historical contexts to the modern situation and human existence, and in personal terms. In his essay "El 'Cantar de Mío Cid' Poema de la honra" ('The Epic Poem of the Cid Poem of Honor'), Salinas marks the crucial place of exile in Spanish literature. He looks back to the medieval poem to define exile as an inherently Spanish condition and to explore universal dimensions of exile. With an inclusive first person plural, Salinas invites his audience to join him in identifying with the heroic solitude of the Cid:

> Es poema de destierro, y la pena del desterrado, en eso consiste: en romper esos vínculos, de los que apenas se tiene en conciencia en el bienestar, con lo nuestro, con nuestra tierra, extendida del modo más ancho. Tierra, y en ella la casa, y en la casa muebles y trebejos usuales, y entre ellos, yendo y viniendo, la mujer y los hijos y los criados, las gentes nuestras, lo nuestro. Desterrarse es arrancarnos de lo nuestro, es decir, dejar de ser nosotros, en una proporción enorme de nuestro ser en todo aquello que hemos preferido para tenerlo alrededor. Es quedarnos solos, y separándonos de nuestro ámbito vital, ya hecho y querido, irse por los mundos en busca de otro casual e imprevisible. (*Ensayos de literatura hispánica*, "El 'Cantar de Mío Cid'..."30)

> It is a poem of exile, and the pain of the exiled, it consists of that: of breaking those ties, those that one is hardly conscious of when experiencing wellbeing, (breaking) with what is ours, with our land, extended in the widest way. Land, and in it, the house, and in the house furniture and the usual things, and among them, going and coming, the wife and the children and the servants, our people, what is ours. To be exiled is to uproot ourselves from what is ours, that is

to say, to cease being ourselves, in an enormous proportion of our being in all that we have preferred to have around us. It is to remain alone, and by separating ourselves from our vital surroundings, now done and beloved, to go out into worlds in search of another accidental and unpredictable one.

These words strike a personal note, as does his assertion that the Cid represents not only the first exile but also the first Spaniard of honor in Spain's first literary monument. Claiming that the key theme of the poem is the recovery of honor, Salinas reflects on the problem of Spain and alludes to his own time and the circumstances of his generation:

> A esta carta de la honra se lo ha jugado España todo, muchas veces. Unas ganó, otras ha perdido. Parece como que el rumbo de la España de los mejores tiempos, su derrota, lo marcaba una brújula con una aguja imantada al norte único de la honra. Así navegamos y naufragamos. (*Ensayos de literatura hispánica*, "El 'Cantar de Mío Cid'..." 43)

> Spain has played out this card of honor many times. Sometimes she has won, others she has lost. It seems that a compass with a needle fixed on the north point of honor was marking the course of Spain's best times and her defeat. In this way we have sailed and shipwrecked.

To conclude the essay, Salinas quotes Cervantes when he questions whether it is wisdom or folly to subject all human action to the ideal of honor. Like the Cid, the character of Don Quixote clearly reflects Salinas's concerns about exile and honor.

In "Lo que debemos a Don Quijote" a speech delivered by Salinas in Bogota and Peru in 1947, he concludes with keen awareness of his separation from Spain and his search for emancipation, apparent as well in his dramatic works, also products of this period of his life. He calls Cervantes's novel an invitation to freedom and a place to build under-

standing among peoples:

> Al *Quijote* debemos ustedes y yo, ustedes los colombianos, los americanos, y yo, y nosotros los españoles, debemos un entendimiento común. En el *Quijote*, amigos míos, nos entendemos todos. Diferiremos en muchas cosas, pero sospecho que nos entenderemos en el *Quijote*, y no es por entender su lengua, no, no es por entender el idioma en que está escrito, sino por entender todo el signo humano que el *Quijote* representa. (*Ensayos de literatura hispánica...* 104)

> You and I owe the *Quixote*, you the Colombians, the Americans, and I, and we the Spaniards, we owe a common understanding. We may differ in many things, but I suspect that we may understand each other in the *Quixote*, and it is not from understanding its language, no, it is not from understanding the language in which it is written, but rather from understanding all the human sign the *Quixote* represents.

Salinas's closing quotation from Colombian Antonio Nariño (1765-1823), writer, statesman, and fighter for his country's independence, gives additional voice to his sense of exile and to his quest for safe haven for those of his generation:

> "Si los destinos han querido que la España se vea envuelta en tantas calamidades, salvemos a lo menos a esta bella parte del mundo para que sirva de asilo a los mismos españoles que no quieren ser esclavos del tirano de Europa." (*Ensayos de literatura hispánica...* 104)

> "If the fates have wanted Spain to see itself involved in so many calamities, may we save as least this beautiful part of the world so that it may serve as a refuge to the same Spaniards who do not want to be slaves of the tyrant of Europe."

The profiles of El Cid and Don Quixote as literary exiles also find their way into the contemporary moment of Salinas and his generation in Salinas's 1939 speech entitled "How Can Culture Survive Exile?," delivered in New York at an international meeting of the P.E.N. writers's club. Salinas takes inspiration from the fact that many of Spain's national heroes gained full stature, immortality, and an opportunity to define a better world though the experience of exile (Newman 209).

A third and poignant example of Salinas's attention to exile as an acutely personal and Spanish circumstance derives from his 1925 critical edition of the poetry of Spanish Enlightenment figure Meléndez Valdés (1754-1817). This work predates Salinas's years in exile but remarkably augurs the experiences of Salinas and his generation. Like Meléndez and his liberal contemporaries, Salinas and his peers were forced into exile by political turmoil and civil strife in Spain. Like Meléndez, Salinas was to die in exile. In his prologue to the volume, Salinas describes the pain and loss of country, home, library, and literary work suffered by Meléndez. According to Salinas, the expatriate's only consolation is the return to poetry. And even with this comfort, Salinas writes, the poet's soul is tortured with longing and nostalgia. To capture these feelings, Salinas cites four lines from Meléndez's poem "Los suspiros de un proscrito" ("The Sighs of an Exile"):

> Cayó desmayado; el alba
> sumido en su inmensa cuita
> le halló otro día en su llanto
> bañándole enternecida.
> (*Ensayos de literatura hispánica...* 237)

> He fell in a faint; the dawn
> plunged into his immense grief
> found him the next day in his weeping
> and bathed him with pity.

To introduce the verses, Salinas envisions the exiled poet looking at his homeland from a precipice, on the night of a full moon, when all is silent except the song of a bird. He suggests that the poet is writing about two lovers, phantoms, all pure illusion. These same elements wrapped in nostalgia appear in the writings of the members of the Generation of 1927 and certainly filter into Salinas's own works in exile. For instance, two of his plays of tragic outcome carry this melancholy and similar imagery. The closing tableau of Salinas's play *Judit y el tirano* features Judit crying at dawn, at the feet of her fallen lover, with a bird singing. In the final scene of *La Cabeza de Medusa*, Lucila ascends a platform to cry at the feet of the isolated Andrenio, who has succumbed after observing an illusion of love.

Besides mournful outpourings, in the creative expression of Salinas and his fellow poets there are resolutely optimistic perspectives from afar reflecting their struggles to balance, to adjust and to adapt, to hold on and to move on, to remember and to forget. The definition of exile as "the metaphorical name for the experience of ambivalence" (Ferguson 277) is certainly applicable to these authors. Writing about this generation of émigrés, Vicente Lloréns, friend of Salinas and also an exile from Franco's Spain, confirms this sense of opposing and contradictory forces and emotions. Of the stifling and alienating effects of exile he writes:

> El desterrado en país de lengua ajena es un ser que se encuentra sin posibilidad de comunicación humana cuando más la necesita; apenas se abre para él un nuevo ámbito de vida, la extrañeza del idioma le intercepta el paso. Situación penosa y desconcertante que le obliga a recluirse en sí mismo y a enmudecer. (Lloréns, "El desterrado y su lengua" 46)

> The exile in a country of a another language is a being who finds himself without possibility of human communication when he most needs it; barely is a new sphere of life open to him when the strangeness of the new language intercepts his passage. A painful and disconcerting situation that forces him to shut himself away and become silent.

And on the brighter side, Lloréns suggests potential positive outcomes from the physical separation from one's country:

> El recuerdo podía conducir, sin embargo, a una revaloración nueva y más justa de lo español. Cuidades, pueblos, paisajes, todo adquiría otro relieve, visto desde lejos y con perspectiva diferente. A veces eran las cosas más pequeñas, los detalles nimios, los que asumían de repente significación insospechada. El redescubrimiento de lo propio necesita, al parecer, del contraste con lo ajeno. (Lloréns, "Memorias..." 77)

> The remembrance could lead, nevertheless, to a newer and more exact revaluation of the Spanish experience. Cities, towns, landscapes all acquired another relief, seen from afar with a different perspective. Sometimes it was the smallest things, the trivial details, that suddenly assumed unsuspected meaning. The rediscovery of what is one's own, apparently, requires a contrast with what is alien.

Bellver also points to a diversity of possible reactions to the condition of exile and cites Claudio Guillén's distinction between two major literary responses. These are "literature of exile, which assumes the elegaic mode and dwells on the subject of exile itself and literature of counter-exile, which includes a sense of triumph over separation and often takes the form of hopeful odyssey" (Bellver 77-78, Guillén 272). In her study of Alberti, Bellver identifies five antidotes—"poetry, painting, the sea, friendship and political commitment"—that "arrest Alberti's spiritual desintegration and help integrate him into the progressive flow of the present moment" (Bellver 69). In another vein, Ugarte's analysis of Cernuda's poetics of exile uncovers profound ambiguities and opposing relationships inherent in the experience of expatriation, and specifically in Cernuda's conception of desire, oblivion, and land.

Looking at immigrant identity and the adaptation process of the individual in exile through the lens of nostalgia, Ritivoi traces the concept of nostalgia back to its origin as a term defining a "medical condition developed by people who were away from home and yearned to return but were somehow unable to do so" (Ritivoi 4). She goes on to characterize nostalgia as "a genuine *pharmakos*, both medicine and poison" (Ritivoi 39). Not unlike what Bellver calls antidotes in Alberti, nostalgia can lead to the search for a remedy in one's exile or, like what Ugarte sees in the poetics of Cernuda, it can cause a toxic obsession with one's separation. "It can express alienation, or it can replenish and rebuttress our sense of identity by consolidating the ties with our history (Ritivoi 39)." Further examination of Salinas's sense of separation from Spain will show that in a strong sense, Salinas's nostalgia takes more the form of remedy than poison. While at times he mourns his separation from Spain and assails oppressive obstacles in his personal communications with family and friends and in some of his creative production, he engages affirmatively in the acculturation process. He makes his theater one significant vehicle for the expression of his nostalgia and his search for adjustment. In part, his theater fulfills the remedial function Ritivoi ascribes to nostalgia: "it is a way of realigning the past with the present (Ritivoi 6)." While Salinas's theater provides a way of connecting with the past and his life before emigration, it does not propose a preservation of status quo or an iconization of time gone by. Rather, his theater and poetic figures serve to unite past with present and point toward a better future.

While Salinas always exhibits strong affinities for his native literary heritage, in exile he appears to feel and demonstrate increasingly the significance of Spanish tradition. There is strong evidence of this in his writings in exile, both in his many critical studies and in his own literary creations, into which he channels the forces of tradition with an abundance of explicit and implicit allusions. Chapter Seven of the present study will examine more closely these manifestations in his dramatic works and the role of the poet as a bridge between tradition and modernity.

SALINAS'S SEPARATION FROM SPAIN
Years before he leaves his homeland, Salinas sees that the ideal world he

believes an essential creation for a poet is certainly not the everyday reality he is experiencing in the early thirties in Spain. In a letter to Guillén, dated April 2, 1931, he virtually shouts on paper in frustration against the terrible political situation:

> Todos estos meses han sido muy fastidiosos. Causa: LA POLÍTICA. Así con todas las mayúsculas y espacios posibles. No se puede vivir. (PS/JG *Correspondencia* 134)

> All these months have been very bothersome. The cause: P O L I T I C S. Like this with all capital letters and possible spaces. One cannot live.

He foresees civil war and expresses a desire to leave Spain:

> ¿Cómo escaparse? No lo sé. Con mucho gusto me iría a vivir fuera de España. Es ya un deseo, quizá sea pronto un propósito. Estamos hoy en España en un estado espiritual de guerra civil. Y creo que pronto se llegará al estado real. (PS/JG *Correspondencia* 136)

> How to escape? I do not know. Gladly I would go to live outside of Spain. Now it's a desire, perhaps soon it will be a purpose. Today in Spain we are in a spiritual state of civil war. And I think that soon it will become an actual state of civil war.

When in 1935 he receives the invitation to teach at Wellesley College, he is most enthusiastic. He accepts the offer by Alice Bush with a cordial reply indicating he is keenly attracted to and curious about the United States, and that he had hopes to visit for some time (Salinas, *Cartas de viaje* 59). To Guillén, he indicates how greatly he desires this chance to free himself from the discord in Spain. Before the trip turns into a permanent exile, he deems it explicitly a salvation:

> ...conoces mis ilusiones por ir a América, y no puedo ir en mejores

condiciones que las que me ofrecen. Va a ser un año de descanso, de cambio, de alejamiento de esta orilla de grillos rabiosos, estupendo. Porque aparte del atractivo de América me encanta el poder salvarme de este ambiente hispánico, cada día más envenenado, más sembrado de odios y rencores, más hostil a los gustos nobles y al trabajo alegre. Yo tengo la impresión de que todo va ¡aún! a empeorar, y ese viaje es una verdadera salvación, yo así lo siento. (PS/JG *Correspondencia* 171)

...you know how I have looked forward to going to America, and I couldn't be going under better conditions than the ones they are offering me. It will be a year of rest, of change, of distance from this shore of rabid crickets, marvelous. Because aside from the attraction of America, I love being able to save myself from this Hispanic environment that each day is more poisoned, more sown with hate and resentment, more hostile toward noble tastes and happy work. I have the impression that everything is going to get *even* worse, and that this trip is a true salvation, that is how I feel about it.

Juan Marichal indicates that Salinas began to realize the impact of exile after he arrived in the United States for the academic year 1936-1937, though he was helped by the fact that he did not have to change languages to conduct his classes: "Pero para él el exilio significó luego lo que representó para muchos, el abandono." (But for him exile meant what it represented for many, abandonment; Cruz 84).

It is noteworthy that even his letters to Margarita from the ship to the United States and from New York on his first days in the host country show the sensibilities of an exile and connect with the evolution of his theater. Salinas's activity as a playwright colors these earliest moments of his departure from Spain. In a speech to the Wellesley Club at Middlebury College after his arrival in the United States, Salinas relates how Spanish soldiers examined his baggage and found the mystical, symbolic drama he had written. This work, *El director*, attracted their attention. Salinas mused about how he would explain the mystical, symbolic work to an inspector. For a moment he imagined himself in jail, but the work passed inspection and the relieved Salinas was permitted to board the U.S. warship Cayuga on August 31, 1936 (Bou and Soria Olmedo 83, 85; Salinas, *Cartas de viaje* 62, n. 66).

During the transatlantic voyage, he writes to Margarita of his deep preoccupation with the situation in Spain, something that appears to him forgotten or certainly unaddressed openly on the ship:

> He pasado de estar rodeado exteriormente por la preocupación de lo español todos los minutos, como en Santander, a tener que vivirlo yo en mi interior sin nada externo que aluda a ello. (*Cartas de viaje* 64)

> I have moved from being surrounded on the outside at every moment by a concern with the Spanish situation, like in Santander, to having to live it all alone inside of me without anything external that mentions it.

He marvels at the busy hive of activity on board the ship. He comments on the loud and uncontrolled behavior of some of the Americans he sees, but acknowledges they are likeable and straightforward, with an unaffected cordiality. Of the difficulty of communicating with his cabinmates from the United States he writes, ¡Pero apenas si me puedo entender con ellos! ¡Qué catástrofe, el idioma! (But I can hardly understand them! What a catastrophe, the language!; *Cartas de viaje* 64). A few days later his letters to Margarita from his first days in New York are colored by his fatigue and loneliness. Salinas juxtaposes his impression of the explosiveness, violence, noise, and dirt of the city with his perception of its marvelous shop windows and its quiet tranquility from the vantagepoint of a hotel room high in a skyscraper (*Cartas de viaje* 64-65). The efforts to balance remembering and forgetting home, to weigh the attractive and repellent features of the new culture, and to face problems of language and communication are constants during his exile.

On numerous occasions with many people, Salinas expresses his sentiments about Spain and life apart from his country, his views of the host culture, and his attention to language and communication. Salinas's search for the positives and negatives in a broad sense and also through little details characterizes his attention to his circumstances. Guillén describes most articulately how Salinas "el atento" (the attentive man) took in the world around him:

> Salinas's attentiveness was constant, meticulous, quite variable, and he focused it on... what? Everything, for everything affected his sensibility with the illumination of understanding. He was a master of delight. For him great constructions and sublime aspects were not the only things that existed. There are also everyday things that are so exquisite that they seem insignificant, subtleties that one must define with great care, for they elude eloquence. (Salinas, *Reality and the Poet...* xvii).

Friends, family members, students, and scholars share abundant recollections, anecdotes, and personal perspectives on his life in the United States, Puerto Rico, and other places in the Americas (Alonso, Bell, Blecua, Borrás, Ciplijauskaité, Cruz, Del Río, Fernández de Lewis, Guillén, Gullón, Marichal, Miras, Newman, Salinas de Marichal, Soria Olmedo, Torre). They complement Salinas's own words about the delights and difficulties he encountered. "Salinas's years in exile were his most fertile ones," writes Guillén (Salinas, *Reality and the Poet...* xii). In a dynamic blending of wonder, fascination, playfulness, and indignation, Salinas the émigré lived what Newman has called "Spain hunger" in America (Newman 31ff), where according to Gilman, the poet-playwright developed the "elemental humanism of his creative position":

> ... Salinas investigates the suffering, the bewilderment, the possible consolation, and all the intricate meanderings of life in our world, not just America, but the modern world in which the evil of sin against man is so often unaccompanied by guilt. (Gilman 148)

Twelve years into the exile, when Blecua asks Salinas what absence from Spain means to him and to his work, this is part of the response:

> Ha supuesto, en primer lugar, la falta de España, su habla viva, excepto el período que pasé en América Hispánica, los amigos, los compañeros de generación y el público. Es decir, España como realidad, que no puede nunca compensarse con nada. He tenido la suerte de poderme dedicar a la enseñanza de la literatura española, y he concentrado en esas clases todo mi trabajo y mi afán y mis soledades de España.... Además he aprendido mucho viviendo en los Estados Unidos. Sus formas de la vida, tan distintas de las nuestras; la imponente grandeza extensiva y numérica con que todo se ofrece; el campo de observación sin par que brinda al interesado en la sociología de la literatura, en ese juego que tan benéfico o tan letal puede ser para las letras, de acciones y reacciones entre el autor y las fuerzas sociales que le rodean.... Por otro lado, la vida norteamericana, que aunque en el extranjero pase por ser ruidosa y agitada, es, por el contrario, si se la desea, tranquila y recogida, me ha dejado muchos ocios que he llenado escribiendo y leyendo. Mis viajes por la América Hispánica me han abierto los ojos a la imponente realidad de ese mundo. (Blecua 2)

> It has meant, in the first place, missing Spain, its living speech, except for the period I spent in Hispanic America, (missing) friends, peers of my generation, and the public. That is, Spain as a reality, that can never be compensated for by anything. I have had the luck of being able to devote myself to the teaching of Spanish literature, and I have concentrated into these classes all my work and zeal and loneliness.... Also I have learned a lot living in the United States. Its ways of life, so different from ours; the imposing, extensive, numerical grandeur with which everything is offered; the unparalleled field of observation afforded to those interested in the sociology of literature, that game that can be so beneficial or lethal to the field of letters, of actions and reactions between the author and the social forces that surround him.... On the other hand, North

American life, although abroad it may seem noisy and agitated, is, on the contrary, if one desires, calm and quiet, it has allowed me much free time that I have filled by writing and reading. My travels through Hispanic America have opened my eyes to the imposing reality of that world.

There is no doubt that Salinas's plays are well-fueled by the sorrows and consolations of his displacement. His comments to others through the years about high points and low points of his circumstance away from Spain further help contextualize his theater. They reflect a complex multiplicity of feelings about loss of land and language, about life in the United States and in Spanish-speaking parts of the Americas, about freedom and oppression, and about love and loyalty, all of which filter into the composition of his dramatic works.

A letter to Margarita in December of 1936 contains an early expression of his consciousness of exile and strong delimiting of the crucial part language plays in his sense of disconnectedness. He acknowledges that being out of Spain means freedom from the violence and oppressive political circumstances, but when he contemplates Margarita's comment that he give up the idea of returning to Spain, he confronts a special pain when thinking about his loss of language. Like a memory, language preserves for him the essence of his country. Though his work as a Spanish professor allows him to hold on to this memory, he is extremely distressed by the possibility of not hearing spoken Spanish in its natural living setting:

> Tú quizá no comprendas lo horrible que es para mí hacerme la idea de no oír estas palabras españolas dichas por cualquiera, en la calle, en el campo, ya más. Siempre, después de vivir en el extranjero me ha emocionado al volver a España, el oír mi lengua, el encontrarla otra vez, hablada por el que sea, por el vendedor de periódicos, por el ser más humilde. (*Cartas de viaje* 77)

Perhaps you may not understand how horrible it is for me to accept

the idea of not hearing these Spanish words spoken by anyone, in the street, in the countryside, what have you. Always, after living abroad, it has thrilled me to return to Spain, to hear my language, to encounter it again, spoken by whomever, by the newspaper seller, by the humblest of beings.

He feels daunted by the prospect of launching a new professional life and laments losing the career, money, and reputation for which he has worked during the past forty years, but what he misses most are the less tangible things buried in his language and memory: "…eso es lo peor, ese algo impalpable, del aire, de la luz, del modo de hablar, de los paisajes y los cielos, que se llama España." (…that is the worst thing, that impalpable something, from the air, the light, the way of speech, the landscapes, and the skies called Spain; *Cartas de viaje* 78). Writing plays is one way to reach for these elusive memories, an attempt to deal with the pain of rupture in its various senses. In plays he could recreate this world he had lost.

Salinas was profoundly disturbed by the events in Spain and the divisions exacerbated by the civil war. He laments deeply the separation of the members of his generation and the change in Spain that mean the end of things past. In his letter to Germaine Cahen, wife of Jorge Guillén, dated March 8, 1937, he communicates his acute sense of loss and also his drive to identify redemptive counterforces to the negatives. He seeks solace in the positive values of truth, friendship, and genuine affection among loved ones:

> Yo vivo como en una pesadilla. Me duele todo lo de España; lo nacional, lo general, lo primero. ¡Pero cuánto me tortura la idea del grupo de amigos, deshecho, Dios sabe para cuándo!…. Ni el país, ni Madrid, ni la gente, volverán a ser lo mismo. Nuestra vida, fatalmente está escindida en dos pedazos: el de ayer sabemos cómo fue, y del mañana no sabemos nada. Por eso mismo yo me aferro a lo único que no puede naufragar jamás: a los seres queridos siempre y para siempre. Hay una cosa que no se puede llevar la guerra, o por lo

menos que a mí no me puede llevar: la verdad, la necesidad y la voluntad de la amistad, y el compañerismo y el cariño. Todo eso se refuerza más y más. (PS/JG *Correspondencia* 178)

I am living as if in a nightmare. The entire situation of Spain pains me; the national, the general, first. But how much I am tortured by the idea that the group of friends is pulled apart, for God knows how long! ...Neither the country, nor Madrid, nor the people will be the same again. Our life is fatally split into two pieces: that of yesterday we know how it was, and that of tomorrow we know nothing. Therefore I cling to the only thing that can never be shipwrecked: to beloved ones always and forever. There is one thing that the war cannot take away, or at least cannot take away from me: the truth, necessity and will of friendship, and companionship and affection. All of that strengthens more and more.

A few weeks later, in letters to Margarita of April 1937, while he again bemoans the hardship of building a new social and professional life and seeking a new spiritual atmosphere (*Cartas de viaje* 78), there is evidence that he is confronting the sadness of separation with determination and hope. From a letter dated April 7, 1937, Newman cites his expressed desire to fight in Spain, or if unable to serve actually as a soldier, to stand with patience against divisive forces (Newman 156-57). Later that month, recounting to Margarita a visit with his new colleague Leo Spitzer, linguist and exile from Nazi Germany, Salinas describes an evolving personal sense of exile that connects with a romantic Spanish past:

...he vuelto a tener la sensación del *emigrado*. ¡Palabra romántica, palabra nacida desde hace 150 años y que ahora se pone de moda otra vez! Yo lo leía siempre con la sonrisa un poco irónica, como si fuese una palabra *literaria*. Y esta noche, hablando con Spitzer me vi, como en un espejo, en ella. No me ha dolido. Me he hecho cierta gracia melancólica. Me he acordado de la locución española: "¡Las

> vueltas que da el mundo!" Y me he dicho, para mis adentros: Que siga, que siga dando vueltas mientras haya como hay hoy, motivos y ganas de vivir en él. (*Cartas de viaje* 92)

> ....I again have the sensation of the *émigré*. A romantic word, a word born 150 years ago and now back in fashion! I always used to read it with a somewhat ironic smile, as if it were a *literary* term. And tonight, speaking with Spitzer, I saw myself in the word as in a mirror. It has not hurt. It has caused me a certain melancholic amusement. It has reminded me of the Spanish expression: "How the world changes!" And I have said to myself: May it continue, may it continue to change as long as there may be like there are today reasons and desire to live in it.

Resolve and bittersweet self-examination are attitudes that flow through his dramatic works, where characters seeking freedom or connection stand firm against aggressors and endure ups and downs with smiles and tears.

A year and one half later, in a letter to Katherine Whitmore dated November 27, 1938, Salinas assesses his state of exile with a positive fighting spirit. Though never dismissing his hunger for Spain, he recognizes his good fortune and embraces affirmatively his new situation. He writes of having lost his career, his social position, his house, and in it the many possessions dear to him. In the United States, he is grateful for the employment he has found, and above all, for a new place to live. Life in America does not compensate for his losses, but it does offer a safe and supportive haven for him, and one where he seeks harmony and tries to make the best of things:

> No soy un desterrado. América no es para mí un destierro, donde viva por obligación, y a disgusto, no. América es para mí un país bueno, generoso, donde me rodea una atmósfera agradable y serena. Es muy difícil, Katherine, vivir a gusto en un país extranjero. Hay muchas cosas arraigadas en el fondo del alma, a mi edad, que le

llaman a una, hacia su patria. Y sin embargo, vivo a gusto aquí. Conforme pase el tiempo, en vez de aumentar mi sentido de la diferencia, de la extranjería, lo que aumenta es mi simpatía por esta nación, y mi deseo de convivir con lo suyo, hasta donde es discreto y posible. Estoy contento, Katherine, porque veo que mi espíritu todavía no está cerrado, helado, y fijo, como suele ocurrir con los años, y que continúa abierto a lo nuevo y deseoso de recibirlo y entenderlo. (*Cartas a KW* 333)

I am not an exile. For me America is not an exile, where I may live by obligation and unhappily, no. For me America is a good, generous country where a pleasant and serene atmosphere surrounds me. It is very difficult, Katherine, to feel at home living in a foreign country. There are many things rooted in the depths of one's soul, at my age, that call one toward one's homeland. And nevertheless, I live at home here. With the passage of time, instead of increasing my sense of the difference, of the foreignness, what increases is my sympathy for this nation, and my desire to live together with what is hers as far as it is reasonable and possible. I am content, Katherine, because I see that my spirit is not yet closed, frozen, and fixed, as usually occurs with age, and that it continues open to what is new and desirous of receiving and understanding it.

Unwilling to release his grasp of the tragedy of Spain and its impact on him, Salinas projects tenaciously a strong bond with his homeland: "No sé cómo acabará lo de España: pero sé que no me robarán mi España, la que llevo en mí, desde que nací, que es sólo mía, y que la defenderé en el fondo de mi alma. (I do not know how the Spanish situation will end: but I know that they will not steal *my* Spain from me, the Spain I carry in me, since I was born, that is mine alone, and that I will defend deep down in my soul ; *Cartas a KW* 334). While thankful for his new environment, he downplays neither the problems of his personal adjustment nor those of the world context to which he connects himself. He identifies difficulties and looks inward to find the reason and will to

persevere:

> ...si una lluvia cae sobre mí a ratos, al pensar en las ignominias e infamias que los hombres cometen, otras veces siento lo bello y eterna que es la chispa y la llama de un alma dentro de un ser humano, y que sólo en eso hay un motivo para vivir. (*Cartas a KW* 334)

> ...if a rain falls on me at times, when I think of the ignominies and infamies men commit, other times I feel how beautiful and eternal is the spark and the flame of a soul inside a human being, and only in that is there a reason to live.

This mindset can be linked to Salinas's theater and to the missions he sets for the poet heroes of his plays. For example, Salinas's allusion to the opposition between the redemptive spark in the human spirit and the evils perpetrated by humankind reverberates in the question posed by Abel Levya, the protagonist of *Caín o una gloria científica,*. Abel is a scientist who suffers a personal and professional dilemma when he is ordered to apply his creative genius to make a weapon that threatens to destroy the world:

> ¿Se merece el hombre el mayor don que le dieran, la chispa de inteligencia, el don de crear, si con ella enciende las lumbres del mal? ¡No, no, y no! No nos merecemos lo mejor, el alma, si en ella se forja la traición del alma. (Salinas, *Teatro completo* 185)

> Does man deserve the greatest gift that may have been given to him, the spark of intelligence, the gift of creating, if with it he kindles the lights of evil? No, no, no! We do not deserve what is best, the soul, if in it is forged a treason of the soul.

After the civil war ended in Spain, although troubled by the postwar conditions there, Salinas maintains a positive perspective from exile. In

a letter dated March 5, 1940 to Guillén, Salinas writes:

> Yo no soy tan pesimista como tú sobre España. Es decir sobre su futuro material inmediato. De la escritura de *Arriba* se saca la conclusión de lo mal que anda todo. La Falange desesperada, rabiosa, dando dentelladas a diestro y siniestro, desconfía de medio mundo, insulta y amenaza, síntoma de debilidad y de recelo. *Esto* no puede sostenerse. La monstruosidad ingénita del movimiento lo condena al no ser, al no poder ser. (PS/ JG *Correspondencia* 224)

> I am not as pessimistic as you are about Spain. That is to say about its immediate material future. From the writings of *Arriba* one draws the conclusion about how badly everything is going. The Phalange desperate, angry, leaving teethmarks right and left, mistrusts half the world, insults and threatens, symptom of weakness and suspicion. *This* cannot be sustained. The inherent monstrosity of the movement condemns it to nonexistence, to an inability to exist.

From his distance, Salinas recognizes that use of threat of force can show lack of confidence and persuasive ability. From a nonpropagandistic, universal, and broadly human perspective, Salinas later dramatizes in his play *Judit y el tirano* this postwar atmosphere and the search for deliverance from repressive dictatorship.

Salinas's withdrawal from Spain increases his desire to retain aspects of Spanish daily life. Jaime and Solita Salinas have reminisced about their father never succumbing to drinking Coca-Cola or having it in the house. According to Solita, in exile her father became much more Spanish than he had been before leaving Spain, and even took *siesta*s (Cruz 84). In a letter dated November 21, 1939, Salinas describes to Guillén his delight in perusing drawings and engravings of sixteenth century Spain from the museums of Boston and New York. He recognizes that exile enhanced his appreciation of things Spanish:

> Pero es curioso, de verdad, cómo este trabajo, que en España no me

habría dicho nada, aquí me entusiasma y aprovecha profundamente. Acaso porque es una de los pocos modos de hacer pie, que le queden a uno, en el eterno y necesario fondo español. (PS/JG *Correspondencia* 212)

But it is curious, really, how this work, that in Spain would not have meant anything to me, here profoundly excites and gratifies me. Perhaps because it is one of the few ways that one has left to stand oneself on the eternal and necessary Spanish ground.

Newman shares numerous anecdotes about Salinas's hungering for tastes of Spain: the quince paste and marzipan, its water and wine, as well as for the buildings and the sites of his boyhood in Madrid, and the songs and sounds of his past (Newman 32-46). "During his exile," she writes, "when he could not hear these accents around him, he would imitate the jargon of the *barrios bajos,* of the *chulo,* for the amusement of fellow *emigrados* who understood. He often sang *coplas* from *zarzuelas;* to do so was like going home" (Newman 41). Many of these touches of home inspire the dialogues and settings of his plays, particularly *La fuente del arcángel,* "*La Estratoesfera,*" and *Los santos.* His daughter Solita writes about the remedial, nostalgic value of her father's theater, especially the plays explicitly set in Spain:

Podríamos decir que Pedro Salinas creaba personajes españoles con quienes poder hablar, y claro, escuchar también sus voces propias. Y hasta cierto punto podría decirse que las dos obras "castizas" del teatro de Salinas (la andaluza y la madrileña) fueron en primer lugar, obras de "entretenimiento." Y así mi padre se divertía, verdaderamente, leyendo en voz alta a su familia y a sus visitantes españoles *La fuente del arcángel* y sobre todo, "*La Estratoesfera.*" (Salinas de Marichal, "Tradición y modernidad..." 3)

We could say that Pedro Salinas created Spanish characters with whom one could speak, and of course, also listen to one's own voice.

And to a certain extent one could say that the two 'most authentic' dramatic works of Salinas (the one set in Andalusia and the one in Madrid) were in the first place works of "entertainment." And so my father enjoyed himself, truly, reading aloud to his family and Spanish visitors *The Fountain of the Archangel* and especially, *The Stratosphere*.

Salinas's frequent travels in exile to lecture and teach stir in him strong associations with Spain. The deserts of the southwestern United States remind him of Castille. The marvel of the Grand Canyon overwhelms him, and in his effusive description of it to Margarita, he repeatedly identifies with his Spanish roots. He sees the fantastic creations of Goya in its awesome geological formations, the mystical delirium of Santa Teresa in the *paisaje puro* or pure landscape, and the sights and smells of El Pardo, the Casa de Campo, and El Escorial in the impressive vegetation and topography (*Cartas de viaje* 108). Ever reaching to hold on to his Spanishness, Salinas feels a special bond with fellow Spaniards in the United States. This sense of unity crosses social and economic boundaries. Of an evening spent in San Francisco with a diverse group of Republican sympathizers that bring together working class people and academics, Salinas writes to Margarita,

> ¡Ay España, España! Sólo una enorme ausencia, vaga, lejanísima y borrosa, España, que sin duda cada uno interpretábamos de una manera, que para cada cual de nosotros era una cosa distinta, nos servía de lazo. Algo fuerte y profundo tiene que ser, para hacer el milagro que gentes que en nada se parecen sientan por dos horas algo común. Quizá todo español lleva en su habla, en sus ademanes, en su (sic) de mirar, algo que es *tierra* española. Y nos sentimos como pisando en mínimos suelos españoles, con la ilusión, en las voces, en los gestos o las entonaciones. ¡Valga para un rato! Quizá eso sea el pueblo. Quizá todo tengamos, por encima de profesiones y sensibilidades, de ideas o educación, algo que es de todos, lo que nos hace pueblo, una *humanidad española*, arraigada. (*Cartas de viaje* 168-

69)

Oh Spain, Spain! Only an enormous, vague, very distant and blurred absence, Spain, that without a doubt each one of us interpreted in a way that for each one was a different thing, served as a tie. It has to be something strong and profound that makes the miracle that people who in no way resemble each other feel something in common for two hours. Perhaps every Spaniard carries in his speech, in his gestures, in his (way) of looking, something that is the Spanish *land*. And we feel that we are stepping on a little bit of Spanish ground, with hope, in our voices, in our gestures, in our entonations. May it help for a while! Perhaps that may be the people. Perhaps all we may have, above professions and sensibilities, ideas and education, something that is all of ours, that makes us a people, a *Spanish humanity*, rooted.

Salinas's visits in exile to Spanish-speaking places draw him even closer to his roots. While motivating strong nostalgic outpourings, they bring him considerable fulfillment by reconnecting him with living Spanish language and culture. During his trip to Mexico during the summer of 1938, he writes to Katherine that he feels reborn and in a state of *adquisición constante* or constant acquisition (*Cartas a KW* 309). Mexico evokes for him a sweeping, encompassing reencounter with his Spanish past:

Y lo más curioso es que no recuerdo partes determinadas de España, sino algo de todo, mezclado. México es una síntesis de lo español: no es lo andaluz, ni lo castillano, ni lo levantino, en estado puro, sino una sutil combinación de temas varios. (*Cartas a KW* 309)

And the curious thing is that I do not remember specific parts of Spain, but rather something of everything, mixed. Mexico is a synthesis of what is Spanish: it is not what is Andalusian, nor what is Castillian, nor what is Levantine, in a pure state, but a subtle combination of varied themes.

In Mexico, Salinas experiences the ambiguity of separation and connection. At the same time he is feeling himself a foreigner in Mexico and recognizing his difference from the Mexicans he meets, he is experiencing a deep sense of homeland:

> La gente, su carácter y habla son una variante, a veces muy alejada, de lo nuestro; pero las calles, las costumbres, lo mudo y tradicional, me acercan a España a cada paso. (*Cartas a KW* 313)

> The people, their character and speech are a variation, at times very removed, from ours; but the streets, the customs, what is mute and traditional, draw me closer to Spain with every step.

He is charmed by the details of the customs and language. He is much amused, for example, by the Mexican shops bearing creative names. He delights in repeating the examples to Katherine and shares his plans to write an essay about the entertaining commercial signs (*Cartas a KW* 347). Two signs from the list he names for Katherine—*"Atlántida. Sombrería"* or "Atlantis. Hatshop" and *"Las emociones. Cervezas y refrescos"* or "Emotions. Beers and refreshments"—may have inspired the composition of two of his plays, *"La Cabeza de Medusa"* "The Head of Medusa" and *"La Estratoesfera. Vinos y cervezas"* "The Stratosphere. Wines and Beers." In each play, a colorful sign bearing the name of the establishment is prominent in the set design. The first setting is a hatshop of mythical name where a detached observer confronts the truths of life's loves and disappointments. In the second play, the scene is a lively neighborhood bar on the outskirts of central Madrid of the 1930s. Here Salinas brings to life the colloquial language of his native city and casts a poet character into a quixotic plot. This play also reflects clearly the enthusiasm Salinas has communicated about Mexico to Guillén. A few months after his trip, Salinas writes to Guillén of the special joy of being in an environment where Spanish is spoken and especially in a milieu of café conversation (PS/ JG *Correspondencia* 190-91).

Significantly, Mexico also puts Salinas back in touch with a Spanish-speaking audience. In this same letter to Guillén in October of 1938, Salinas is ecstatic about reaching a public that understands him. He confides somewhat diffidently that after spending some two years in New England, Vermont, Maryland, and New York, he feels like he is in *Nueva España* or New Spain, the label Cortés has given Mexico (PS/JG *Correspondencia* 191).

Back in the United States, there are times when the pressures of exile slow or impede his productivity. Though persistent in trying to improve his English, he continues to feel frustrated and describes himself to friend Catherine Centeno as "English-proof" (Bou and Soria Olmedo "PS Cartografía..." 114). At the beginning of 1942, although he writes to Guillén of having many ideas, a literary history of the twentieth century, other articles, and a play already completed in his mind, he feels despondent about the world situation, unproductive, and caught in a labyrinth of distractions (PS/JG*Correspondencia* 271). The opportunity to reenter a Spanish-speaking environment, to live and and work in Puerto Rico between 1943 and 1946, proves to be the oasis or Eden during his separation from Spain (Ciplijauskaité, Newman 221ff).

His daughter Solita describes Salinas's years in Puerto Rico as the happiest of his exile (Bou "Descubrimiento'..." 451; Salinas de Marichal "Cronología" 43). His son-in-law Juan Marichal uses the neologism of José Gaos to refer to Salinas no longer as an exile, but as a *feliz transterrado* or happy transplant in Puerto Rico (Marichal in Salinas *El defensor* 11). Though early in his stay Salinas confesses to colleague and friend from Vassar College Margarita de Mayo that he is having trouble working in the beautiful, tropical environment and that he has worked better in the United States, this soon changes (*Cartas de viaje* 179). His letters, especially those to Guillén between 1943 and 1946, have shown how in Puerto Rico he composes the poetry of *El contemplado* (*The Contemplated Sea*), many of the poems of *Todo más claro* (*All Things Made Clearer*), and *Confianza* (*Confidence*), numerous essays including his works on Rubén Darío and Jorge Manrique, and much of his theater. By 1946, toward the end of his stay in Puerto Rico, Salinas writes to Katherine that he is working regularly and more than ever (*Cartas a KW* 369).

While ideas for and about drama were germinating in him for many years, it is in Puerto Rico that Salinas composes ten of his fourteen plays. The comforts of Puerto Rico and its Spanish-speaking milieu facilitate Salinas's engagement with theater and conversational Spanish. For Salinas, the island is a *fecunda frontera de tensión*, a fertile frontier of tension between the English language and Spanish language and their civilizations and cultures (Marichal in Salinas *El defensor* 11). These tensions he addresses quite explicitly in several essays, notably in his speech "Aprecio y defensa del lenguaje" ("In Appreciation and Defense of Language") to the graduates of the University of Puerto Rico in 1944, and they inform many juxtapositions found in his plays, where characters seek to adjust and to carve an ideal space, sometimes in playful and sometimes in serious response, to the pressures of modern life and communication.

Experiencing a kind of rebirth in Puerto Rico, Salinas is able to amplify his lyric voice and to reencounter his Spanishness. What he writes to describe the relationship of Rubén Darío with his native Nicaragua captures the empathetic mentality of Salinas the exile seeking contact with his roots:

> Era su tierra, tierra patria. Lugar de los orígenes; allí se le abrió la vida de los sentidos y de la razón a sus primeras, las más inolvidables, experiencias elementales. Patria sencilla, la que va descubriendo tanto puro y sin estrenar, casa y familiares, paisajes y juegos de niño, flores primeras, rostros primeros que se le asoman a una a la mirada, los sones primeros que enseñan a distinguir en el instinto el ruido de la melodía, el torrente del ruiseñor, y a desearlos o temerlos. (*La poesía de Ruben Darío* 34)

> It was his land, homeland. Place of origin; there were opened to him the first, most unforgettable, elemental experiences of the world of the senses and reason. Simple homeland, that which he goes on

discovering so pure and unreleased, home and relatives, landscapes and childhood games, the first sounds that teach the instinct to distinguish noise from melody, torrent from nightingale, and to desire them or fear them.

Through writing plays, Salinas is able to transform and give special definition to these sorts of fundamental details of dailiness, personal history, home, family, and nature and to affirm his attachment to his land and living language.

In Puerto Rico Salinas does not escape world happenings or his separation from Spain. Rather, the experience of the island contributes to his appreciation of the redemptive power of exile, as exemplified by what he writes to Américo Castro soon before returning to Baltimore:

> Entretanto, lo único posible, vitalmente, moralmente, es hacer lo que V. hace, pensar, escribir, trabajar profundamente. No comprendo como un español pueda oír sufrirse su ocio vacío, a no ser que él mismo esté vacío, o lleno de politiquerías baratas. El que vuelva a España con las manos tan sin nada como cuando salió, o cargado de combustible para la nueva hoguera sacrificial, no merece volver. Sólo nos justificará lo que llevemos, cada cual según su capacidad y medios. Si el destierro es bueno es por lo que tiene de espoleo y de purificador. Por lo menos nosotros hemos tenido la inmensa suerte de haber podido seguir pensando sin tener que ahormar nuestro pensar y nuestro hacer a modelos de Estado, como aquellos pobres que viven y sufren en España. (Bou and Soria Olmedo "Cartografía-..." 129)

> Meanwhile, the only thing possible, vitally, morally, is to do what you are doing, to think, write, work profoundly. I do not understand how a Spaniard can hear suffering in his empty leisure, unless he himself is empty, or filled with cheap petty politics. He who returns to Spain with his hands as empty as when he left, or charged with a combustible for the new sacrificial bonfire, does not deserve to

return. Only what we may be carrying, each according to his capacity and means, is what will justify us. If exile is good it is for what it is as a spur and a purifier. At least we have had the immense fortune to have been able to continue thinking without having to mold our thought and our doing to the model of the State, like those poor people who live and suffer in Spain.

Appropriately, Juan Marichal calls the circumstance of exile a fortune in the sense that many people discover in exile talents they did not know they have (Cruz 84). Salinas appreciates greatly the freedom of thought and movement he enjoys outside of Spain, and sees the condition of exile not only in personal terms but also as part of the modern human condition and an inspiration for linkage and salvation. This perspective connects with the goals of his poet characters seeking a liberating unification with others.

After leaving Puerto Rico, Salinas returns to the United States to teach and his work takes him to Latin America and Europe. During his trips to lecture in Colombia, Ecuador, and Peru in 1947, he finds frequent reminders of Spain. His letters to Margarita, Solita, and Juan carry vivid descriptions of the bustle of the center of Bogota, the congregations of people, the bus-stops, the lottery sellers, and the food, all of which Salinas associates with Spain, especially Madrid: (*Cartas de viaje* 191-92). In 1949, Salinas visits France, Italy, and other European countries, but not Spain. He writes to Guillén of the pain of not being able to enter Spain (PS/JG *Correspondencia* 477).

During the last years of his life, as Salinas encounters challenges to the staging of his plays and becomes ill, at times he expresses his sense of exile with more distress than bittersweet nostalgia. In a letter to Guillén of January 1950, after his children and grandchildren leave Baltimore for Cambridge, Salinas writes of his profound attachment to his family and his intense need for them. Sharing with Guillén his suffering, melancholy, and feelings of detachment, he attributes this need to his condition of exile:

> ...se me figura que el destierro, el vivir en una situación extraña íntimamente a mí, es causa de esa situación, y que en España las cosas serían de otra manera.... Pero no puedo por menos de ver acumularse las desventajas, las adversidades, del destierro, se suman a las esenciales, la vida familiar y de amigos, las otras, importantes también, las de mi vida como escritor y sus ilusiones. Contraste: esta calma, este bienestar material, esta atmósfera materialmente satisfactoria, y la insatisfacción interior. (PS/JG *Correspondencia* 518)

> ... it occurs to me that exile, living in a situation intimately strange to me, is the cause of that situation, and that in Spain things would be different.... I can't help but see the disadvantages, the adversities of exile accumulating, they add up to the essentials, family life and life with friends, the other things, also important, those of my life as a writer and its hopes. Contrast: this calm, this material wellbeing, this materially satisfactory atmosphere, and the internal dissatisfaction.

In empathetic response, Guillén expresses his own melancholy and shows his understanding of the obstacles Salinas is facing as a dramatist:

> De ese destierro, de esa falta de tierra provienen muchos males particulares. En tu caso de dramaturgo, la casi imposibilidad—¡casi!—de ver representadas tus obras. (¡Cuánto la habría gozado yo, amigote del autor, en los estrenos de esas obras en Madrid, en el otro Madrid!...) (PS/JG *Correspondencia* 520)

> From that exile, that lack of land comes many specific evils. In your case as a dramatist, the almost impossibility—almost!— of seeing your works staged. (How I would have delighted, as good friend of the author, in the premieres of those works in Madrid, in the other Madrid!...)

Later that year, Salinas reacts unhappily to the rejection of his work by Editorial Sudamericana. He notes the irony of the press citing economic difficulties and lack of paper, while back in the United States he is seeing newspapers with some eighty pages, filled with ads for the approaching Christmas season (PS/JG *Correspondencia* 546). He is feeling acutely the problem of suviving in Spanish outside of Spain, especially as a writer and a dramatist. After six weeks in Latin America and unsuccessful attempts to make the necessary contacts to see his theatrical works move toward production, he laments to colleague Guillermo de Torre the "doble condición del desterrado" or double condition of the exile. He is suffering not only the broadly human condition of a person in exile but also the special frustration of the exiled dramatist (Torre 16). Long deeply concerned with the problematic relationship between the artist and society, Salinas again bemoans his distance from Spain and his detachment from Spanish-speaking cultural centers, a circumstance Torre has evaded by living in Buenos Aires. Writing plays is a means of combatting his feelings of removal from Spain and a Spanish-speaking public, but the difficulty of finding an audience for them exacerbates his sense of separation.

As letters to Guillén and family have shown, Salinas's living to see the production of *La fuente del arcángel* was immensely gratifying to him. "Con Pedro Salinas" ("With Pedro Salinas"), the article published by Dámaso Alonso to describe the playwright's delight, generated a letter of thanks in which Salinas links his self-definition as an exile, his yearning for connection, and the function of his theater:

> …Yo no soy más que un pobre desterrado, lejos de sus nietos y de su patria, que escribe por desesperación, y que le quiere mucho y le da un gran abrazo, y no se resigna a que se vaya usted por esos aires sin verle otra vez. (Alonso, "España en las cartas…" 5)

> … I am only a poor exile, far from his grandchildren and his homeland, who writes out of desperation, and who loves you very much and gives you a big embrace, and does not resign himself to your leaving without seeing you again.

Echoing in a way what he had written in his essay "El 'Cantar de Mío Cid' Poema de la honra," Salinas goes on to identify with the banished hero. Though he cannot allow himself the luxury of weeping with grief like exile exemplar, he is inclined to do so since he is now seeing himself without an exit in the midst of an alien world (Alonso, "España en las cartas..." 5).

Salinas's nostalgia and so-called desperation enter with strong positive force into his theater. With a timelessness that touches the everyday world and reaches beyond it, his theater raises questions about past, present, and future, and is part of his search for remedy. The experiences of exile as rupture and exile as redemption can be connected to the ways the plots unfold in Salinas's fourteen plays. Separation and connection, restriction and freedom, these are the concerns that shape his dramatic corpus. His plays can be viewed in the light of his conception of exile as a heartfelt separation from Spain, a part of the modern human circumstance, and a stimulus for redemptive reconnection.

Part II

The Poet in the Theater

4
Poet and Plot: Salinas's "Fabula" of Confinement-to-Freedom

> Es inútil tratar de convertirla [la poesía] en un ave doméstica, subyugada, confinada, pronto a servir en cualquier momento, transformándose en el plato familiar de cada día. No admite jaulas ni corrales.
> SALINAS, "Prólogo a una traducción de sus poemas,"
> *Ensayos completos III* 430
>
> It is useless to try to turn it [poetry] into a domestic bird, subdued, confined, ready to serve at any moment, by changing it into an ordinary, everyday dish. It does not allow cages or corrals.

IN THE PREFACE TO *Reality and the Poet in Spanish Poetry*, Guillén wrote of Salinas's dramatic works, "For him they were 'reality in fable form' (xxi)." Guillén then concurred, "Precisely: an action situated on a normal level, so to speak, rises little by little, leaving behind the first level, until it reaches the heights of fantasy (xxi)." These words serve as a point of departure for offering a preliminary account of the structure of the dramatic works as a guide to poetic action. It can be established that each of Salinas's fourteen plays conforms to a basic *fabula*, or fundamental story-line, and that his dramatic corpus stands as a unified body. At the same time, every play might be considered a representation of a particular configuration of narratable events into a plot, in Russian formalist terminology *sjuzet*, the arrangement of the "narration" which includes omissions, changes in sequencing, flashbacks, incidental comments, etc. that do not contribute directly to the dynamic chain of events (Elam 119). A particular story could be communicated through any number of plots. Each different arrangement of the same story elements would result in a new plot. An overview of Salinas's fourteen different plot lines will show that each constitutes a kind of variation of the same fundamental action, that is, the movement by a character or characters out of confining isolation toward liberating contact with another or others. His protagonists, initiators of the process, are the key contributing factor to this basic unity. Employing these figures to shape his creations of "reality in fable form," Salinas constructs a body of drama that reflects his unique blending of contemporaneous currents of realism and antirealism in the modern theater. On the one hand, Salinas shows with realism ordinary people and commonplace settings to reflect truths about human life. On the other hand, he reaches for a timeless perspective and probes beyond everyday routine to enter the world of hopes, dreams, and visions and to explore significant intangibles of existence. Moreover, Salinas's artistic blending combines this universal, humanistic outlook with immediate circumstances that touch him personally and profoundly.

Persistently adhering to the unifying, underlying confinement-to-freedom framework, Salinas joins his characters in a variety of thematic spheres. Most often, he sets their pursuits in a predominantly romantic context, for example, in *La isla del tesoro*, *La fuente del arcángel*, and *El chantajista*. In other plays, he casts his freedom seekers in a political context (*Caín o una gloria científica*, *Los santos*), the business world (*Sobre seguro*), or in a sphere involving artistic endeavor or intellectual and existential pursuit (*Ella y sus fuentes*, *El precio*). In some of his works, he blends the romantic with other contexts, for example, the political (*Judit y el tirano*), the commercial (*La Bella Durmiente, La Cabeza de Medusa*), or the existential (*El Director*). Spatially and geographically, he locates them in environs which suggest contemporary yet universal contexts: in a restaurant (*El parecido*), a mountain resort (*La Bella Durmiente, El Director*), a café (*"La Estratoesfera"*), a park and garden (*El chantajista*), a hotel room (*La isla del tesoro*), a boutique shop (*La Cabeza de Medusa*). The majority of the plays take place in imaginary countries in urban or rural locations, but even the works with specific local color such as *La fuente del arcángel,* "*La Estratoesfera,*" and *Los santos* transcend immediate surroundings to project a universality connected to the fundamental action.

Salinas also employs variety in his choice of characters and key character combinations. Although the majority of works depict the pairing of a male and female in a developing amorous relationship, there also exist prominent interactions among groupings such as mother and son (*Sobre seguro*), brothers (*Caín o una gloria científica*), writer and invented character (*Ella y sus fuentes*, *El precio*), fellow prisoners (*Los santos*), employer and employee (*La Cabeza de Medusa*), and divinity and worshiper (*El Director*). His characterizations typify what Scanlan has categorized as the four chief macroconflicts in modern drama: male versus female, the individual versus social injustice, human consciousness versus the mystery of life, and personal dream versus the real world (136-42). Salinas projects these struggles in a variety of formulations and combinations, all initiated and driven by his poet heroes' quests for freedom. In his frequent male-female pairings, Salinas emphasizes the search of the protagonists for outlet for their individuality and creativity, for example, in *La fuente del arcángel* (Florindo-Claribel), "*La Estratoesfera*" (Alvaro-Felipa), "*La isla del tesoro*" (the journal writer-Marú), *El chantajista* (Lisardo-Lucila), and *El precio* (Jáuregui-Melisa). In some of the male-female conflicts, Salinas highlights the characters' search for emancipation from the social context [*Judit y el tirano* (Andrés-Judit), *La Bella Durmiente* (Carlos-Soledad)], the desire to penetrate the mysteries of life [*El parecido* (Roberto-Julia), *El director* (Gerente-Mecanógrafa)], or the confrontation of personal dreams with the "real" world [*Sobre seguro* (Angel-Petra), *Ella y sus fuentes* (Merlín-Julia), *La Cabeza de Medusa* (Andrenio-Lucila)]. In the conflicts of *Caín o una gloria científica* and *Los santos*, Salinas also incorporates male-female interactions while focusing on the heroic characters' expression of humanity and truth as they struggle with sociopolitical pressures.

Salinas's plays move horizontally, with a causal structure propelled principally by the aspirations and movements of dominating poet characters. The motivational force of these characters in the emancipation process forges connections and advances toward a fulfillment. After surveying the fundamental *fabula* and its two variations, confinement-to-freedom with felicitous outcome or with tragic resolution, this chapter will examine the structural components of Salinas's plot creations to show the essential motivating force of the poet heroes in the action.

"REALITY IN FABLE FORM":
  THE *FABULA* OF CONFINEMENT-TO-FREEDOM

The structure common to the diverse plot lines of the fourteen plays, the *fabula* of confinement-to-freedom, is a dynamic progression of actions and events involving poet heroes as chief agents. In general terms, it appears that initially, characters function apart from one another or in solitude with an unenlightened view of their circumstances. The fundamental redemptive action begins when the guiding "poet" successfully sets forth to the character or characters to be transformed a vision that prods their self-discovery and desire for freedom. The process develops as the evolving character or characters show a predisposition to enter the orbit of the leader character. The union is realized when the one comes to define himself or herself through the lens of the poet. Their vital connection often stands in sharp contrast to the negativity and confinement in relationships other than their own. The plays end in one of two ways. Either the redeemed characters "exit" from the plays together, in an auspicious poetic union, or they are separated, usually through the death of one of the characters, after the experience of a climactic, liberating revelation. Eight plays conclude in the more optimistic and open-ended manner. The other six culminate in a transformation possessing tragic overtones. All demonstrate the crucial impetus of the poet hero in the redemptive process.

In the first group, the primary poet figures exhibit an influential confidence in their own identities and the emerging identities of their counterparts. Exercising an energetic independence that enables them to open relationships with those so far confined, these poets are able to combat the circumstances threatening to their liberating unions. Before they initiate the action of redemption with their chosen kindred spirits, they have already experienced a spiritual emancipation from the sorts of repressive, divisive obstacles they will encounter freeing others. Their successful interactions and ultimate unions take place outside the oppressive milieu that therefore can only touch them slightly. At the conclusion of these plays, the united characters exit transformed and free to pursue together their happiness in keeping with the original stance of the poet initiator. This happy open-endedness shows that even the structure of these plays suggests the outcome of transcendence.

In the second group, the main poet characters are extremely preoccupied with self identity and with the identity of their kindred characters, but successful affirmation along with liberation from confinement is tragic because one or both characters have been impeded by obstacles that must be faced through painful struggle. Ultimately, they are compromised or remain trapped in a highly limiting, spiritually oppressive environment that outlives the success of their discovery process. The communicating characters achieve a liberating understanding and measure of fulfillment, but identity problems and the related overburdening circumstances determine the unhappy conclusions of these plays.

A typology of the plays based on the outcome of the confinement-to-freedom process points to the following two groupings:

FREEDOM AND FELICITOUS OUTCOME

La fuente del arcángel	comedia
"La Estratoesfera"	escenas de taberna en un acto
La isla del tesoro	comedia
Ella y sus fuentes	comedia
El chantajista	fantasía en un acto y dos cuadros
El parecido	comedia
Sobre seguro	comedia
Los santos	

FREEDOM AND TRAGIC OUTCOME
La Bella Durmiente	comedia
Judit y el tirano	drama en tres actos
La Cabeza de Medusa	comedia
El precio	fantasía en un acto y dos cuadros
Caín o una gloria científica	comedia
El director	misterio en tres actos

While all the works except *Los santos* bear subtitles, these denominations do not demarcate the two variations, though they indicate each play's broad dramatic form or structure. Salinas's earliest play, *El director*, a mystery in three acts, with its enigmatic Divinity figure, its puzzled, soul-searching creatures, and symbolic touches, shares features of the allegorical *autos* or eucharistic plays of Spanish Golden Age theater. *"La Estratoesfera,"* subtitled "tavern scenes in one act," approximates the *sainete*-like, slice-of-life exchanges Salinas admired in the works of Carlos Arniches. His final two compositions, *El precio* and *El chantajista*, "fantasies" in one act and two scenes, both represent dreamlike, metatextual creations by poet characters in search of counterparts; but these works stand in different groups because the *fabula* of confinement-to-freedom concludes painfully in one and blissfully in the other. His other full-length work, *Judit y el tirano*, as well as the majority of the shorter pieces, carry more the generic subtitles of *drama* or *comedia*. Different from the English word "comedy," the term *comedia* reflects a broader scope and the more traditional Spanish definition of play or dramatic work. Salinas's plays contain both humorous and serious elements. The subtitles mark the works' theatrical shape and composition, but do not signal the nature of the resolutions of the plays. An overview of the two variations will illustrate their key similarities and differences.

FREEDOM AND FELICITOUS OUTCOME
With the exception of *Los santos*, in each play of this first group, the redemptive communication develops essentially between two characters,

a male and a female. The man successfully seeks and guides the woman in *La fuente del arcángel* and "*La Estratoesfera*"; the woman pursues and breaks the confinement of the man in *La isla del tesoro* and *Ella y sus fuentes*; and in *El chantajista*, *El parecido*, and *Sobre seguro*, there occurs between the male and female a more mutual, interactive liberation process. In *Los santos*, there is no single poet figure. Instead, Salinas augments the basic couple construction to focus on the transcendence of the six principal characters in concert with their saintly counterparts. These plays all develop according to the same pattern: characters emerge from isolation or constricting surroundings. Often, Salinas contrasts the evolving successful relationship with other deficient relationships. The following situations illustrate the fundamental movement and transformation out of oppressive circumstances toward emancipation.

In *La fuente del arcángel* and "*La Estratoesfera*," both Claribel and Felipa escape from extremely cloistered lives. Claribel boards ten months a year at a convent school, and for the remaining two months vacations at the home of her aunt Gumersinda, who carefully arranges and inspects every activity in which Claribel and her sister participate. Felipa, after having to leave her town in disgrace, is the constant companion of her blind grandfather, with whom she sells lottery tickets. Each young woman finds newer, richer meaning for her life with the aid of a young man, a poet character, who charms her out of her rigid, sterile environment. Florindo the magician (and later, the come-to-life Eros statue of the fountain) communicates with Claribel, awakening within her the imaginative spirit that is longing to emerge. Alvaro the poet restores Felipa's sense of honor and opens for her a happier future. In both plays, Salinas incorporates the physical gesture of hand holding to mark the unions. At the conclusion of *La fuente del arcángel*, Claribel, transformed into the Byzantine empress Teodora, now believing in the authenticity of illusion sees some of the falseness of her sheltered existence. In the final scene, she exits hand in hand with the Archangel-turned-Eros figure (*Teatro completo* 241). "*La Estratoesfera*" ends with a similar transformation. Leaving her past experiences behind, Felipa smiles and gives her hand to Alvaro as they move toward the door (*Teatro completo* 211).

Salinas even utilizes the stage design in these two plays to complement his plot development, focusing on isolation versus liberating communication. He creates in *La fuente del arcangel* a set with three divisions: the parlor in the home of Gumersinda, the stage for Florindo's performance, seen through a picture on a wall of the parlor, and, just outside the house, the main square of the town, in which the fountain of the Arcángel is located. Claribel functions as the only character in the family capable of linking with Florindo and the Arcángel, and therefore inhabits all three environments. Gumersinda remains enclosed within the parlor setting. Estefanía and Sergio attend the magic show but return home to stay there. "La Estratoesfera" is furnished with at least five separate tables. One group of customers, Julián and his friends, remains forever isolated in the play, because they never interact with any of the characters at the other tables. In addition to portraying their withdrawal from everyone else, Salinas satirizes the inability of these few men to communicate with each other. They argue incesssantly, and their discussions about social justice are filled with meaningless jargon and malapropisms. Only the patrons who move away from their tables to visit others achieve some degree of meaningful communication. Alvaro, the most mobile character, is the one who communicates most effectively, and who, in turn, influences Felipa, César, and even Luis, to reach beyond their narrow spheres.

In *La isla del tesoro* and *Ella y sus fuentes*, the female protagonists Marú and Julia share the goal of identity clarification with relation to a particular individual, the writer of the mysterious notebook, and Desiderio Merlín, respectively. Their pursuit of successful interaction with these men constitutes the driving force behind the action of each play. Once Marú finds the notebook and discovers its contents, she feels compelled to know the identity of this person whose ideas so perfectly match her own, and with whom she feels destined to share her life. Once Julia learns that she is being so grossly misinterpreted by someone reputed to be an expert about her and her life, she feels driven to make Merlín see his errors. Both women accomplish their aims, and at the end of each play, Salinas links the characters in a poetic, spiritual union. In

La isla del tesoro, Marú, certain that the young man will read her newspaper advertisement the following morning, confidently awaits his reply. In *Ella y sus fuentes*, even though Julia cannot change her image within the national heritage, she does bring the truth to Merlín, and finds a way for him to remain by the truth. Merlín chooses to die, to follow Julia to the afterlife, and an idealized connection in the world beyond. Salinas's concluding portrayal of them, as well as his concluding representation of Marú awaiting her young man, thus suggest a transcendent union between each pair.

The formation of these ties underlines the breakdown or falseness of other interactions in the two plays. In *La isla del tesoro*, the relationship between Marú and Severino proves to be extremely weak and confining to Marú, as well as devoid of any special magnetism like that which exists between Marú and the mysterious writer. In fact, their differing interpretations of what constitutes true communication lie at the heart of their fragile match. Severino demands a rational explanation about the notebook and insists on remaining within the bonds of conventionality, but Marú sees a valid place for the inexplicable and for free imagination, which, to her, in no way hamper communication, and, in fact, allow for a necessary limitlessness in the interpretation of events.

In *Ella y sus fuentes*, the reason Julia, dead for one hundred years, is granted permission to return to earth for a short while, is to correct an error that has been communicated widely during the century, perpetuated through cold, rigid, written sources, to which Merlín is bound. Merlín discounts too much the validity of more colorful human sources and of the oral tradition, those more imaginative sources that could possibly tell more than dry documents. The interview with the one surviving man who said that he knew Julia, and certainly the appearance of Julia herself, prove to be more liberating forms of communication than all of Merlín's written research.

The female protagonists lead the action in *El chantajista*, *El parecido*, and *Sobre seguro*, though in these works there is much more developed reciprocity on the part of the male principals than in *La isla del tesoro* and *Ella y sus fuentes*. In *El chantajista*, Lucila's planting of the love letters activates Lisardo to co-create a relationship that draws them out of their respective states of isolation. In *El parecido*, once the Incógnito piques Julia's curiosity and she arouses Roberto's preoccupation with the identity of the Incógnito and the initiation of the confessions about the past, Roberto takes as great a part as she does in unlocking his sentiments and increasing their intimacy. In *Sobre seguro*, the initial view of the mother-son relationship focuses on the fierce attachment of Petra to her missing son, but is soon broadened to include Angel's return and a look at their transcendence beyond the opresive worlds of family and insurance.

The individuals in each of these three plays emerge from relative isolation or from a frustrating environment to attain fulfillment as part of a pair. At the end of each play, Salinas points to the continuation of their transformed status. Lisardo and Lucila fall in love to escape loneliness, and after a series of mysterious encounters, explain their charades, uncover their true feelings, and look ahead to a promising future. Lucila, in the final moments of the play, recaps her movement out of solitude:

> El amor es el que hace al amante. El me hizo a mí, primero... Y como me dejó sola yo tuve que buscarte..., que hacerte (Sacando las cartas.) así..., Lisardo. Te he engañado para la verdad. (*Teatro completo* 306)

> Love is what makes the lover. It made me, first... And since it left me alone I had to look for you..., and make you (Taking out the letters.) like this..., Lisardo. I have deceived you in order to arrive at the truth.

The couple shares the contents of one of the letters to begin their idyllic alliance. In *El parecido*, Roberto and Julia leave the restaurant freed from harboring secrets from their pasts and having undergone a kind of renewal. Trying to discover the identity of the Incógnito intensifies their mutual understanding, elicits significant personal confession, and brings them to harmony.

A confinement-to-freedom process is also evident in *Sobre seguro*, in the bonding between Petra and Angel. Although the insurance men and the other family members presume he is dead, Petra refuses to accept his death. The scene in which the others try to convince her to sign the paper in order to receive the insurance money contains the best examples of their failure to reach her. Petra makes her position perfectly clear to them, but they are utterly ineffective with her and cannot speak her language. When one of the men attempts to explain the situation, she laments to her husband:

¿Qué dicen? ¿Qué es eso? ¿Por qué me hablan tantas y tantas palabras y no se entiende nada? (*Teatro completo* 152)

What are they saying? What is that? Why are they speaking so many words to me and nothing is comprehensible?

In the scene of Angel's return, Salinas emphasizes the exclusivity of the mother-son relationship from which everyone else is distanced. Angel looks to Petra for love, protection, and guidance. After destroying the insurance money, they escape together, hand in hand, "los dos solos" (alone together; *Teatro completo* 162). Their union is the enduring, authentic spiritual interaction upheld in the play, and it provides stark contrast with Petra's lack of rapport with the rest of the family and with the insurance agents.

In *Los santos*, Salinas expands the first basic plot variation beyond the male-female pairings to represent solidarity among an archetypical body of three men and three women. A generous act by the prisoners to save one of their group provokes the miraculous force of the saint statues. The icons represent poetic counterparts to five of the characters whom they replace and save. This play, with its six interacting characters against the backdrop of a historical event, is the most compelling among the eight plays that represent the movement from confinement to freedom with a happy outcome. While underlining the catastrophic effects of disconnection, Salinas expresses his hope for a sustained union among divided peoples, regardless of position or politics. All eight plays end on a positive note, suggesting ongoing relationships among characters. In *Los santos*, Salinas most forcefully shows the redeeming value of genuine fellowship contrasted with the consequences of its desintegration.

FREEDOM AND TRAGIC OUTCOME
In the other six plays, Salinas also demonstrates how certain characters emerge from isolation to share a liberating connection with others. Likewise usually the communication occurs between a pair, though the male-female coupling prevalent in the first group of plays is by no means the general rule for this group. In two of the plays, *La Bella Durmiente* and *Judit y el tirano*, Salinas develops the relationship between a single man and woman. In *La Cabeza de Medusa*, the principal communication exists between one male character, Andrenio, and three women, although perhaps viewable as one (Cowes, "Relación..."; Maurín). In *El precio*, in addition to the bond between the writer Jáuregui and his character Melisa, a strong link develops between Melisa and Alicia. In *Caín o una gloria científica*, the primary bond is between two brothers. In *El director*, the key interaction is between a female, the "Mecanógrafa" (Typist) and the "double male divinity" figure, the "Director-Gerente" (Director), with numerous subplots involving one man and one woman, or two women. While Salinas exhibits more variety in combining his communicating characters in these six plays, what really sets this group apart to form the second variation of his basic plot is the outcome: the redemptive process culminates in tragedy.

The characters strive toward and achieve some measure of freedom, but in all six plays, for one of two reasons, their escape from confinement is curtailed. One reason, found in *Caín o una gloria científica* and *Judit y el tirano*, is that a character cannot disengage himself or herself sufficiently from external circumstances in which restrictions persist. The other cause of separation, present in *La Cabeza de Medusa*, *La Bella Durmiente*, *El director*, and *El precio*, is that there remains a lingering disconnect in the relationship of the characters involved in the transformation process.

This group of plays contains the same movement toward emancipation found in the first eight plays, but with obstacles enduring.

Both in *Caín o una gloria científica* and *Judit y el tirano*, a pair of characters gains essential, mutual understanding, only to be separated by the circumstances that have drawn them close together. Abel, unable to cope alone with the dilemma concerning his nuclear research, engages his brother Clemente. With total commitment, Clemente accepts a full share of the burden, but in doing so, is forced to kill Abel. The total absence of understanding between Abel and his superiors tests the relationship of the brothers and proves their unity in the quest for redemption, but paradoxically separates them with the death of Abel, and leaves open the question of the fate of mankind.

Similarly, in *Judit y el tirano*, the Regente, a completely solitary figure, seeks to emerge from isolation with the help of Judit. She gives him the courage to reenter the world and engage in life outside his office, to leave behind the reclusive existence in which he communicates with his people only as a faceless entity. The circumstances of his past are too powerful to overcome, and they cause the tragic separation of Judit and the Regente. The Regente's police kill him because they see him as a man who threatens the life of the official Regente. Salinas underscores the irony of this apt description of what he has become. The police do not recognize him to be the Regente himself, because of the previous, secret, inhuman manner of interaction with his people. The liberating connection between the new man and Judit cannot overcome the forces of his former life.

In the four remaining plays, successful sharing among characters is likewise interrupted, but this time it is due to some deficiency within the relationship itself. The characters are transformed in their achievement of some significant communication, but ultimately separate because one of them is unable to transcend certain self-imposed boundaries, or because one of the characters feels compelled to hold back from the relationship a part of himself or herself.

In *La Cabeza de Medusa*, Andrenio ventures from the shelter of his upbringing to attain a deeper knowledge about life from Lucila and the visitors to her shop. Andrenio is sadly ill-equipped, however, to participate in life, and merely absorbs everything before him as a passive listener. He follows the instructions of his father to the letter: to get to know life by observing it from the outside, objectively, and by not getting carried away in its whirlwind (*Teatro completo* 122). Seeing the disillusion present in life, yet unprepared to cope with it, Andrenio chooses death as the only real solution for himself. The consummation of Andrenio's liberating understanding of those he observes is marked by his exclamation that everything is clear, and his sudden death (*Teatro completo* 136).

In *La Bella Durmiente*, *El director*, and *El precio*, an unhappy escape from confinement for the central characters is most directly related to the clarification of the identity of one of them. In *La Bella Durmiente*, Carlos Rolán and Soledad, the famous model of his mattress advertisements, each ignorant of the other's identity, flee from the superficial relationships they have with people in their public lives. They fall in love at the mountain retreat, "La Cima Incógnita" (The Hidden Summit). Their candid self-expression of feelings for one another holds promise of a happy future together, but after the full confession of Soledad, Carlos feels he must maintain the lock on the secret of his identity in order to preserve any of Soledad's affection. Believing that he pities her more than he loves her, Soledad misinterprets the reason for the impossibility of their marriage. Carlos prefers to stay trapped in his past rather than allow emergence of the truth, which he believes would totally destroy their relationship. Either way, they are destined to separate, but now Carlos believes that at least he can carry within him a union of their sufferings.

In *El director*, the separation of the divinity figure from the typist and the rest of the people he oversees is also tied to the problem of his identity. The director is able to transform the typist and to draw her close to him by explaining how he brings happiness to others, but he fails to convince her that the "evil" Gerente is an integral part of his being. Her close-minded refusal to believe the truth about him and the meaning of happiness leads to the tragic conclusion in which she sees the unity of his two parts too late.

In *El precio*, although Melisa exerts a strong influence over Alicia and successfully injects more poetry into the life of her new friend, a bothersome insecurity plagues their relationship. All the while Melisa gropes for her identity, Alicia fears that its discovery will mean Melisa's departure. The union of the girls necessarily dissolves when Jáuregui appears and the mystery is solved. Through her interaction with Melisa, book character come to life, Alicia undergoes a significant transformation, but their connection is severed when Melisa must pay for her survival in a literary medium with her physical life.

The preceding review of the design of the *fabula* of confinement-to-freedom has introduced both the diversity and unity across the plays. Whether, as in the second group of plays, the characters find freedom but also tragic separation, or, as in the first group, their transformation perpetuates a happy union, Salinas traces the same development in their relationships. The characters seek to escape the emptiness and restrictiveness of an isolated existence, and whether or not they are able to sustain union with others, all experience, due to the impetus of the idealist characters, a close and emancipating contact with another figure or figures, which Salinas has set forth as an aim to be pursued.

The chief difference between the two groups may be understood in terms of the intention and purpose of the actions in which the poet figures engage. In both variations, the poet agents perform with success their intended actions of bonding with and transforming certain co-agents or patients; that is, they initiate and advance the process. Also in both groups, to some extent, the coherent sequences of distinct actions and interactions governed by the desired ends or purposes of the leading characters are achieved; in other words, the agents realize linkage and transcendence. The separating feature is found in the macro-purpose or long-term outcome of the actions. "The dynamism of the drama derives from the suspension—and thus projection into the future—of the purpose-success/purpose-failure of the sequence, so that every distinct act is replete with the possible global result: '[The drama's] basic abstraction is the act, which springs from the past, but is directed towards the future, and is always great with things to come (Langer

306)'" (Elam 124). In both variations, Salinas elevates the spiritual force of the poet liberator. Social circumstances and identity issues impact upon the global results.

The macro-purpose and resulting success of the *fabula* of confinement-to-freedom signify rupture with the depersonalizing, restrictive forces of modern life which provoke human division by causing spiritual blindness, deterring creative invention, and impelling conformity with the dull and commonplace. In casting his poet activists both as boundary-breakers and bridge-builders, Salinas endows these liberators with creative capacities to rework old blueprints and design new ones. He envisions new constructions, erected with poetic purpose. As the poet attempts to inhabit a concrete social realm, his or her inner animating force upholds an identity of independence, an identity celebrating its opposition to obstacles in the material sphere. The ultimate success depends on the degree to which the force of their identity of independence overpowers the opposing forces met in the social realm.

The grouping of Salinas's plays according to their felicitous or tragic outcomes does not diminish the heroism of the poet. Both variations evidence the poet's strong spiritual stance, humanistic outlook, and fundamental idealism. Moreover, many actions of Salinas's characters have autobiographical significance and suggest the circumstances and world-view of Salinas the poet. While the first group celebrates the promise in human relationships, the latter group underscores the enormous tensions and pressures in the confrontation with modernity. In both variations, Salinas accentuates the search for liberation and the crucial importance of the poet's mission, and there is a persistent, optimistic affirmation of the poet's enterprise.

THE POET IN THE PLOT

Functioning as crucial links, the directive role of Salinas's poet heroes is connected to the key narrative events of the *fabula* of confinement-to-freedom. Their actions advance the narrative logic and constitute major story events. Translating Barthes's term *noyau*, Chatham describes these events as "kernels... narrative moments that give rise to cruxes in the direction taken by events" (53). "Kernels cannot be deleted without destroying the narrative logic" (Chatman 53). This terminology, though applied primarily to analysis of the genre of narrative, lends itself as well to discussion of the structure of fundamental story events in the drama. The actions of the poet figures configure the logical sequence of consequential events and form the nucleus of the playwright's "narrative." In addition to constituting the *kernels*, their movements often give rise to minor plot events that Chatman, interpreting the French structuralist term *catalyse*, calls *satellites* (Chatman 54-55). *Satellites* are elaborations that enrich and flesh out the skeletal narrative. A further look at story construction in Salinas's plays will illustrate in more detail this structural significance of his poet heroes, whose sharing of self and circumstance determines the propitiousness and permanence of the emancipation attained.

A convenient organization for examining the form of their action in the confinement-redemption *fabula* derives from Smiley's *Playwriting The Structure of Action* and his discussion of the structure of story and action in drama. His typology of ten basic story elements—balance, disturbance, protagonist, plan, obstacles, complications, sub-story, crisis, climax, and resolution—is not intended to be formulaic, but does suggest the means for construction of a story and a method for a playwright to organize actions, characters, and thoughts (Smiley 53-61). The components enforce no pattern, and a playwright may use them or not, or use some of them. A sub-story, for example, may be absent, as could almost any other element, except crisis and climax (Smiley 61). Though a fully developed story is not absolutely necessary for every play, most sets of dramatic materials are better organized for having one. The story construction across Salinas's fourteen dramatic works is solid, and the following presentation of the happenings in his plays will show that he is a purposeful story builder. Even into the short pieces, Salinas incorporates most, if not all of the basic elements. Though inclusion of these story components does not automatically create story, in Salinas's case, their representation and combination produced vivid illustrations of the basic *fabula* in its two principal variations. A survey of the components in Salinas's plays will highlight the core movements of the poet heroes and will help differentiate the two groupings—freedom with happy outcome and freedom with tragic overtones. Distinguishing features of the two groups appear especially in Salinas's composition of obstacles, complications, crises, climaxes, and resolutions. The following overview of the key story components in the plays will clarify the differentiation, mark the dominance of the poet figures in the dramatic structure, and precede comprehensive attention to one work of each variation—*El chantajista* and *Caín o una gloria científica*. A close look at these two compositions will further elucidate their dramatic structure and sharpen the definition of *kernel* and *satellite* dramatic moments hinging on the actions of the poet figures, the crucial initiators and promoters of communication.

Throughout his plays, the structural dominance of Salinas's poet characters and their actions stands firm. In his design of story elements, from initial balance through to resolution, Salinas sustains their anchoring function. A view of the role of the poet characters in the balance or opening situation of the plays reveals that they are essential to the establishment of an initial dynamic stability that leads into the central actions. They are an integral part of a tense equilibrium between contrasting forces that holds the potential for subsequent conflict. In *Ella y sus fuentes*, for example, the guiding force Julia Riscal is key inspiration to the biographer Desiderio Merlín, who is claiming to dispute the lies and exaggerations of other studies in his definitive work of her life and deeds. In *La Bella Durmiente*, Soledad and Alvaro have just returned from an idyllic walk they have both enjoyed. Her simple and sincere bearing has captured his interest and piqued his curiosity about her. While cherishing her privacy, she points to the tension between their position of retreat and their other lives outside the resort.

When the story yields to a first disturbance, an event that upsets the balanced situation and initiates the action, the poet characters are again crucial factors. They either effect or inspire an agitation in the world of the participants in the play. Such disturbances take place in both variations, and often constitute a first step by the poet hero on his or her idealistic course. For instance, early stable circumstances are agitated when Julia Riscal appears to the confident Merlín, and when the drawing of Judit's lot makes her the assassin of the tyrant. The initial disturbance represents a kind of specialized complication in the story. Later complications in the story structure present new obstacles to the protagonists, and figure more significantly in the distinction between the two variations.

As protagonists, poet characters are clearly focal because they cause or receive most of the action, they are most affected when the disturbance causes imbalance—even when they themselves cause the upset, and usually it is they who set about to restore order in the situation. Smiley differentiates between main characters that are volitional and force the action and those who are less volitional. The latter are central but more victimized by opposing characters or forces (55). Even though powerful obstacles thwart their attempts to retain a joyous emancipation, Salinas's primary poet heroes of the second variation are no less volitional than their more successful counterparts. In the six plays with tragic outcomes, they are greatly, if not most affected by the misfortune. Soledad the Sleeping Beauty, Judit the tyrant slayer, Lucila the proprietress of *La Cabeza de Medusa*, Alicia the autonomous character of author Jáuregui, Abel the physicist and glory of science, and the Regente, divinity figure of *El director*, all suffer the oppression of an overwhelming power. It is they, nevertheless, who chiefly propel the action and advance it to resolution. Less volitional are the proximate poets, or characters transformed by the main poets. These are often co-protagonists or complementary central figures whose function bolsters the position and authority of the guiding poet heroes. Drawn into the action and carried along by the principal poets, their circumstances and fate, whether favorable or ill, converge with those of their guiders and mirror them. In good fortune, Claribel thus accompanies the Florindo/Eros/Archangel figure of *La fuente del arcángel*, and Felipa follows Alvaro in *"La Estratoesfera."* Likewise, in somber conclusion, Andrés the tyrant both comes to life and dies with Judit, and the typist sees happiness fulfilled and doomed in her association with the divinity figure.

Normally, when the protagonist begins the activity of reestablishing the balance, he or she has a plan. While founded upon creative inspiration and idealistic motivation, the plans of Salinas's poet heroes are most often conscious and carefully formulated. Also, the plans frequently involve a goal or stake (a person, place, or thing desired by the protagonist and usually wanted also by his opposition; Smiley 55). In *Ella y sus fuentes*, Julia's plan is to communicate to Merlín the truth about her identity. Merlín, initially Julia's opposition, is also desirous of this same goal. In *La isla del tesoro*, Marú's plan is to find the journal writer, or creator of the treasure. Her oppositions are, on the one hand, members of the hotel staff who want to keep secret his existence, and, on the other hand, her fiancé Severio, who cannot reach her in the same way as the mystery notebook writer. The plans of Judit are more complicated and changing because when she is about to execute her plan to kill the apersonal, faceless tyrant, she discovers the man. Salinas incorporates a number of key speeches to elaborate her adaptations, establish the credibility of her actions and uphold her axial position.

As protagonists attempt to restore balance by carrying out their plans, they meet with obstacles or factors that oppose or impede their progress. An obstacle generates the most tension and is strongest when it imposes two conditions upon the protagonist: it aims a threat toward the protagonist and it causes conflict when the protagonist tries to remove it. Consequently, the obstacle will lead to a major or minor climax in the story. For Smiley, the plays with the best stories are those which combine use of four kinds of obstacles: physical obstructions; antagonists, or other characters in the play who oppose the protagonist; obstructions within the personality of the protagonist himself or herself; and mystic forces, or elements such as accidents, god figures, or moral and ethical codes (56). Into many of his works, into the plans of his poet characters, Salinas incorporates all four types of obstacles. In *Los santos*, for example, the prisoners must contend with their confinement in the church basement, with the enemy soldiers, with their own fears, and with the accidents of war that have brought them to confront death. In *Sobre seguro*, Petra experiences threat and conflict from the insurance agents, from her persistent refusal to accept the death of Angel, and from the insurance money, both in its realistic containment in an envelope and in her vision of its colorful personification.

Complications may appear at any point in a story in the form of "characters, circumstances, events, mistakes, misunderstandings, and best of all–discoveries" (Smiley 56-57). They set new obstacles for the protagonists, and provoke a change in the course of the action. They can be positive or negative forces for any of the conflicting aspects of the play. These elements in Salinas's plays are numerous, and while aiding or hampering progress, they showcase the creative genius of the confronted poet characters. In *El precio*, when the inspector of police arrives to connect Melisa with an unsolved murder, she totally dominates the conversation with lyrical explanation about buried jewels and surprising fruits that strangely coincide with details of the case but soar beyond the scope of the everyday world and exemplify her imaginative flight (*Teatro completo* 274-75).

Builders of tension and surprise, the obstacles and complications encountered by the poet characters also help mark the distinction between the two variations of Salinas's *fabula* of confinement-to-freedom. In the plays of felicitous conclusion, these factors exert vitally positive force. Whether or not they augment a work's humor, they solidify the dominance of the poet's vision. In *"La Estratoesfera,"* for instance, the death of Felipa's grandfather generates an expression of feeling by her that proves she has been transformed by the poet's influence (*Teatro completo* 210-11). In *Sobre seguro*, the reappearance of Angel and his attraction to the insurance money moves Petra to share her vision of their retreat to "la casa clara" (the bright house; *Teatro completo* 160). Obstacles and complications built into the works of tragic outcome carry chiefly negative force. They contribute to the continuation of an anti-poetic environment that survives beyond the interrupted success of the redeemed poet characters. When, in *Judit y el tirano*, the secret police who have never seen the tyrant face-to-face hear him say he has killed the "other," they do not understand that he has been liberated from his former guise. Their actions, ultimately provoked by Judit and her weapon, end the life of the tyrant, terminate the relationship of the protagonists, and perpetuate the system that has separated them.

An element to mirror the main story of a play or contrast with it is the sub-story, or secondary story. In his twelve one-act plays, by ascribing to tenets of unity, brevity, and economy, Salinas retains focus on the central figures, and does not compose sub-stories with any intricacy. At times, to highlight or reflect the position of the protagonists, he includes a scene or fragments of scenes that appear as a vivid flash or series of flashes. In *La Cabeza de Medusa*, the episodes involving Gloria and Rosaura are more extended segments, and possibly viewable as sub-stories to the extent that they may be representations of earlier moments in the life of protagonist Lucila, but they are not really subordinate to the main story. Their inclusion is central to the bonding between Lucila and Andrenio. In *La fuente del arcángel*, the scene of lovers Honoria and Angelillo at the fountain echoes briefly Claribel's growing connection to the fountain figure. In the three-act *El director*, Salinas weaves into the central relationship of the typist and the director a more detailed subordinate story of the minor characters in search of happiness. The pursuits of Juan, Juana, Inocencio, and Esperanza intertwine with the quests of the Typist and Director. They reach crisis and climax just before the major climax in the main story to thus complement it and affect it.

Crisis is a story component that demonstrates the concentrated activity of the poet protagonists and forces significant change. Crises, or turns in the action that mark conflict during which the outcome is uncertain, may be scenes of progressively heightened struggle. They may transpire throughout a play until the occurrence of a major crisis scene, followed by a culminating moment that settles the conflict either intermediately or permanently. Related structurally to obstacles and complications, crises, like these components, also serve to distinguish between the two variations of Salinas's *fabula* of confinement-to-freedom. The major crises of the works of happy conclusion portray the primary and proximate poet characters in triumphant acts of unmasking and co-discovery. As the ensuing climaxes indicate, once these characters reveal their true identities, any threats to their union dissolve. Accordingly, after the prisoners share their sufferings, the saint statues come to life to save them in *Los santos*. Similarly, in *La fuente del arcángel*, after Florindo awakens Claribel to the power of illusion, the fountain figure comes to life to emancipate her.

The crises in the works of tragic conclusion generally depict more violent conflict and change. In the freedom-seeking process, the major crises of uncovering or co-disclosure by poet heroes and their counterparts push them to face a final opponent who endeavors to interrupt their success. This final opponent may be one of the poet characters themselves, forced by constricting circumstances to withhold definitive identification, as occurs in *La Bella Durmiente*, or driven by misunderstanding to eliminate an enemy to their unity, as in the case of the typist who kills the director. Or the fatal force may be one other than a protagonist, a power of the oppressive system, such as the secret police who confront the tyrant in *Judit y el tirano*, or "¡la vida!" (life!; 137) in *La Cabeza de Medusa*.

The climax, or result of a crisis, is the point at which a conflict is settled. In all his plays, Salinas creates a series of minor climaxes to lead to a major climax in which the final outcome is determined. Across his two groups of plays, the conclusive climactic moments constitute a key distinguishing element. In the works of the first variation, the final climaxes show the protagonists having won their goal or "stake" of freedom. They join together to realize a transcendant union beyond any contact they have experienced with an everyday, mundane, constricting milieu before this moment. They are about to take a victorious first step toward an idyllic fulfillment. Salinas thus constructs final climaxes in which transformed characters respond to the beckoning of the primary poet figures: Claribel takes the hand of Florindo; Claribel accepts the invitation of the fountain figure; Desiderio Merlín joins Julia Riscal; Angel leaves with Petra. Or Salinas depicts the promise of a felicitous alliance resulting from the impetus of potent poetic entities. In *La isla del tesoro*, for example, Marú advertises to find her ideal mate, the notebook writer; in *El parecido*, the *Incógnito* encourages the unity of Julia and Roberto; and in *Los santos*, the animated statues redeem the prisoners. These climaxes of the first variation portray optimistic moments of decision or discovery, and in the case of *Los santos*, a happy reversal of fortune.

In contrast, the final climaxes of the six plays with tragic outcome all depict reversals of circumstance that interrupt the transformation of poet characters and separate them from their idealistic course. Close to or as part of the major climax, Salinas portrays them claiming or about to claim their "stake" of redemption, but inserts an ultimate clash with their definition of self or with outside forces. Salinas upholds these characters as moral and spiritual champions, but in their search for wholeness and emancipation grounded in truth and happiness, he does not discount the hostility of their social context. By way of illustration, one can witness the parting of Soledad and Alvaro in *La Bella Durmiente*, the defeat of Judit and the tyrant, the separation of Melisa and Alicia in *El precio*, and the typist's erring elimination of the director.

After the final climax, the resolution of a play sets the situation of the characters and restores a kind of balance to the work. Like the crises and climaxes from which they follow, the resolutions of Salinas's dramatic works differ. Underscoring the idealisim and positive expectations of the poet protagonists, the resolutions of the works of the first variation tend to indicate the fortune of these characters without providing an absolute close. In contrast, the final circumstances of the more tragic works set the destiny of the characters more firmly, usually with a death (for example, of the tyrant, Melisa, Andrenio, Abel, and the director) or some definitive separation (Alvaro and Soledad).

If the plays do not end with close focus on the poet protagonists themselves, then whatever the outcome, the final scene measures their effects or contains an assessment of the relationship by others. A journalist in *Ella y sus fuentes* thus reports the coincidental death of Merlín near the statue of Julia Riscal; and at the conclusion of *La fuente del arcángel*, the family's discovery of the pieces of the Eros/Archangel statue is connected to the disappearance of Claribel.

The pivotal role of poet heroes in pursuit of a redemptive unification with kindred figures provides Salinas's dramatic corpus with a structural unity. As key supports of the framework of the plays, these characters stand at the core of his organization of his *fabulas* to embody spiritual and social attributes exalted by Salinas. Whether the plays end happily or unhappily, whether Salinas allows that the ideal may or may not be immanently achievable or sustainable, he upholds the quixotic virtue of patience he had praised in his essay "Lo que debemos a don Quijote" ("What We Owe Don Quixote"; *Ensayos de literature hispánica* 101). This patience is the resolve to continue. The happy conclusions exhibit with sunny optimism the virtues advocated by the poet. The unhappy outcomes do not suggest the passive acceptance of defeat, but rather they imply the necessity of converting failure into a stage or step toward a desired future triumph.

5
Poet and Plot: Two Variations

La faz del mundo tiene muchos admiradores, hasta adoradores: todos esos que contemplan la primavera o las noches de luna, diciendo "¡Qué bonito!" Pero hay también otros seres que al ver el rostro de las cosas y las personas miran siempre más allá, y se preguntan, angustiados, cómo será el revés de todo eso.
    SALINAS, *Teatro completo, El director* 354

The face of the world has many admirers, even adorers: all those who contemplate the spring or moonlit nights saying "How pretty!" But there are also other beings who when they see the face of things and people always look beyond, and ask themselves, distressed, how the reverse of all that might be.

STUDY OF THE CONSTRUCTION of *El chantajista* and *Caín o una gloria científica* will further distinguish the two variations of Salinas's *fabula* of confinement-to-freedom and demonstrate the powerful unifying force of his poet characters. Lucila of *El chantajista* and Abel of *Caín o una gloria científica* are both creative visionaries and directive forces who touch profoundly their counterpart characters Lisardo and Clemente. Moreover, examination of the actions of these leading figures will point to correspondences with circumstances in the life of Salinas the poet and support a view of his plays as autobiographical discourse. The relationship between Lucila and Lisardo in *El chantajista* and the play's places, interior spaces, and voices echo Salinas's *Cartas de amor a Margarita*, and represent a nostalgic recreation of Salinas's own experience of a vivid past reality at the beginning of his life with Margarita. The struggle of Abel and Clemente in *Caín o una gloria científica* communicates Salinas's anguish in the 1940's over the threat of atomic destruction, an anguish resounding in the compositions of *Todo más claro*, in his letters to Guillén, and at the end of the decade in his "fabulación" *La bomba increíble*. While *El chantajista* harks back to capture the pretty, moonlit, romantic moments of Salinas's past, *Caín o una gloria científica* confronts the ugly face of immediate reality to reach beyond it.

A NOSTALGIC TRANSPLANTING: *EL CHANTAJISTA*

The plot of *El chantajista*, of felicitous outcome, involves a blackmail situation and the creation and claiming of love letters in a woman and a man's search for love. The play begins at dusk with a strong aura of mystery. Eduardo, the victim, cloaked in a long raincoat and concealing hat, waits nervously on a park bench for the arrival of Lisardo, the "blackmailer." Lisardo has found the love letters written to Eduardo by Lucila, and will return them only if Eduardo accedes to his demand for the key to Lucila's garden gate so that he may assume the place of Eduardo during the nightly, appointed hour with the incomparable Lucila. In the hour he has won, Lisardo hopes to steal Lucila's heart. Eduardo does relinquish the key, but soon after, at the end of the first part of the play, the audience learns that Lucila has been disguised as Eduardo during the conversations with Lisardo. She has written and planted the letters. In the second part of the play, set in Lucila's garden, the lovers uncover the blackmail and forge a bond of love through various manipulations and confessions.

The play's opening situation is an elaborate exposition that holds implications of all impending conflict and defines the primary poet figure Lucila as the creative inspiration and force behind the redemption process. In the park at dusk, Lisardo meets Eduardo, who has acceded to the former's request for a meeting. Eduardo maintains silence while Lisardo begins to explain his identity. Lisardo intimates his role as the proximate poet as he explains how he has become a novice blackmailer. A groping figure, Lisardo states that he is taking a path signaled by

Eduardo, who, later, it will be discovered, is the disguised Lucila, the primary poet figure:

> Usted me señala la línea entre el mundo que llaman del bien y el del mal. Es usted la frontera, como quien dice, por la que voy a dar mi paso. (*Teatro completo* 292)

> You point out to me the line between the world of good and evil. You are the border, as it is said, through which I am going to take my step.

Also, Lisardo associates finding Lucila's letters with good fortune, and lacking comprehension, he introduces the earliest suggestion of their unification:

> Tengo a mi lado a ella, a la gran compañera de los grandes pasos, ya sabe usted, la suerte... Soy yo y no soy yo, somos la suerte y yo. (*Teatro completo* 292)

> I have her at my side, the great companion of great steps, you know, luck... It is I and it is not I, it is luck and I.

Lucila's letters stir Lisardo to feel vividly the reality of their past in the present, and his physical hold on the packet, the instrument of his blackmail, intensifies this sensation. There is explicit reference to the palpable power of the artistry of Lucila and to all the possibilities that this balanced situation, grounded in the product of the poet heroine, holds:

> ¡Pero son tan hermosas, tan vívidas! Se siente la realidad pasada tan presente, que lo va dejando, de un día a otro, y las lleva encima, atadas con su cintita (...), sin separarse de su tesoro... Nadie sabe lo que puede suceder... (*Teatro completo* 294)

But they are so beautiful, so vivid! The past reality is felt so present, that it keeps producing, from one day to the next, and carries them on it, tied with their ribbon (...), without separating from their treasure... No one knows what can happen...

Through the opening scene, Salinas also draws attention to the work's narrative design and specifies the process whereby narrative moves into dramatic form. Lisardo chooses to fill in the background for their meeting by giving Eduardo a deliberate, third person account of how Lisardo discovered the letters. Lisardo forewarns him that he reserves the right to transform his "impersonal" version of the story into an immediate dramatic scene that will draw them together. This narrative nevertheless is highly personal not only from the standpoint of Lisardo's participation, but also because of its connection to the amorous correspondence between Salinas and Margarita. Lisardo relates with detail how, by chance, a young man found the letters in a movie theater, took them home, read them, and delighted in their passion and grace. The letters awaken his loneliness, and a yearning to come into contact with the romantic ideal expressed by the writer. Curiously, they contain only her name and address, but since the finder is a gentleman, he manages to set up a meeting with Eduardo. The letters would certainly upset the writer's disapproving parents. They contain the outpouring of her soul, of a lover separated from her beloved.

In his letters to Margarita, Salinas had explored many places that they had experienced sometimes together, but more often apart, milieus where he sought spiritual communion with her. In *El chantajista*, most notably he reproduces and further transforms the settings of a movie theater, a park, and Margarita's garden. It is in a movie theater that Lucila plants the love letters for Lisardo to find, thus manipulating him into thinking that he is the blackmailer. Lucila inspires his demands to meet in a park and in her garden and engages him in her pursuit of a romantic ideal. In his early and later descriptions of these places, Salinas, with an enduring artistry, fuses physical and spiritual realms.

In a letter dated 1913, at the beginning of their courtship, Salinas relates to Margarita his experience in a movie theater. Seeing a French film with a seascape triggers a profound nostalgia for Margarita and the beach of Santa Pola, and arouses his fantasy about future encounters:

> Y eso me hizo pensar, largamente, en los paseos que daremos este verano por junto al mar, y me hizo soñar en esa noche que iremos a ver la luna desde el huerto de las palmeras. Margarita, mira por qué encadenamiento de cosas triviales y banales como una impresión vulgar de un cinematógrafo, se va mi espíritu volando hacia ti. Y cuando salí del cinema había una luna hermosa, hermosísima, llena de ideales esperanzas. Parece que me decía: 'Espera, espera, una noche me verás no tú solo, sino con ella; os besaré a los dos en la frente, os envolveré de pureza. Ya me verás en los ojos de ella.' Y parece que me consolaron estas palabras imaginarias de la luna creciente. (*Cartas de amor* 52)

> And it made me think, for a long time, in the walks we will take this summer near the sea, and it made me dream of that night we will go to see the moon from the palm grove. Margarita, see through what chain of trivial events such as a common expression of a film projection that my spirit flies toward yours. And when I left the movie theater, there was a beautiful, a very beautiful moon, full of ideal hopes. It seems as if it were saying to me: 'Wait, wait, one night you will see me not alone, but with her; I will kiss both your foreheads and envelop you in purity. Now you will see me in her eyes.' And it seems that those imaginary words of the rising moon consoled me.

Salinas here exhibits early sensitivity to the blendings of sense and spirit. Out of what he recognizes to be a trivial experience in a movie theater, he conceives the imaginary words of a full moon, words suggesting to him the possibilities of an exceptional reality full of ideal hopes and his beloved.

Salinas's poetization of that evening at the movies and the planting of letters reverberate through *El chantajista*. He makes a movie theater showing a French film the site of Lisardo's spiritual ignition, and later envelops the lovers in a moonlit garden scene where the meaning of the letters is uncovered. Some of the details from the *Cartas de amor a Margarita* have changed or are fused, for example, the place where the poet places the letters, the reason for the lovers' separation, and the title of the film. In *El chantajista*, the title of the film, *La invención de Romeo*, more pointedly foreshadows the budding romance. Early versions of the play and manuscript notes of Salinas indicate that the work held a number of different titles and spelling variations before *El chantajista: La invención de Romeo, El chantagista o la fuerza de amor, El chantagista, o las cartas* (Houghton Library, BMS Span 100 (975-976). Also, in his correspondence with Guillén, dated 16 June 1949, Salinas mentions he has just completed a new work with title yet uncertain: *El chantajista o la invención de Romeo* (421).

In the opening missive of the collection addressed to Margarita, Salinas imagines his beloved finding the letters near a tree in her garden, and has begun this narrative of the found letters as well as his story to Margarita about the movie experience with talk of youth, innocence, and the erasure of boundaries between ordinary and extraordinary circumstances. To explain the story of his first letter, Salinas writes:

Perdóname estas cosas de chico, pero es que me pongo a pensar, y pensando llego a ese maravilloso mundo de infancia donde todo lo imposible y extraordinario es natural y cotidiano. ¡Vida, alma, y sigo soñando, ya ves si soy tonto, en la alegría que tendría la novia de mi alma hallando allí, junto al árbol las cartas esperadas!

Pardon these boyish things of mine, but it is that I put myself to thinking, and thinking, I arrive at that marvelous world of infancy where all the impossible and extraordinary is natural and daily. Life, soul, and I continue dreaming, now you see I am foolish, in the happiness that the bride of my soul would have, finding there, next to the tree, the wished for letters! (*Cartas de amor* 32)

Lisardo's monologue in the opening circumstances of *El chantajista* carries forward these memories. The persistent silence of Eduardo provokes Lisardo to interrupt his narrative and move to more direct personal encounter. It is at this point that the plays initial balance yields to a first disturbance, enacted by the disguised Lucila. Her curt "¿Cuánto?" (How much?; 293), uttered in a stage voice ("voz de teatro"; 295), perturbs Lisardo and pushes him to confront Eduardo with his demand of Lucila's key. The creator of the letters has agitated his imagination and awakened his desire to know her, see her, hear her voice, and speak to her:

> La persona que ha escrito esas cartas, esa mujer que a usted le quiere, me ha trastornado la imaginación.... Quiero conocerla. Ni más ni menos. Verla, ver su cara, oírla su voz, hablarla si fuera posible. (*Cartas de amor* 296)
>
> The person who has written those letters, that woman you love, has upset my imagination.... I want to meet her. No more no less. To see her, see her face, hear her voice, speak to her if possible.

It is quite understandable that Salinas has displaced the role of letter writer to a woman, although his letters, and not Margarita's, stand as a source text for the dramatic work. In the initial balance, Lisardo asserts: "Y hay que reconocer que escribe a maravilla, con toda su alma. Las mujeres son, para esto de las cartas, únicas" (And one must recognize that she writes marvelously, with all her soul. Women are, in this matter of letters, unique."; 293). Salinas reaffirms this talent of women as letter-writers with a number of specific examples in his essays (*La responsabilidad del escritor* 67-69, *El defensor* 52-58). Moreover, throughout the *Cartas de amor*, Salinas defines Margarita as his principle source of inspiration and self-definition. She motivates his life and dreams, his writing, his loving, his being: "Soñar, vivir, tú eres el motivo de mi sueño y de mi vida" (To dream, to live, you are what motivates my dream and my life"; *Cartas de amor* 103).

When Salinas himself engages in activity as a correspondent, in addition to seeing himself created by his beloved, he also emphasizes the notions of co-creation and self-discovery. In his key essay on letter writing, Salinas highlights this idea. He likens the letter-writer to a Narcissus who unwittingly encounters his own reflection:

> ...el que escribe se empieza a sentir viviendo allí; se reconoce en estos vocablos... surge de entre los renglones su propio reflejo, el doble inequívoco de un momento de su vida interior. Todo el que escribe debe verse inclinado,—Narciso involuntario—sobre una superficie en la que se ve, antes que a otra cosa, a sí mismo. (*El defensor* 25)

> ...he who writes begins to feel himself living there; he recognizes himself in these words... his own reflection emerges from between the lines, the unmistakable double of his interior life. Everyone who writes must see himself bent,—an involuntary Narcissus—over a surface in which he sees himself before he sees any other thing.

Lucila's provocation of the blackmail situation reflects well this theme of letter writing and self-discovery. Lucila disguises herself as Eduardo and as one who loses the letters to initiate and develop her creation of a beloved. She thus conveys a tangible self-representation as part of a union. Once Lisardo presents himself as a blackmailer desirous of moving into the place of Eduardo, Lucila uncovers her disguise for the audience, who can now see that she the mail-writer is also a blackmailer, that they are both extortionists, each exacting a contribution from the other in a kind of under-cover process of self-discovery and co-discovery.

This situation recalls a number of passages from Salinas to Margarita about letter writing and the uncovering of souls. In the second letter of the collection, Salinas describes the secrecy: "Sigues dándote a mi alma en esas palabras, y te das a mi alma de la manera más pura y más delicada en una secreta y continuada ofrenda" ("You continue to give yourself to my soul in those words, and you do so in a secret and continuous offering in the most pure and delicate way"; *Cartas de amor* 33). A letter from late in 1914, continues the theme, carries the persistent garden motif both of the play and the letters, and also suggests the image of Narcissus found in his essay. Eagerly in search of her soul, Salinas bends over the pages of Margarita's letters just as Narcissus peers over the water. His discovery of her leads him to find himself. His explanation of her words guides him to understand his own. To discover Margarita is to realize authentic happiness and deep truth:

> Margarita mía, qué bien comprendes esta avidez con que *me inclino sobre tus cartas para recoger tu alma*. Me dices que yo me explico tus palabras ¡mejor que tú misma!.... Margarita mía, ... tu belleza ha dormido ignorada de todos. *Y yo ahora la voy descubriendo, y al descubrirla, mi felicidad se hace, porque al descubrirla en ella, me descubro a mí mismo.* Si yo te explico tus palabras es porque *tus palabras me explican a mí mismo*, es decir, porque son mías. Y así este amor es como un cambio de las ideas nuestras, que nosotros nos vamos dando *bajo distintos matices*. Margarita mía, todo, todo tiene su significación, y *como a mí lo que más me interesa es la raíz de las cosas, su verdad oculta, yo busco tu alma en todas las palabras, y al explicarlas, me explico mi amor y el tuyo. Sabes, es como si oyendo el ruido de las hojas del árbol, se pensase en las raíces, en la interna vida que fuera vibra en las hojas. Margarita mía, toda la vida no es más que una explicación de nosotros mismos; vivir es explicarse a sí mismo.* (Cartas de amor 160-61, emphasis added)

> My Margarita, how well you understand this eagerness with which *I bend over your letters to recognize your soul*. You tell me that I explain your words better than you yourself!.... My Margarita,... your beauty has slept ignored by all. *And I now am discovering it, and upon discovering it, my happiness is made, because upon discovering it in your beauty, I discover myself.* If I explain to you your words it is because *your words explain me to myself,* in other words, because they are my

> words. And thus this love is like an exchange of our ideas, that we go on giving to each other *under different shades*. My Margarita, everything, everything has its meaning, and since *what interests me most is the root of things, their hidden truth, I seek your soul in all words, and upon explaining them, I explain my love and yours. You know, it is as if hearing the rustling of the leaves of a tree one were to think of its roots, of the internal life that vibrates outside in its leaves. My Margarita, all life is no more than an explanation of ourselves; to live is to explain oneself to oneself.*

It is at the end of the first part of the play, upon removing the Eduardo disguise, that Lucila introduces her plan, the fundamental one of the work, and the one which intersects with the plan of novice extortionist, Lisardo, whose immediate stake is the key to Lucila's garden. Ultimately, for both Lisardo and Lucila, the stake or goal is emancipation from a state of incompleteness and loneliness through union with a beloved.

The play's early scenes that introduce the stake of the main characters are interrupted by the search for a lost kite by a young girl. The child's appearances add an abbreviated sub-story that presents a quest parallel to that of Lucila and Lisardo. Her three brief entrances reflect the early intrigue of the work and intersect with the dialogue and goals of the protagonists. The girl's complaints about the robber of her kite suggest the underhandedness of the blackmail situation and also invite characterization of Lisardo, the supposed blackmailer. When she asks "¿La han visto ustedes?" (Have you seen it/her?; *Teatro completo* 293), Lisardo first responds to the ambiguity of her question with mind focused on his female ideal: "¿A quién jovencita, a quién?" (Seen whom, little girl, whom?; *Teatro completo* 293). His telling her to follow the thread or string ("seguir el hilo"; *Teatro completo* 293) to untangle her problem points to the intricacies of the main story of extortion. Advising her not to worry, wishing her good luck, and disavowing this sort of dirty activity help define him as a nonruthless character. When the girl appears for the second time to inform the pair that she sees the kite and implores them to run with her to reclaim it, it is Lisardo who turns impulsively to follow her. When he sees that Eduardo has not moved, he resumes his immediate course of action: to recover Lucila's key.

The child's third and final appearance brings the sub-story's early resolution and prefigures attainment of the protagonists' ideal. In place of an early speech in which primary poet Lucila sets forth her plan, the young girl gives it symbolic voice. Just after Lucila has removed her disguise, the little girl uncovers the identity of Lucila and enjoins her to reclaim the kite:

> ¡Si no es el caballero de antes! ¿Ve usted qué bonita? Ya la estoy enrollando... Ayúdame a bajarla. (*Teatro completo* 297)
>
> Oh you are not the gentleman from before. See how pretty? Now I am winding it up. Help me to lower it.

Lucila will wind up with Lisardo just as she draws in the kite. Her exclamation, an exact echo of the girl's, joins sub-story to main story:

| NIÑA | ¡Ya está aquí! ¡Ya está aquí! |
| LUCILA | ¡Ya está aquí! (*Teatro completo* 297) |

| LITTLE GIRL | ¡Now it's here! ¡Now it's here! |
| LUCILA | Now it's here! |

The rest of the work unravels her plan of mail creation and male creation. As primary poet figure, her plan is the basis for the layering of plans in the play and propelling what has generated Lisardo's plot, along with ensuing obstacles and complications.

In the second part of the play, Lucila both plants and removes many obstacles and complications on the way to solving the blackmail puzzle. Taking a cue from the letters in which Lucila identifies with Juliet, Lisardo, now in Lucila's garden, takes off his cape and appears dressed as Romeo. Lucila enters dressed as Juliet. These added masks of archetypal, young, first loves suggest in general terms the relationship of Salinas and Margarita and parts of letters such as the following:

> ¡Qué dulce es, amada, hallar en la primera novia, la esposa única! .... somos también, Margarita, hermanos en pureza: yo soy tu primer amor, tú eres mi primer amor. (*Cartas de amor* 39).

> How sweet it is, beloved, to find in the first sweetheart, the one and only wife! .... we are also, Margarita, matched in purity: I am your first love, you are my first love.

In the dream-like ambiance within the garden, Lucila and Lisardo advance toward their goal as they don and shed the guises of blackmailer, Romeo, Juliet, and Eduardo. In pursuit of a transcendent union, Lucila has led Lisardo from the theater, to the park, to her garden on a moonlit night. Before their love blossoms in the garden, Lisardo appears an outsider entertaining hope: "Así, ella a plena luz, luna en la cara.... yo en la sombra..." ("She in full light, moonlight on her face.... I in the shadows"; *Teatro completo* 298). Lisardo's words are reminiscent of Salinas's to Margarita in letter from the fall of 1913, after a summer in Santa Pola:

> Margarita, vida y dulzura, por este camino de la luna voy hacia ti, por esa maravillosa escala de plata. Y tú te vistes de luna, y eres todo blanca y fragante, todo pura y honesta, recogida, silenciosa e íntima, alma de luz de luna. (*Cartas de amor* 111-12).

> Margarita, life and sweetness, I come toward you along that path of the moon, that marvelous silver ladder. And you are moon-dressed, and you are all white and fragrant, all pure and honest, gathered, silent and intimate, soul of moonlight.

Lucila's directions engender fear in Lisardo, who laments he will be recognized as an impostor. Yet she constantly pushes him to overcome this obstacle, to see the truth in his deceit, and to move toward a full identification with the beloved. Through explicit references to truth and falsehood and to Salinas's ever prominent *yo/tú* (I/you) pronominal system, Lucila urges contact and steers Lisardo toward a "truth of two." She inquires, "¿Por qué me hablas así esta noche? ¡Ella! Tercera persona. ¿No somos tú, tú, y yo, yo?" (Why do you speak to me in this way tonight? She! Third person. Are we not you, you, and I, I?"; *Teatro completo* 209). Lisardo replies, "¡Tú..., tú..., tú...! ¡Qué palabra tan hermosa!" ("You..., you..., you...! What a beautiful word!"; *Teatro completo* 209).

Lucila also guides the fearful Lisardo through the creation of the "memory" of their first kiss, a kiss that each imagines has taken place. A confusion of garden, desert, island, sand, sun, and solitude arises from their hopes and the words of the letters. In the play's one concrete geographical reference to the home of Margarita, Lucila names the place where the kiss occurred: Bou Saada, a town near Maison-Carré, where Margarita was born and grew up (Moraleda, *Teatro completo* 301, note 14). Inside the garden, the lovers are an island unto themselves, and Lisardo recalls:

> Todos cercados de arena..., los dos solos..., aislados, allí en el mar de arena, y sin isla, porque nosotros éramos toda la isla, estábamos en nosotros. *(Teatro completo* 300)

> All surrounded by sand..., the two of us alone..., isolated, there in the sea of sand, and without an island, because we ourselves were the whole island, we were within ouselves.

Salinas's letter-texts entertain a similar solitude that he desires via and beyond the garden. Early in 1913, he writes of yearnings kindled by the sight of a house with a garden during his walks through the city at night. Like Lisardo and Lucila, he dreams of the immeasurable happiness of a seclusion alone with Margarita:

...Soñando en esto paseo por la ciudad a la noche, y viendo alguna calle silenciosa y apartada, una casa con un jardín, una casa donde haya una ventana iluminada sueño que allí podría estar nuestro hogar, que detrás de aquella ventana tú y yo podríamos estar gozando de este placer infinito de sentirnos solos, solos en el mundo, el uno para el otro, aislados en medio de toda la ciudad, de todo el mundo. (*Cartas de amor* 63).

...Dreaming on this I walk through the city at night, and seeing some street silent and removed, a house with a garden, a house with a window iluminated I dream that there could be our home, and behind that window you and I could be enjoying this infinite pleasure of feeling ourselves alone, alone in the world, for each other, isolated in the midst of the city, from everyone.

In a letter of 1914, more than a year later, these thoughts reappear, intensified. Salinas deems most authentic the interior world that Margarita and he share. He describes life outside of their eternal spiritual communication as one with events that might impress them momentarily. Quickly, however, they would return to their private dialogue. Salinas even internalizes Margarita's garden and makes it theirs to share:

No nos contamos nada de la vida externa, de lo que sucede en torno nuestro, sólo nos contamos lo que nace y vive dentro de nosotros. Parece que ahí se detiene la vida, y que la única verdadera vida es ésa, alma de mi alma.... Tú, vida, cuando me hablas de tu jardín, no me parece a mí que me hablas de nada de fuera, creo que es algo bien de nosotros. (*Cartas de amor* 168)

We do not tell each other anything of the external world, of what happens around us, we only tell each other what is born and what lives within ourselves. It seems that here life stops, and the only real life is that one, soul of my soul... You, life, when you talk to me of your garden, it does not seem to me that you speak of anything from the outside, I believe it is something quite ours.

Additional obstacles and complications continue to solidify the dominance of the poet Lucila's vision. Guiding Lisardo to remember the outfit she wore the day of the kiss, she describes a fulfillment within her soul that surpasses the borders of measurable space and deepens the roots of the lovers in their ideal ground. Her dress is a wearable, living, nourishing, spiritual garden. She does not know how it has occurred to her to put it on for their excursion to the desert, but as their surroundings dry up more and more, she senses the flowers not on the fabric, but more internally, in her flesh, as if they were seeking earth in which to take root, wanting to flower on her, from her life (*Teatro completo* 301). While the stage directions indicate Lisardo's discomfort and distress, his response conceives a grafting of the lovers with the life-giving potential of their kiss. As he sees Lucila brimming with freshness, there in the total dryness, he leans toward her for the kiss. What happens to the flowers happens to him: he needs to feel the substance of the earth through her, or he will wither in the dryness:

> ...si tú no me dejabas sentir a través de tu cuerpo el jugo de la tierra, la esencia de la vida, me rendiría agostado, de tanto seco sol... (*Teatro completo* 301)

> ...if you did not let me experience through your body the substance of the earth, the essence of life, I would surrender withered, from so much dry sun...

Salinas, in a letter well into their courtship, attributes similar powers to Margarita. He knows of no one who might have experienced the beauty and meaning of her garden as she has. Before she begins to tend it, the gardener has watered the garden and it produces roses, but that is all. Margarita endows the garden with a soul, a voice, and a being:

Margarita, ¿quién, vida, habrá mirado, habrá sentido la belleza y la significación de ese jardín como tú, vida? Hasta ahora no ha vivido: el jardinero le daba agua, él daba rosas, y eso era todo. Pero ahora ya tiene un alma, ya tiene una voz que le has dado y que tú escuchas a tu vez. Alma, le has sacado del no ser al ser... (*Cartas de amor* 168)

Margarita, my life, who might have seen, experienced, the beauty and meaning of that garden as you have, my life? Until now it has not lived: the gardener watered it, it produced roses, and that was all. But now it finally has a soul, now it has a voice that you have given it and that you listen to in turn. Soul, you have brought it from not being to being...

In an intermediate crisis at the end of the scene of reminiscing, Lucila forces a trembling Lisardo to kiss her, after which she runs off and he agonizes that she has discovered he is an impostor. This turn in the action arouses suspense before the major crisis of their triumphant co-discovery at the conclusion of the play. In the scenes leading up to the work's final climax and resolution, Lisardo still must confront the physical obstructions or complications Lucila embodies or imposes: Eduardo, the one hour time limit, Eduardo's revolver, and the ten-minute extension on condition Lisardo tell her the truth.

When Lucila returns dressed again as Eduardo to tell Lisardo that his hour has expired, Lisardo reveals that she has sucessfully transported him to the realm of her romantic ideal. His hour is not measurable according to conventional time. His love and its time frame are boundless. Lisardo returns the key, but his passions remain unlocked. When Eduardo tries to force Lisardo's compliance by taking out a gun, Lisardo defies him and gains an additional ten minutes to tell Lucila the truth. This minor climax and Lisardo's literal unmasking or removal of the Romeo costume precedes the final identification scene in which the protagonists win their stake. Lucila also appears without disguise, and shows Lisardo the elements of her composition of Eduardo, of a beloved, both the physical and the epistolary. Through their conversation, Salinas reenacts an embrace of soulmates that pairs with much of the discourse of a letter to Margarita about their adoption of *tú*, the informal, intimate pronoun "you." Parts of the letter seem transplanted into the dialogue of Lisardo and Lucila, for example:

> Es decir, que yo no quería darme cuenta de que aquello era cosa de juego, de que aquello era mentira, y para ello suprimía mi razón y me entregaba enteramente a aquella ilusión tan dulce de llamarte *tú*…. Aquel "tú" de mentira era verdad; nos engañamos creyendo que era de mentira; nosotros, nuestra razón nos decía que todo aquello era un juego, pero el corazón nos decía en aquel momento divino de llamarnos "tú," que aquello era verdad… (*Cartas de amor* 42)

> That is to say, I did not want to realize that that was something of a game, that it was a lie, and for that I suppressing reason and succumbing to that illusion so sweet of calling you *tú*…. That *tú* of falsehood was truth; we deceived ourselves believing it to be false; our reason was telling us that all that was a game, but our hearts were telling us in that divine moment of calling each other *tú*, that it was truth…

These words of the young Salinas echo through the disclosure of Lucila:

> en mi amor… Eres tú…. Acaba de nacer… en ti… Y ya podemos ponerle nombre, ¿verdad? Eduardo lo llamaba mientras no sabía cómo se llamaba… Ahora se llama Lisardo, tú. …. A ti, al que ibas a ser tú… (*Teatro completo* 305)

> in my love… It is you…. He has just been born… in you… And now we can give him a name, can we not? Her name was Eduardo as long as I did not know his name. Now his name is Lisardo, you. …. (I was writing) to you, to the one who was going to be you…

In the final climax, Lucila admits her role in the deceit, which Lisardo interprets to seal the authenticity of their connection. The resolution depicts the promise of their transcendent union, free from obstacles. In the garden, at the end of the play, as Lucila and Lisardo join together in the reading of the letters, definitions of letter-writers, poets, blackmailers, innocents, and lovers are fused. The work concludes with resplendent optimism and balance restored. Lisardo reads aloud one of Lucila's letters and signals the lovers' cohabitation in an ideal reality where the voices of love and poetry flourish. The scenic effect of a beam of light focusing on the letter further clarifies the blackmail situation with echoes of a letter from Salina to Margarita: "Me parece tan pura, tu carta, tan buena, como hecha por rayos de luna..." (Your letter seems to me so pure, so good, as if made by moonrays...; *Cartas de amor* 58). The final poetry of Lisardo, which is Lucila's illusion, replicates the voices of Salinas and Margarita in a return to the physical settings of garden and summers by the sea, and to spiritual coverings and uncoverings:

> Apenas te has marchado, y ya te siento, otra vez, mañana, el portillo que se abre, y la arena de la senda, que te reconoce los pasos, y no dice nada, como yo, que te espero vestida, como de sombra de esperanza, a la del mirto aquí en el banco... (*Teatro completo* 306).

> You have barely left, and already I feel you again, tomorrow, the gate that is opened, and the sand on the path, that recognizes your steps, and says nothing, like I, who awaits you dressed, in a shadow of hope, in the shade of the myrtle, here on the bench...

This idealistic and open-ended resolution further recalls an impassioned Salinas's words to Margarita:

> Y el jardín, el jardín inolvidable, mi vida, aquel jardín que nos llenó el corazón del presentimiento de nuestra vida futura, que nos hizo vivir un momento, como si no nos fuésemos a separar nunca. (*Cartas de amor* 111)

And the garden, the unforgettable garden, my life, that garden that filled our hearts with the presentiment of our future life, that made us live a moment, as if we were never going to separate.

Salinas places poet creator Lucila at the heart of *El chantajista*, a play of felicitous outcome that returns to his own youth, correspondence, and developing relationship with Margarita. It is Lucila who engineers the conception of the beloved, fabricates the instruments, explains the process, specifies a provisional name, identifies the true participants, and marks their birth. The positive, idealistic perspective of the heroine carries through to the resolution of the work, which opens optimistically to their promising union and reflects the nostalgia of the poet in exile.

The play's representation of a poet correspondent's involvement with a "blackmailer" and their self definition through love, nostalgia and a liberating *búsqueda hacia un más allá de la materia* (search toward a realm beyond the tangible; *Cartas de amor* 23) has unmistakable roots in Salinas's *Cartas de amor a Margarita*. Salinas's return to the collective paradigm text of his own letters through his creation of a fittingly named Lucila, illuminator of a path to love, marks the consistency of his aesthetic. Salinas continued to be an avid letter writer throughout his life, and the voices of poet and correspondent shape the form and content of his expanded literary production. With his early love letters to Margarita, Salinas begins the discourse of a poet epistler forging a love relationship and initiates the definition of an aesthetic that comes full circle and into full bloom in his final dramatic work. *El chantajista* provides a look at a mature Salinas recreating the extraordinary reality of a budding romance from a formerly experienced and epistolized love relationship.

Seeking a wondrous realm within everyday reality and to fuse reason and sensation, letter writing and poetry, Salinas appears to ascribe to a traditional aesthetic goal in his quest to celebrate love. In *The Ideology of the Aesthetic*, basing his characterization on the theories of the father of modern aesthetics, German philosopher Alexander Baumgarten (1714-62), Eagleton identifies the traditional aesthetic ideal as "a unity of spirit and sense, reason and spontaneity" (265). Baumgarten formulates the notion of a confusion or "fusion" of elements, that "in their organic interpenetration... resist discrimination into discrete units," elements that become clearer "the more 'confused' they are" (Eagleton 15). Salinas approximates this ideal. In a number of letters from the collection to Margarita, Salinas describes the fusion of reason and sensation in the process of artistic production. He refers to various philosophers of aesthetics and to the complicated nature of the topic, and ultimately believes that there can be as many systems of aesthetics as there are artists.

Relatedly, and perhaps more significant to the germination of the happy *fabula* of confinement-to-freedom of his drama with the poet as standard-bearer, the letters also contain a number of the earliest of Salinas's passionate references to the rights and privileges of the poet with respect to freedom of expression. Exposed in the Paris of 1914-1915 to a multitude of artistic traditions, schools, and currents, Salinas writes to Margarita of his utmost regard for the artistic soul and his contempt for any restrictions to its free exercise:

> La libertad de expresar lo que se tiene en el alma, es la más sagrada de todas. Y esa libertad no se respeta si se encierra al arte en jaulas de preceptos y de reglamentos. (*Cartas de amor* 194)

> The freedom to express what is held in the soul, is the most sacred of all. And that freedom is not respected if art is enclosed in cages of precepts and regulations.

He reiterates his powerful devotion to free expression in art in another of his letters:

> El principio de la libertad artística es innegable: cada hombre tiene derecho a escoger el medio de expresión que más le convenga, y a usarlo a su modo. (*Cartas de amor* 196)

The principle of artistic freedom is undeniable: every man has the right to choose the means of expression that is most suitable to him, and to use it in his own way.

Not only through his artistic expression or poetry does the poet lead the pursuit of freedom and grasp it. The poet leads and attains redemption through love. When Salinas defines his love to Margarita as an expansion of interrelated thoughts and feelings, of new realms and desires, of clarity and spiritual freedom, he is also setting forth an aesthetic ideal that will permeate his work:

> Queriendo mucho, alma, los sentimientos se aclaran, se enoblecen, porque queremos dar al ser amado lo más puro de nosotros. Y queriendo mucho, alma, el campo de las ideas, los horizontes espirituales se ensanchan enormemente y se piensa en cosas que nunca se habían pensado. El alma siente una libertad nueva, un anhelo nuevo, y los pensamientos se hacen como los círculos en el agua, cuando algo cae en ella, más anchos en torno al centro cada vez. (*Cartas de amor* 222-23)

> By loving much, soul, feelings become clear, ennobled, because we want to give to the beloved the purest of ourselves. And by loving much, soul, the field of ideas, the spiritual horizons widen enormously and one thinks about things that had never been thought. The soul feels a new freedom, a new desire, and thoughts become like concentric circles in water, when something falls into it, each time wider around the center.

In the final letter of the collection, dated October 31, 1915, two months before their wedding, Salinas's outpouring of affection to Margarita reveals an intimate portrait of the poet. Enraptured and emancipated, Salinas treasures the sweetness of their connection and offers himself as Margarita's own path or co-path to freedom:

Yo veo en ti, alma, una alegría de libertad, y yo siento, mi Meg, que esa libertad la represento yo acaso, verdad, vida. Y eso quiero siempre ser tu libertad, ser aquello hacia lo cual tú vayas con impulso de todo tu ser, con espontánea alegría, como vienes en esta carta, mi Meg. Margarita, tú vas a escapar, alma mía, conmigo, a un destino, a una fatalidad que ha querido ser dueña tuya. Alma, ahora vas a tu libertad, y yo no pido otra cosa, Margarita, sino darte siempre, siempre motivos para que me mires como tu libertad, y tu destino juntamente, es decir, como el destino dentro de tu libertad. *(Cartas de amor* 266-67)

I see in you, soul, a happiness of freedom, and I feel, my Meg, that perhaps I represent that, freedom, truth, life. And I always want to be your freedom, to be that toward which you may go with the impulse of all your being, with spontaneous happiness, as you come to this letter, my Meg. Margarita, you are going to escape, my soul, with me, to a destiny, to a fate that has wanted to be your companion. Soul, now you go to your freedom, and I do not ask any other thing, Margarita, that to give you always, always, reasons so that you look at me as your freedom, and your destiny, together, that is, as your destiny within your freedom.

It is this powerful, long-term identification with liberty, love, redemptive union, and happy destiny that Salinas reproduces in *El chantajista* and in the other plays of the first variation. With a triumphant confidence, the poet crystallizes the definition of their alliance and is able to guide the kindred spirit to a promising future. Independent of opposition or transcending it, the poet hero firmly plants himself or herself to flourish with the counterpart. The resolution signals their enduring success, a bright "always" that promises to continue unimpeded by counterpoetic obstacles.

AN ANGUISHED PROPHECY: *CAÍN O UNA GLORIA CIENTÍFICA*

In *Caín o una gloria científica* and other plays of the second variation,

Salinas likewise centers on the visionary leadership of a primary poet figure seeking redemption, but its tragic outcome represents a Salinas with poetic voice preoccupied with powerful destructive forces. The oppressive situation in which the protagonist struggles reflects Salinas's own anguish over world events of the 1930's and 1940's as well as broader, more universal moral exhortation.

The plot of *Caín o una gloria científica* depicts the struggle of physicist Abel Levya, who is on the verge of an important discovery that would give nuclear capabilities to his country's odious, repressive regime. At the beginning of the play, it is revealed that Abel has been absent for twelve days from the laboratory, where he feels compelled, both by his superiors and by his own genius, to complete his work. Worn down by the strain of a terrible inner struggle to withhold for ethical reasons this idea burning in his mind, he looks to his wife Paula and brother Clemente for help. As the pressure increases, Abel entrusts his hope for a better world to his brother. Clemente promises not to allow Abel to destroy his fellowmen under any circumstances. At the conclusion, when General Ascario decides to imprison Abel in the lab until he completes his research, Clemente, in total solidarity with Abel, agrees there is only one escape from increasing evil in the world and therefore kills his brother.

In the first scene of the play, an immediate and powerful pressure is established with poet character Abel as the focus. The secretary of Professor Fontecha, director of the National Institute of Physics, informs Paula of Abel's crucial role in research of great interest to the Institute and tells her that the director is impatient for Abel to return to his laboratory. The opening situation is prolonged with a mounting tension when Paula hides her agitation and surprise about this absence and assures the secretary that her husband will return from his trip that day. The anxiety of Paula might be viewed as a minor disturbance that is incorporated into the initial equilibrium which continues into Scene Two, when Paula sobs to Abel's brother Clemente that lately her husband has been acting strange, distracted, and withdrawn. Clemente's attempt to dispel Paula's fears about her husband's infidelity help introduce the impending conflict and define the poet's stance vis-à-vis the regime in power and the odious war toward which it is pushing them. His early justification of Abel's behavior connects with the views of Salinas himself, haunted by the threats around him in the world of the 1940's. Clemente tells Paula:

> No es extraño. Esa amenaza de la guerra, cada vez más encima. Y Abel, como tú, como yo, odia a este régimen y a la guerra adonde nos lleva, una guerra infame. (*Teatro completo* 171)

> It is not strange. That threat of war, ever more upon us. And Abel, like you, like I, hates this regime and the war toward which it is taking us, a frightful war.

Finished sometime before February of 1945, before the dropping of the first atomic bomb in August of that year, the play is an anguished presentiment of nuclear destruction and a vehicle through which Salinas gives voice to a poetic search for a redemption for mankind. The correspondence of Salinas and Guillén strongly supports this definition of the work. Their letters also offer a clear trajectory to trace the creation and composition of two other works linked thematically as manifestations of Salinas's anguish over world conflict and the possibility of nuclear destruction: the poem "Cero," and the narrative fable, or "fabulación," *La bomba increíble*. A look at a number of the letters helps establish the context for *Caín o una gloria científica* and the role of the poet in search of a redemptive emancipation.

From the early years of the World War II, Salinas writes of his abhorrence of the Nazis and Fascists. From the perspective of a human being and a man of letters, he feels tortured by the horrors they are perpetrating. In a letter dated October 5, 1940, he expresses to Guillén how unendurable he finds not only their atrocities, but also the verbal expressions through which they justify their acts. The idea of crusading is not natural to him, but their extremes are pushing even him to suggest a suspension of all else in order to put an end to their evil doings:

De lo del mundo no quiero hablar. Porque cada día me siento más desesperado; y más firme, al mismo tiempo, en mi odio absoluto, creciente y yo creo inagotable al nazismo y al fascismo. A veces llega a lo obsesivo, y me exalto como no quisiera, ante la diaria avalancha de atrocidades, mentiras, y estupideces que producen y vierten sobre el mundo, sin cesar. ¡Si por los menos no hiciesen más que la guerra, a secas! Pero lo intolerable son los discursos, las declaraciones, los artículos, las posturas, en que arrastran por los suelos todo, lógica, decencia, esperanza. Se me está metiendo en la cabeza que todo lo que los hombres hacemos hoy debía suspenderse, para predicar, sí, para predicar la cruzada del aplastamiento total, sin compasión de esas dos monstruosidades. Y comprenderás que no me hace gracia el sentir en mí ningún espíritu de cruzada, por lo demás. (*PS/JG Correspondencia* 241)

About what's going in the world I do not want to speak. Because every day I feel more desperate; and firmer, at the same time, in my absolute hatred, growing and I believe inexhaustible of Nazism and Fascism. At times it approaches the obsessive, and I get worked up like I wish I didn't, in the face of the daily barrage of atrocities, lies, and stupidities that they produce and pour over the world, without stopping. If at least they just made war and only war! But what is intolerable are the speeches, the declarations, the articles, the postures, in which they drag everything, logic, decency, hope. It is occurring to me that all we men do today should be suspended, in order to preach, yes, to preach, a crusade of total crushing, without compassion, of those two monstrosities. And you must understand that I am not keen about feeling any spirit of crusade, moreover.

These same sentiments he repeats in more general terms in *La responsabilidad del escritor* in his plea for contemporary people to arm themselves against imposters who exploit the linguistic incompetence of others to push them to erroneous action (18).

One year later, on October 29, 1941, Salinas complains to Guillén of

France's complicity in the war, and indicates that he cannot sleep in response to the lack of protest by Churchill and Roosevelt. Dismayed by so much evidence of inhumanity, Salinas expresses shame at being a member of the human race having to follow the abominable events. He dreads the effects on human sensibility, of continuing with one's daily activities when such things are occurring. He fears how human sensitivity will emerge from the war (PS/JG *Correspondencia* 263).

While Salinas continues to condemn specific current events in his letters, he is engaging in a highly personal and morally charged crusade that is less politicized and more universal. Newman underscores this perspective of Salinas:

> Indeed, the question of morality had always stood at the core of Salinas's thinking—morality which was national and universal as well as individual. The world's dilemma he saw as essentially a moral one, and had failed to comprehend national reticence in the face of commitment, observed during the Civil War when major European powers like England and France had not helped Republican Spain, and in the forties when the United States was delaying participation against the same forces which had been ranged against the Republic. (185)

This is the stance ultimately translated with poetic voice into "Cero," *Caín o una gloria científica,* and *La bomba increíble.* In his letter of January 4, 1942, Salinas writes of Japan and Hitler, of Russia and the United States, and entertains a variety of possible scenarios and outcomes. He expresses trouble understanding the course of world events, but he tries to explain it in terms of the inevitable, fatal course of a tragic hero, seen in theater from Aeschulus to O'Neill (PS/JG *Correspondencia* 269). Greatly disturbed by the forces of harm and evil, when Salinas writes a year later of his fears of the growing menace of Hitler and for Spain, he does so in Miltonian terms. He perceives the world to be astounded by the incredible destruction resulting from politics, from the Nazi burnings, and from a Satanic Hitler whose evil offers no possibility of a Miltonian redemption (PS/JG *Correspondencia* 295-96). Salinas indicates that he is optimistic, but not unconditionally so (PS/JG *Correspondencia* 269). This perspective emerges in *Caín o una gloria científica* and the other dramatic works of tragic outcome in which poet heroes are ultimately overcome by unrelenting counterforces.

Salinas's optimism fades somewhat as the war continues. A couple of years later, soon after the composition of "Cero" and close to that of *Caín o una gloria científica,* Salinas writes to Guillén that he has little hope for peace. He sees events as a terrible drama in which a frightening combination of forces co-exist. On the one hand there is progress in the production and use of materials, and there is precision, organization, and power in their implementation. And on the other hand there is an extremely disoriented way of thinking characterized by crudeness, self-centeredness, and smallmindedness. According to Salinas, only a war with the proportions of the one they are witnessing will fill the immense distance between the extremes. On November 29, 1944, he tells his friend that one must be patient, and he cites the words of Georges Duhamel, the French novelist who has decided to return to Paris after the Nazi occupation: "No suicidarse; no huir; no esconderse. Trabajar" (Do not commit suicide; do not flee; do not hide. Work; PS/JG *Correspondencia* 341). Not discounting the power of the counterforces, Salinas injects this fighting spirit into his poet characters, but he does portray the setbacks of Abel and the protagonists in his other plays of tragic outcome.

The Salinas-Guillén correspondence through 1944 and 1945 continues with frequent reference to the increasing menace of the bomb and its relation to the creative production of the poet, to the poem "Cero" and to the play *Caín o una gloria científica*. In March of 1944, when Salinas seeks his friend's evaluation of "Cero," Guillén lauds the poem's organic accumulation of images, its insistence, and its dramatic tension (PS/JG *Correspondencia* 322). He praises especially the poem's explosive contemporaneousness that at the same time transcends the temporal and conveys a profound eternity. He is particularly moved by the passages about time undone ("el tiempo deshecho 322") and about treading on fragments of time ("Piso añicos de tiempo 322"), and he identifies closely

with that host of staunch defenders of their dreams ("esa hueste de tercos defensores de sus sueños 322") that can be pulverized in an instant. These images and the prophesy reappear in *Caín o una gloria científica* in the form of the little crystal boat and in the dream scene. The "instant" of destruction that takes place in August of 1945 occasions a couple of gripping letters by Salinas to Guillén at the end of the month.

In a letter dated August 28, 1945, Salinas laments to Guillén that he has not published the play before the bombing, and he expresses feelings of shame and diminishment as a human being who lives in a time that can produce such a horror:

> ...el fin de la guerra, bien de magnitud incalculable. Pero ¡lo que ha dejado atrás! El archi "Cero," si me permites que me aluda inmodestamente. No sé si recordarás que en la lista de piezas de teatro en un acto que te mandé hace tiempo había un título: *Caín o una gloria científica*. Pues es precisamente lo de la bomba atómica. Siento no haberlo publicado, porque se creerá que se me ocurrió por un suceso de actualidad, y no por un pensar del presente. Te aseguro que desde que me enteré de la invención y uso de la tal bomba, me siento como avergonzado y disminuido en mi calidad de humano. Sí, la guerra ha terminado, pero antes de morir se deja puesto ese huevo monstruoso, del que pueden salir horrores nunca vistas. Por otra parte, el invento es exactamente lo que había que esperar, es el coronamiento de la época más estúpida de la historia humana. ¡Y qué comentarios, los de alguna gente! Demuestran que la historia estaba a punto para que la bomba naciera, que es la descomunal forma simbólica de la brutalidad y la estupidez del hombre del automóvil, de la radio, etc., del hombre del progreso. Se inaugura la era del terrorismo mundial. Ahora ya vivimos bajo una amenaza vaga, difusa, superior a todos los temores de antes. No sabes hasta qué punto me ha perturbado el tal invento, y lo desconrazonado que me tiene. (PS/JG *Correspondencia* 357)

...the end of the war, of quite incalculable magnitude. But what it has

left behind! The arch "Zero," if you permit me an immodest allusion. I do not know if you will remember that in the list of one act plays that I sent you some time ago there was a title: *Caín o una gloria científica*. Well, its subject is precisely the atomic bomb. I regret not having published it, because it will be thought that it came to me as a result of a contemporary event and not as a contemplation of the present. I assure you that since learning of the invention and use of such a bomb, I feel ashamed and diminished in my human condition. Yes, the war has ended, but before dying this monstrous egg is left in place, this egg from which can emerge horrors never seen before. On the other hand, the invention is exactly what was to be expected, it is the crowning of the stupidest period in human history. And the comments of some people! They demonstrate that history was ripe for the birth of the bomb, that it is the colossal symbolic form of the brutality and stupidity of the man of the automobile, the radio, of the man of progress. The age of world terrorism is inaugurated. Now we live under a vague, diffuse threat, superior to all fears before this. You do not know to what extent this invention has upset me, and how bewildered it has me.

These are the sentiments that echo throughout the play, with emphasis on the themes of fratricide and spiritual ruin, as well as physical devastation.

The following day, August 29, 1945, Salinas writes more about his torment over events, about his inability to write, about how the aftermath of war leaves one knocked down, dismantled, and on a path of nothingness: "…las gentes se quedan más descaminadas, más asombradas que nunca" (…the peoples are left more on the wrong track, more frightened than ever; PS/JG *Correspondencia* 361). Can there be any solace in groping through this confusion and pain? At the end of his letter the day before, Salinas indicates how in the midst of this social crisis and uncertainty about the future, he has been struck and consoled by the voice of the poet Valéry. He sees in Valéry's words from *Histoire d'Amphion* an expression of the horrific, but also a crystallization of a powerful potential, and he makes protagonist Abel the mouthpiece of this sentiment: "Egaré dans mon âme, et maître autor de moi! Et je tremble comme un enfant devant ce que je puis" (Lost within my soul and master creator of myself! And I tremble like a baby before what I am able; PS/JG *Correspondencia* 357).

Abel is terrified and tormented by the power he holds, and as Salinas's principal poet character in the play, his words and actions explode with moral and poetic force. In Scene Three, Abel's assurances of love remove Paula's agitation and extend the play's opening balance into Scene Four, into his conversation with Clemente. He mentions to Paula that he is preoccupied with something, and in Scene Four he creates the first major disturbance to set the action in motion. Abel explains to Clemente how he has been wandering about during the past days, unable to free himself from the idea consuming him. He cannot escape from his discovery of the simple solution that will lead to nuclear capabilities then to be abused by an odious dictator who can thus terminate what freedom is left in the world (*Teatro completo* 177-78). The disturbance intensifies as Abel describes the inescapability of his idea:

> Está como una luz radiante en el centro de mi inteligencia, y no se apaga nunca, igual que esas luces de torturadores de la Gestapo. (*Teatro completo* 177-78)

> It is present like a radiant light, in the center of my intelligence, and it is never extinguished, like those lights of the Gestapo torturers.

The reference to the Gestapo and the portrayal of General Ascario reflects Salinas's hatred of Nazism and Fascism, of Hitler and the atrocities of war, topics about which he writes repeatedly to Guillén and others in the early years of World War II, before the composition of "Cero" and *Caín o una gloria científica* and subsequently. Although the letters allude specifically to how deeply world events disturb him, haunt him, and leave him sleepless, this play, like "Cero" and the other poems of *Todo más claro*, transcends a specificity and partisanship to uphold a more broadly social and humanistic ideal. Abel's ethical ideals supersede the deadly, narrow afiliations of the socio-political settings of the twentieth century.

Physicist Abel is more a poet visionary and less a politician. His illustration of the consequences of the total destruction is a delicate glass boat figurine, what Paula later describes in the sub-story of Abel's dream as the epitomy of the fragility of matter (*Teatro completo* 187). The fragile object and all the creative refinement it represents will return to a dust as fine as the sand from which it was formed and will disappear without a trace. Tying this image to the genius's suffering and dreams and to the protagonist's plan, Salinas carries it through the play. At the end of Scene Three, when the plan of protagonist Abel first emerges in vague form, he impresses upon Paula and Clemente his need to pursue his dream and his refusal to increase evil in the world, and he holds out the ideal of finding a beach haven for them to be shadows in the sand (*Teatro completo* 179). In Scene Eight, Abel's dream forms a sub-story which reflects the main conflict and manifests a poetic ideal again expressed in terms of the extreme delicacy of the glass. Abel's vision of Paula's wish that their son be a creator of useless ("inútiles"; *Teatro completo* 187) glass objects is the poet's response to the pressures and dangers of war and misguided power. They are the artist's weapon against the bomb. These ultrasensitive countercreations to violence inspire ultimate peace and tranquility:

> No aceptan la violencia, ni resisten el choque. Piden delicadeza. Ellos son lo primero que se rompe si se los maltrata, si se los oprime torpemente. Son las avanzadas de lo frágil en la materia. No pueden existir más que en un mundo de paz. Despiertan ternura en los que viven junto a ellos. Para ellos el aire tiene que estar en calma, ser bueno. Ellos enseñan a las manos a tener precauciones, a tomar delicadamente las cosas, a templar la rudeza de los músculos que tienden a oprimir, con una voluntad de no romper nada, de no hacer daño. Siempre se vive mejor rodeado de seres de vidrio. En la guerra lo primero que cae, que se quiebra, que gime, son ellos. Son las primeras víctimas... de... el explosivo. (*Teatro completo* 187-88)

They do no accept violence, nor do they resist shock. They ask for delicacy. They are the first to break if they are mistreated, if they are pressed clumsily. The are the epitomy of the fragility of matter. They cannot exist except in a world of peace. They awake tenderness in those that live near them. For them the air must be calm and good. With a will not to break anything, to do no harm, they teach hands to be careful, to take things delicately, to temper the rough motions of muscles that tend to oppress. One always lives better surrounded by entities of glass. In war, they are the first to fall, to break, to moan. They are the first victims... of... the explosive.

In the scenes before and after the dream, Salinas's construction of obstacles, complications, crises, and climaxes accents the tragic force of the work and marks Abel as the impetus that advances the play to its resolution. In Scene Five, Abel opposes Ascario and Fontecha's insistence that he return to work. The physicist thus provokes an interim crisis and climax in which he stands firm and is then placed under house arrest. In Scene Six, Abel continues to offer hope to Paula though he tells her that they must postpone leaving the country. He directs her to be calm and think twenty years beyond the current situation to a world in which their child may live in peace. In the crisis and climax of Scene Seven, Abel elaborates to Clemente the current dangers, implores him to help in escaping them, and elicits Clemente's promise to save them. After the dream scene, in the fast-moving Scenes Nine and Ten, Abel reminds Clemente of his promise, Abel refuses the orders of the General, and then instructs Clemente to carry out his promise.

In his construction of the tragic augury, Salinas makes Abel a poet visionary and a driving moral force who seeks to carry his fellow human beings beyond the threat of world destruction and the pressures and dangers of misguided power. Abel rejects his fated role as an ultimate contemporary Cain, and agonizes over the possible eradication of freedom and humankind. He desperately seeks the ideal island not unlike the sphere visited by Lucila and Lisardo in *El chantajista*, but it appears less accessible in his tortured vision:

Los sueños de los hombres tienen forma de isla. Cada vez que se forja un sueño, se asoma a la superficie de algún mar, a esperarlo, otra isla más. Todas inaccesibles, todas destinadas a ser islas desiertas. ¡Si se encontraran los sueños con sus islas! (*Teatro completo* 178-79)

The dreams of men have the form of an island. Every time a dream is forged, another one looms up to the surface of some sea, to await it. All inaccessible, all destined to be desert islands. If only dreams could find their islands!

When he decides that his death must be his response to political superiors and must serve as the means to the redemption of others, he casts his brother Clemente into the role of a heroic Cain, one who is his brother's as well as his brothers' keeper, allied with Abel in a mutual commitment to humanity. Abel's dream just before the fratricide charts the route to his utopian island. The minute glass boat that Paula shows to the fairy is the means of arriving at Abel's desideratum, a pacific milieu which would permit the survival of even the most fragile of beautiful creations.

Though Abel bonds his brother and frees himself in the final crisis and climax, the work's outcome does not communicate the promise of his poetic ideal. In a conclusion unlike those of the open-ended, happy plays, a violent act fixes the tragic destiny of Abel, and the resolution emphasizes the menacing opposing system. Though Abel refuses to participate personally in promoting the negative forces, he recognizes his fate when he hands Clemente the gun and tells him to use it without hesitation. Forced to see that the world could always be worse, he chooses to remove himself rather than contribute to the evil: "Lo malo del mundo es que siempre puede ser peor. ¡Que no lo sea, hermano, que no lo sea, por mí!" (The bad thing about the world is that it can always be worse. Don't let that be, brother, don't let that be, because of me!; *Teatro completo* 188).

In this prophetic play and others of the tragic variation, Salinas fuses with the existential anguish of the poet the hopes for a better world that transcend national and ideological boundaries. In his preface to *Todo más claro*, lamenting the dehumanization of modern man and the paradox of modern progress which have produced "el más definitivo regreso del ser humano: la vuelta del ser al no ser" (the most definitive regression of the human being: the reversal from being to not being; *Poesías completas* 595), Salinas indicates that he feels the distressing events attacking him from many sides. He carries this burden in universal as well as particular terms, as a man, a European, a Spaniard, and an exile living in America (*Poesías completas* 595).

In writing about "Cero" and other poems of *Todo más claro*, Carlos Feal has summarized well the Salinian stance: "Un asomo de la angustia existencial de nuestro tiempo: la angustia de la libertad" (an appearance of the existential anguish of our time: the anguish for freedom; 243). This is the posture that maintains the tragic rhythm of the fable of *Caín o una gloria científica*. The brother with the name Clemente (Clemency) becomes Salinas's contemporary Cain who by committing the fratricide frees his brother Abel from the agonizing role of murderer of all his brothers. With this freedom comes a sense of fulfillment of a tragic destiny that may lift the poet hero above his defeat, but there is also relinquishment of power to the pressures of the social sphere. Still, there is hope envisioned in the dream of Abel for his unborn son into a world that can protect fragile glass creations.

Salinas the man and the poet stands among humankind and faces immediate circumstances that press upon him and his position in the modern world. Subsequent to the dropping of the bomb, Salinas's letters to Guillén underline these sentiments. Amidst mention of specific world events and criticism of the conduct of individual leaders, he accents broadly humanistic ideals. On January 26, 1946, Salinas injects a frustrated sarcasm into his perspective when he complains to Guillén about the "better world" being designed by forces of mediocrity that have given in to narrow nationalistic, economic or class self-interests: "¡Vaya un mundo mejor que nos están fabricando todas esas medianías..." (What a better world all these mediocrities are making for us...;

PS/JG *Correspondencia* 372-73). In his letter of December 3, 1946, Salinas again communicates his perspective as he justifies his motivation for writing *Judit y el tirano* in May of 1945 and also *Los santos* in 1946, both composed shortly after *Caín o una gloria científica*:

> ...nuestra común condenación de la política tiene la misma base: una moral y una sensibilidad comunes. Sobre todo, eso; que para ti y para mí, no hay más que problemas morales y situaciones humanas, sin que las unas ni las otras tengan que ser sacrificadas a la abstracción política. (De ahí, *Judit y el tirano*. De ahí, *Los santos*.) (PS/JG *Correspondencia* 408)

> ...our common condemnation of politics has the same base: a common morality and sensibility. Above all, that; that for you and for me there is nothing more than moral problems and human situations, without either having to be sacrificed to political abstraction. (From that, *Judith and the Tyrant*. From that, *The Saints*.)

Though never unburdened happily from the negative weights of modernity, the poet protagonists of the plays of tragic rhythm reach to uphold an exemplary morality, sensibility, and humanity. Salinas presents their sufferings as a necessary consequence in the process of salvation and liberation, and through to the end of his life, he sees the exigency of this sacrifice in the disturbing world around him. On January 1, 1951, the first day of his last year, he composes a poignantly fateful letter to Guillén. Having enjoyed immensely a day with his grandchildren, he writes, "Los 364 días que me restan traerán lo que traigan" (The 364 days that I have left will bring what they may bring; PS/JG *Correspondencia* 551). This is a day he wants to hold apart from others, a day free from the suicidal blindness of those in the world who persist in making war. Pleading for life, peace, and dignity, he laments not hearing any loud voices to promote these ideals, and he points to the value of sacrifice:

Lo que nadie dice es que habrá que buscar con tanto empeño, con tanta actividad y con tanta energía como se pone en preparar la guerra, caminos de paz, incansablemente, y con los sacrificios necesarios de lo menor, que es todo, en comparación con lo mayor, que es la vida y dignidad de la humanidad, que sucumbirían en una guerra, sin salvación posible. (PS/JG *Correspondencia* 552)

What no one is saying is that it is necessary to seek paths to peace, with as much persistence, as much activity, and as much energy as is put into the preparation for war, tirelessly, and with the necessary lesser sacrifices, which is everything, in comparison with the greater, that is the life and dignity of humanity, that in a war would succumb without any possible salvation.

In the anguished prophecy of *Caín o una gloria científica*, Salinas has made his poet character Abel a strong voice of this ideal and an example of the necessity of sacrifice.

6
Poet and Perception: The Poet as a Visionary

> Eso es lo supremo: una vez escogido lo que nos llama más la atención al corazón, se lo contempla es decir se fija la vista en ello, se pone en la vista la voluntad de penetrarlo con el alma, y así va uno apoderándose de ello.
> SALINAS, *Cartas de viaje* 109

> That is the supreme thing: once we choose what calls most to the attention of our hearts, we contemplate it, that is, we fix our sight on it, and put into our sight the will to penetrate it with our soul, and thus we come to take possession of it.

SALINAS'S THEORY OF TOURISM, which he shares with Margarita in a letter of 1939 at the time of his visit to the Grand Canyon, marks three levels of seeing: "ver," viewing involuntarily what falls in front of us, "mirar," looking by choice and actively, and "contemplar," contemplating with heart and soul to penetrate and take possession of what captures our attention (*Cartas de viaje* 109). Salinas's poet characters are ideal travellers and travel guides through contemporary existence who practice what he deems the supreme level of seeing. These poet characters see beyond surfaces and superficial values. The world views of Salinas's poet figures can be fruitfully examined in part through attention to an elaborate system of references to seeing that Salinas builds into the dramatic discourse of his fourteen plays. The key poet characters emerge as viewer-guiders engaging in penetrating, liberating modes of seeing.

Consequently, the guided-viewers, those characters influenced by the poet guiders, adjust their vision and begin to perceive more fully. Moreover, preoccupations with seeing by peripheral characters or in sub-stories echo these important reconfigurations of seeing or stand in sharp contrast to them. References to eyes, windows, and mirrors support a view of seeing as a kind of discernment beyond the conventional ocular glance.

The role of the poet as a visionary in the dramatic works can be tied to Salinas's conception of the poet as disclosed in his poetry, letters, and essays. Attention to Salinas's views of the poet's special capacity to see will contextualize the exploration of the discourse of seeing found in his plays. Then, examination of prominent patterns of references to seeing in the dramatic works will highlight the spiritual and social force of Salinas's poet heroes. Investigation of character interactions will show how Salinas's poet visionaries see profoundly and enable others to gain access to this heightened sensitivity.

SALINAS'S VIEWS OF THE POET'S CAPACITY TO SEE

Salinas's portrait of the poet possessing powers of vision is hardly novel, yet its appearance is clear, consistent, and explicit throughout his work. The poet is constantly counteracting the enervating habituation attributable to conventional modes of perception. "Seeing" means surpassing ordinary cognizance, reminiscent of the Russian formalist notion of "ostranenie," defamiliarization, or "making strange" (Elam 17, Bennett 53 ff, Hawkes 63). Structuralists such as Terence Hawkes have described the visual prowess of poets in the following terms:

> The poet thus aims to disrupt 'stock responses', and to generate a heightened awareness: to restructure our ordinary perception of 'reality', so that we end by *seeing* the world instead of numbly recognizing it: or at least so that we can design a 'new' reality to replace the (no less fictional) one which we have inherited and become accustomed to. (Hawkes 63).

Salinas defines the visionary capacity of the poet in much the same way, but with even more emphasis on the poet's seeking a liberating reality constituted by a fusion of his or her own inner, psychological reality and ordinary aspects of external reality. In *Reality and the Poet in Spanish Poetry*, he seeks to showcase the potentialities of the poet-creator by defining reality "in a general and comprehensive sense," and by referring to its limiting nature: "Reality, the life of the world that surrounds us and limits us, that gives to the individual the measure, at once tragic and magnificent, of his own solitude and of his creative possiblities" (*Reality and the Poet* 3). For Salinas, the poet's way of seeing transforms ordinary reality by seeing it more fully and lovingly. In turn, Jorge Guillén, in his preface to the lectures, writes of his friend, "How he gazed at his surroundings! His surroundings are loved and assimilated, above all, by his gaze. Vision is our poet's primary faculty. One desires what is real. And in order to convert it into spirit, one must go deep into matter. Not the orange, an easy solution, but its secret: the juice, an internal reality" (*Reality and the Poet* xxiv).

This mention of the orange is clearly a reference to Salinas's poem "El zumo" (Juice) from his second volume of poetry, *Seguro azar*. The poet searches beyond the visible exterior of the orange, which can be misleading:

> Lo que da son disimulos,
> redondez, color, rebrillo,
> solución fácil, naranja,
> a la mirada y al viento.
> (*Poesías completas* 112)
>
> What it gives are deceptions,
> roundness, color, radiance,
> easy solution, orange,
> to the glance and to the wind.

In this poem and many others, not discounting the visible, the poet looks deeper, and pursues a latent, profound, and often deceptive-to-the-eyes truth. Another salient example of this perspective is Salinas's poem "Vocación" (Vocation), from the same volume *Seguro azar*. Here again, the poet employs his sight to the fullest to behold the physical materiality of what is before him; and then, with echoes of a Platonic vision, sees through the eyes of his soul beyond the immediate to discover its essence:

> Abrir los ojos. Y ver
> sin falta ni sobra, a colmo;
> en la luz clara del día
> perfecto el mundo, completo.
> ....
> Cerrar los ojos. Y ver
> incompleto, tembloroso,
> de será o de no será,
>
> —masas torpes, planos sordos
> —
> sin luz, sin gracia, sin orden
> un mundo sin acabar,
> necesitando, llamándome
> a mí, o a ti, o a cualquiera
> que ponga lo que le falta,
> que le dé la perfección.
>
> En aquella tarde clara,
> en aquel mundo sin tacha,
> escogí:
> el otro
> Cerré los ojos.
>   (*Poesías completas* 110)

To open one's eyes. And to see

Without absence or excess, to the limit;
In the clear light of day
the world perfect, complete.
    ....
To close one's eyes. And to see
incomplete, trembling,
of what is to be and not to be,

—awkward masses, deaf planes
—

without light, grace, order
a never-ending world,
needing, calling
to me, to you, or to whoever
can offer what it needs,
who can give it perfection.

On that clear afternoon,
in that world without flaw,
I chose:
the other
I closed my eyes.

The poet considers his calling a process of moving deeper into himself and his surroundings as he endeavors to navigate and connect the complex spheres of perception outside and inside himself.

From a variety of perspectives, numerous critics in addition to Guillén have noted Salinas's attention to visual perception and have studied the role of Salinas the seer, especially in his poetry. Many have emphasized Salinas's rejection of external reality and of what the eyes see in his search for an essential, absolute, or other realm (Cirre 29-30, Dehennin 23, Stixrude 22, Zardoya 106). C. B. Morris describes Salinas's revival of Spain's popular, traditional "ver-no ver" (to see-not to see) conceit, the poet's denial of sight, and his determination to visualize things in his imagination (*A Generation...* 43; "Visión y mirada..." 103-12). Citing poems such as "Vocación," interpreters of Salinas's poetry write of the poet's closing his eyes to the outside world and his preference for an interior, intensely personal realm (Del Río 205-06, Feldbaum 17, González Muela 198).

Other critics see in Salinas's poetry, in the poet's attempt to comprehend reality, a strong attachment to the visible world. Zubizarreta traces a trajectory in the poet's gaze or "mirada" from the early poem "Vocación" ("Vocation") to the later composition "Ver lo que veo" ("To see what I see") included in his final volume of poetry, *Confianza* (*Confidence*). She claims that Salinas moves from an early fixation in "Vocación" on the separation of exterior and interior reality, toward a capacity to extract a redemptive essence from the outside world, to a vehement acceptance of what he sees (Zubizarreta 300). Salinas affirms in "Ver lo que veo" that more than anything else, he wishes to see what he sees: "Quisiera más que nada, más que sueño,/ver lo que veo" (I would like more than anything, more than a dream, to see what I see; *Poesías completas* 777). Rupert Allen, in a detailed analysis of this poem, interprets this to mean that Salinas is concerned with the here and now, with a salvation or a wholeness derived from truly seeing what he beholds (148). Likewise, Crispin denies the idea that poet is seeking to escape his surroundings because he closes his eyes in "Vocación" (*Pedro Salinas* 52); and Luis Vivanco sees Salinas's imagination of reality as an attempt to discover it and explain it, rather than to invent it (*Introducción a la poesía española contemporánea* 118-19). Havard, in his study of Salinas and the poetics of motion, links Salinas's attention to visual perception in part with Ortega y Gasset's theory of perspectivism. Referring to the poem "El zumo" ("Juice"), he asserts that the outward appearance of the orange offers an easy, but deceitful solution to its reality. To see it fully, "we need to adopt a variety of viewing positions by moving from one place to another, or else the orange will have to move as we view it" (*From Romanticism to Surrealism* 152). Carlos Feal ties Salinas's attraction to "lo invisible" (the invisible), the inseparable, other face of "lo visible"(the visible) to Heidegger and Merleau-Ponty. He examines how

Salinas exalts the world of the senses with a poetry "cargada de vista y no de visiones" (charged with sight and not visions) and underlines the poet's search for an illumination of being ("Lo visible y lo invisible en los primeros libros poéticos de Salinas" 182).

A few critics have directed attention to the social significance of the poet as a seer. Soufas argues convincingly that in the poetic process, Salinas affirms the centrality of the intellectual will in the creation of an alternative reality: "Even in the early poetry, Salinas is dissatisfied with traditional representational models and begins to look for a better image of reality, in contradistinction to ordinary experiences in either external, empirical reality, or inner, psychological reality. He subsequently invents a realm that expresses these aspirations and its alternative values. Poetry becomes the vehicle through which to create an alternative world, a better image, of being" (64-65).

Some of those who have studied his later poetry have also pointed to a more socially conscious Salinas. Morris mentions how Salinas felt the horror of his time and the fear of atomic annihilation, and mentions the poet's prediction of the end of mankind reflected in his gazing at his own skeleton in the mirror (*A Generation...* 244-46). Crispin describes the poet's ethical mission to preserve humanity in the face of war, the cold modern world, and technology (*Pedro Salinas* 106-29). Díez de Revenga writes of Salinas's commitment in both *Todo más claro* and in the posthumous *Confianza* to a reality encompassing contemporary society ("la realidad comprometida con la sociedad en la que el poeta vive") (the reality engaged with the society in which the poet lives; Salinas *Poemas Escogidas* 52). Encountering a Salinas open to the world in the poems of *El contemplado*, Feal asserts that Salinas has managed to introduce "un sentimiento colectivo, social, en un canto de naturaleza contemplativa" (a collective, social feeling into his contemplative song to nature; 467-68). Rather than a manifestation of Salinas's isolation, these poems reveal the poet's connectedness with surroundings and fellow beings. Lloréns concurs, and emphasizes the poet's attainment of an eternal vision through his contemplation of the sea, a vision that effects continuity and salvation (192-93).

All three of Salinas's final volumes of poetry—*Todo más claro, El contemplado,* and *Confianza*— exhibit a social sensibility and an attention to seeing that Salinas charges with a more powerful moral-ethical dimension in his dramatic works. In the poems of *Todo más claro,* composed between 1937 and 1947, significantly contemporaneous with the composition of his plays, the poet focuses most intensely on the degeneration of modern life. The volume begins with an exaltation of poetry and its capacity to make things clear and concludes with a condemnation of war. Also contemporaneous with some of the plays, *El contemplado* is a product of Salinas's time in Puerto Rico between 1943 and 1946, at the end of the Second World War and during a parenthesis of special peace during his years of exile in the United States. Employing throughout this work vivid visual imagery and a pervasive pattern of references to vision, Salinas engages in a dialogue with the Sea of San Juan to pursue its serenity and its relationship to nature, reality, tradition, and the material world. From this volume, his poem "Salvacion por la luz" (Salvation through the light) crystalizes how contemplation of the sea enables the poet to see the past and the generations before him, to connect with eternity, and to reach for salvation: "Y de tanto mirarte, nos salvemos." (And from so much looking at you, may we save ourselves; *Poesías completas* 589) In his final poems of the forties and early fifties, collected in *Confianza,* the problems of the modern world become endurable as Salinas experiences with all his senses, sight prominent among them, the pleasures of nature and of communion with his surroundings.

Some of the later poetry especially, as well as his essays that elucidate his poetics of seeing (for example, "Registro de Jorge Carrera Andrade" from *Ensayos de la literatura hispánica* and the essays of *La responsabilidad del escritor*) portray Salinas the poet as a visionary social force in search of liberation from the destructive aspects of human interactions, as a figure addressing certain societal ills and seeking to alter the sensibilities of others. In his dramatic works, these preoccupations receive expanded attention as Salinas assigns similar missions to the poet figures in the plays. Since the dialogic exchanges of the *dramatis personae* reflect everyday life, and the characters function within common social situations, many references to seeing, observing, staring, eyes, and the like represent superficial colloquialisms and conventional phrases. Yet beyond the many context-appropiate, realistic references to seeing in the plays is discernible a larger framework appropriate to the poet characters and their modes of perception. It will be shown that throughout the dramatic works of Salinas, the discourse of seeing and the lack thereof goes beyond ordinary seeing. The poet figures do not deny the significance of the tangible, but seek its profundity—a *dejà vu* of Salinas's perception of the orange in his early poem "El zumo," where the poet probes for the essence of the fruit that appears deceptively tangible.

VIEWER-GUIDERS AND GUIDED VIEWERS
In his dramatic works, Salinas emphasizes the spiritual leadership of his poet heroes who can see the ordinary reality and beyond. Part of the discourse of seeing communicates a removal of the necessity of actual, physiological seeing for significant and meaningful perception—an echo of the "ver-no ver" paradox of Salinas's poetry. The seeing that Salinas attributes to his poet characters involves an uncovering, discovering, creating, and transcending of conventional vision bound by limitation. After a survey of the conventional references to seeing that offer an external coding complementary to the more consequential discourse of seeing, analysis of Salinas's construction of the poet as a visionary will focus on his portrayal of the relationships between viewer-guiders and guided-viewers.

Throughout the plays, many conversations contain recurrent syntactic and rhetorical patterns reinforcing the discourse of seeing. Often, these are lexical iterations or repetitive, simple directive or commissive speech acts through which one character steers or conjoins another character to look, watch, or take notice of something or somebody. In *La fuente del arcángel,* Florindo describes to his audience the rapidity of his transformations as a flash: "un abrir y cerrar de ojos" (an opening and closing of the eyes; *Teatro completo* 231). In *Caín o una gloria científica,* Paula plans an escape and tells Clemente, "*Mira,* la casa la puede venir a vivir mi hermana..." (*Look, my sister can come live at the house...*) and later, "*Mira, mira,* ya tengo el plan del viaje..." (*Look, look, now I have the plan for the trip...*; *Teatro completo* 183, emphasis added here and subsequently). Judit utters "*A ver. A ver. A ver*" (*Let's see. Let's see. Let's see*; *Teatro completo* 383) as she looks for the word to describe her action of preventing the death of the tyrant. In *El director*, saying "Ya lo *verá* usted" (Now *you will see* it; *Teatro completo* 318), Esperanza punctuates her views on dictation and creation to the Mecanógrafa.

A number of utterances reflect the linguistic features of a particular character or location and heighten the local color of the dramatic discourse. The lexicons that Salinas creates for Gumersinda and the town's lovers in *La fuente del arcángel*, for example, reflect their participation in the discourse of seeing and emphasize the visual prominence of the statue. Gumersinda worries that her nieces will cast "una *miradita*" (a *little glance; Teatro completo* 227) through the fence and see lovers kissing at the fountain. Later in the play, the playful exchange between Angelillo and Honoria at the fountain of the Arcángel includes Honoria's "*Mía tú,* Angelillo,..." (*Look,* Angelillo...; *Teatro completo* 238) and Angelillo's "Ahora, San Miguel, *a vé* cómo te porta..." (Now, San Miguel, *let's see* how you behave...; *Teatro completo* 238). In *Los santos*, the rural dialect reappears when the Madre tells Palmito: "Muchacha, *mía* que estás ofendiendo a Dios" (Girl, *look* that you are offending God; *Teatro completo* 255). Salinas's experimentation with regional dialects, especially in "*La Estratoesfera*" and *La fuente del arcángel* clearly reflects his nostalgia for Spain. Of "*La Estratoesfera,"* he writes to Guillén, "Es un solo acto, situado en una taberna de la guindalera. Me he soltado el pelo madrileñista. ¡Ay lo que daría por leérselo! (It is a single act, located in a tavern of the *guindalera* neighborhood. I have let down my *Madrileño* hair. Oh, what I would give to read it! PS/JG *Correspondencia*, 353).

In addition to the common usages and popularisms like the above noted in the dramatic dialogue, there is consistent, frequent, and explicit mention in the stage directions of common postures associated with vision, connection, and love. Emphases on physiognomy focus further on the poet's extraordinary powers of perception. To portray the unity and harmony of lovers, Salinas clearly defines how Lisardo and Lucila gaze at each other in the conclusion of *El chantajista* (*Teatro completo* 304). Similarly, in *El parecido*, he specifies how Roberto eyes Julia (*Teatro completo* 28) and in *Judit y el tirano*, the heroine faces her challenger turned sweetheart (*Teatro completo* 402). In *El chantajista*, to augment the pressure of the ten minute limit in which to tell the truth, Salinas specifies that each character looks at the clock; and to portray the climax and liberating recognition of the truth of their togetherness, the instructions underline Lisardos's anxious yearning and Lucila's assurance of its fulfillment (*Teatro completo* 306). In *Judit y el tirano*, to convey the tragedy of the death of the Regente, it is indicated that Judit covers her eyes with her hands (*Teatro completo* 410). These extra-linguistic actions that accompany the dialogue of the poet characters underline the intensity of their seeing and their powers of vision to discover, create, and transcend a constricting milieu. References such as the aforementioned contribute especially to the rhetorical and stylistic coherence of the plays and complement a more expansive and pivotal discourse centered on seeing, a discourse that highlights the poet's special visual acumen. This faculty leads to a liberating recreation of circumstances for the guiding and guided characters.

The poet protagonist characters' posture and speech activity centered on seeing reinforce significantly their commanding role in orienting the views of others. Their actions and words communicate a preoccupation with directing sight beyond facade, with engaging themselves with others, and with achieving communication that breaks through superficialities. The social settings of the plays often occasion realistic dialogues that incorporate literal or figurative usage of references to a superior level of seeing achieved by these characters.

In many passages, poet protagonists beckon overtly to others to share their viewpoints. With the aim of ultimately discovering what may lie beyond appearances, Florindo, in *La fuente del arcángel*, invites his audience and especially Claribel to share his illusions (*Teatro completo* 236). In the escape scene of this play, the Arcángel/Eros/Florindo figure guides Claribel toward an ideal realm described with vivid visual imagery. When Claribel asks where they are going, the tripartite figure directs her toward the blackbird and the star, to the bottom of crown of the hat of Florindo (*Teatro completo* 240). Acknowledging perception of the magical hat, Claribel demonstrates that she now is prepared to share this special scope of vision, which the poet-guide suggests may have a depth without bounds. Florindo pushes Claribel to transcend the perception of the unidimensional appearance of the statue as Arcángel. His guidance for their shared vision leads to their deliverance: "Puede..., ya lo veremos" (It can..., now we'll see; *Teatro completo* 240). Similarly, in "*La Estratoesfera,*" when Felipa asks Alvaro where they are going and who he really is, he looks to save her by transporting her to a future beyond her lowly life. When he responds "Eso ya lo verás" (Now you will see it; *Teatro completo* 211), he is ready to raise her literally and figuratively out of the bar named La Estratoesfera.

In *Sobre seguro*, Petra serves as the visionary guide of her son. When Angel asks his mother if it is true that he has not died, Petra replies, "No, tonto, no. ¿No los ves? ¿No ves a tu madre?" (No, silly, no. Don't you see? Don't you see your mother?; *Teatro completo* 159). In leading him to an idealized realm where they can be safe together, she points to the moon and its suggestive illumination: "¿No ves la luna tan hermosa...?" (Don't you see the beautiful moon...?; *Teatro completo* 160). She directs him to see what she sees: "¿Tú ves este dinero? Pues es malo, muy malo" (Do you see this money? Well it is bad, very bad; *Teatro completo* 162). Involving him in the burning of the money, she leads him to see and take action: "Mira lo que vamos a hacer" (Look at what we are going to do; *Teatro completo* 162). Instructing him to throw the money into the fire, she rejoices, "Tú verás las llamas tan preciosas que da..." (You will see the pretty colors it makes...; *Teatro completo* 162). Her enjoyment of the spectacle of combusting colors signals a poetic, symbolic recovery of life. With the destruction of each packet, Petra envisions three additional years of life for Angel and deliverance from the cut-throat world of insurance.

In *El director*, Salinas draws a vivid picture of an omniscient, sight-guiding deity. The Director has clearly foreseen the creature who turns out to be the Mecanógrafa even before she arrives in person. He tells her, "...cuando yo puse ese anuncio era justamente para que lo leyese una mujer a quien ya conocía sin haberla visto" (...when I placed that ad it was just so that a woman whom I already knew without having seen would read it; *Teatro completo* 310). One of the most forceful passages that exalts perception beyond superficialities appears toward the end of the play, when the divinity figure undertakes visual counselling of the Mecanógrafa. He warns that a deeper contemplation of things may destroy the contentment derived from fixation on outer appearances. A penetrating gaze toward the reverse side of something and beyond may open the way to painful struggle:

> Sí, hay que reconocer que para los espíritus simples el revés de las cosas es desconcertante. Se prenden ustedes en la apariencia más brillante, la superficial. La faz del mundo tiene muchos admiradores, hasta adoradores: todos esos que contemplan la primavera o las noches de luna, diciendo: '¡Qué bonito!' Pero hay también otros seres que al ver el rostro de las cosas y las personas miran siempre más allá, y se preguntan angustiados, cómo será el revés de todo eso. Ansían verlo, y sueñan con que les gustaría mucho más, que ellos han nacido para mirar por ese lado. (*Teatro completo* 354)

> Yes, one must recognize that for simple souls the reverse side of things is disconcerting. You attach yourselves to the shiniest, superficial appearance. The face of the world has many admirers, even adorers: all those who contemplate the spring or moonlight nights saying: 'How pretty!' But there are also other beings who when they see the face of things and people always look beyond, and ask themselves, distressed, how the reverse of all that might be. They long to see it, and they dream that they would like it much more, that they were born to see that side.

A number of other poet protagonists experience analogous suffering as a result of their penetrating visions during their quests for emancipation. Through these characters, Salinas espouses relationships between seeing and anguish, seeing and self-torment, seeing and suicidal tendencies or death. Judit, needing to be the one to kill the tyrant, explains how much she needs to see him and why:

> Sí, porque necesito verla de cerca, antes de que caiga, por mi mano; sentirla caer delante de mí, ver el embuste, el embeleco, materialmente derrumbada a mis pies.... Necesito verla de cara a cara, por primera y última vez, ser yo la que expulse de la realidad. (*Teatro completo* 366-67)

> Yes, because I need to see it up close, before it falls, by my hand; experience it fall before me, to see the lie, the fraud, physically destroyed at my feet.... I need to see it face to face, for the first and last time, and to be the one who expels it from reality.

In the tense anticipation before the drawing of the lots, Judit is singled out in the stage directions that describe her obsessive stance oriented toward a far-reaching vision and a redemption: "...Judit es la única que pone los ojos en el vacío, como si estuviera mirando a una visión, con ojos ardientes" (...Judit is the only one who stares out into space, with eyes blazing, as if she were looking at a vision; *Teatro completo* 369). Soon before the tragedy that ensues due to the misperceptions of the secret police, Judit explains to the tyrant the significance of the final test in terms of perception and seeing: "Si al acabar tu discurso ves ya claro..." (If upon finishing your speech you then see clear...; *Teatro completo* 372). The ironic and fateful death results from the clarity of vision about himself that Judit has brought to the Regente and that she has insisted he possess.

Like Judit, Abel, the preeminent, self-stated, "observador de oficio" (observer by profession; *Teatro completo* 173), also struggles with the pain of piercing, clear vision. After finding the key to his research, he says, "Parecía increíble, pero pronto vi que era la verdadera. Desde entonces no descanso..." (It seemed incredible, but soon I saw that it was the true one. Since then I have not rested...; *Teatro completo* 177). Though part of him fights fiercely to contain the solution he knows he has within him, Abel sees exactly what the idea is and how it should be carried through to the final discovery: "Veo punto por punto todo lo que se necesita hacer..." (I see point by point all that needs to be done...; *Teatro completo* 178). He agonizes about withholding his insight from a government that will misuse it: "Es porque detrás de ella empiezo a ver algo aterrador" (It is because behind it I am beginning to see something terrifying; *Teatro completo* 176). This painful illumination makes Abel delineate for his brother the one escape he sees from his anguish, an escape inextricably rooted in his view of Clemente: "A ti, que te veo ahora agrandado, infinito, hecho de todos los hermanos inocentes que podrían morir por mi culpa y no morirán" (You, I see you now magnified, infinite, acting as all innocent brothers who, because of my guilt, could die and will not die; *Teatro completo* 185).

Abel's depth of vision is clear in his role as a husband and father as well as in his role as a scientist, brother, and aspiring keeper of all brothers. Trying to protect Paula from the torturous visions that plague him, Abel directs her to look beyond immediate circumstances toward an idealized realm of salvation: "...apartar la vista de esto y ponerla muy lejos.... ¿A ver? Mira muy lejos..." (...remove your sight from this and put it very far away.... See? Look very far...; *Teatro completo* 183). The inclusion of Scene Seven reinforces Salinas's conception of the poet dreamer. Abel daydreams of a visit to Paula by a fairy who grants her wish of a son who makes delicate glass figures. Their fragility constitutes a plea for a world without violence. The dialogue between Paula and the fairy takes place with Abel illuminated, sitting in a corner of the stage, and staring into space. Salinas thus adjusts focus through the mind's eye of Abel and draws in the audience to behold an idealized view of a redemptive future that transcends the more concrete oppressive circumstances outside the dream.

Seeing is to uncover, to discover, and to create, and also to cross through view-obstructing boundaries. It is with the impetus of the poet visionaries that other figures come to share more open fields of view and acquire new powers of vision. The activist poets generate the transformation of kindred characters, who engage in a discourse of seeing that reflects their concentration on empirical verification of their recently enhanced capacity to perceive.

In *La fuente del arcángel*, after entering the realm of illusion created by Florindo, Claribel confirms that "se me veía a mí así" (I was seen like this; *Teatro completo* 237). Also, subsequent to her experience with Florindo, she shows her ability to see and interpret the meaning of the lovers' conversation at the taboo fountain (*Teatro completo* 238-39).

In *El chantajista*, Lisardo's self-liberating view of blackmail springs forth from the letters that Lucila has planted for him to find in the theater. His price is the opportunity to meet her, to see her, to behold her face, to hear her voice, to speak to her if possible (*Teatro completo* 296). Early on, he does not have a full perspective on the simple condition he has demanded, but he is somehow captivated by the significance of seeing. At the beginning of the second scene, though still in the dark, he is intent upon moving forward with his plan: "Por ver a una muchacha.... Y por verla,... " (For the sake of seeing a girl.... And for the sake of seeing her...; *Teatro completo* 298). Also, this preoccupation with vision is apparent in his wearing of the Romeo disguise. Guided into the relationship by the surreptitious Lucila, he is consumed with the desire for her to see him in this new layer of romantic costume.

Lisardo's ability to see grows steadily during their encounter. After Lucila tells him about the first kiss, Lisardo articulates his new way of perceiving solitude: "La soledad, qué hermosa se vio desde entonces, por el derecho" (Solitude, how beautiful it was seen since then, from the right side; *Teatro completo* 300-01). Lisardo begs the disguised Lucila to see Lucila a few minutes more. This final sighting and genuine discovery of Lucila will mean the laying bare of the real truth of his feelings. Complying with the conditions for receiving another ten minutes with the beloved, Lisardo repeatedly utters references to seeing and the truth and articulates clearly his eagerness to share in perception beyond surfaces. He tells Lucila that it is his turn to pass to the side of the light so that she can see him and see the truth, and he directs her to look at his face closely

(*Teatro completo* 304). He stresses the ripeness of the opportunity to seize the truth: "No falta casi nada... para que veas la verdad, aunque no la quieres ver..." (Almost nothing is lacking... for you to see the truth, even though you do not want to see it...; *Teatro completo* 305).

In a number of plays, guided viewers acknowledge pointedly the transformation that their power of sight undergoes. In *El precio*, after Jáuregui tells Alicia and her father about the universal nature of poetry and the poet's special way of seeing, Alicia measures the pervasive influence of Melisa upon her: "¡Es verdad, ella lo ve... y yo empezaba a verlo...!" (It's true, she sees it... and I was beginning to see it...!; *Teatro completo* 287). At the conclusion of *Judit y el tirano*, at the insistence of Judit, the tyrant readies himself to submit to a final proof that will link his capacities to see and to be free. It involves his perception of his own humanity and clear recognition of his release from being a tyrant: "Si ya no creo en lo que digo, si lo veo como mi engaño, ya no podré engañar más a mi pueblo" (If I no longer believe what I say, if I see it as my deceit, I will no longer deceive my people;*Teatro completo* 401).

In *El director*, Mecanógrafa's quest for empirical verification takes a tragic turn. The Divinity figure seriously alters her perceptions, but she misguidedly seeks an ill-fated liberation of the Director from his counterpart. Her deicide confirms her faulty vision and the inseparability of his angelic and diabolical sides. Also, it certifies the guiding figure's earlier espousal of a poetic definition of seeing as the penetration of darkness beyond which true clarity is attainable:

> Sólo las personas a quienes les gustan las cosas claras son capaces de vivir en la oscuridad, entre tinieblas, luchando entre ellas; saben que la verdadera claridad sólo está allí, al fondo de lo oscuro. Usted se quedará conmigo. Vivirá usted entre estas cosas oscuras, precisamente porque aspira a traspasarlas. No a ver la luz esta, que está delante de usted, sino la otra, la que está detrás de las tinieblas, la que yo tengo, la que le tienta sin cesar, la que venía usted a buscar, ahora, hace un momento. (*Teatro completo* 324)

Only those people who like things clear are capable of living in darkness, among the shadows, fighting there; they know that true clarity is there, at the depths of what is obscure. You will remain with me. You will live among these obscure things, precisely because you aspire to transcend them. To see not this light, which is in front of you, but the other one, that which is behind the shadows, the one I have, the one that tempts you unceasingly, that which you came to seek, now, a moment ago.

Salinas's poet visionaries and those they guide are powerful and persistent seekers who experience inevitable struggle on their paths to redemptive, spiritual fulfillment. Often, Salinas represents their confusion, transmits their perceptions, and upholds their depth-seeking contemplations via imagery focused on or through eyes, windows, and mirrors. These all constitute lenses that magnify the special positions of the poet protagonists and help expose their world views oriented toward the rescue of humanity.

EYES, WINDOWS, MIRRORS AND THE SCOPE OF THE POET
A significant part of the discourse of seeing in the dramatic works involves images of reality explicitly framed through eyes, windows, and mirrors. Repeatly, Salinas makes explicit associations between his characters and these apertures to emphasize their capacities to penetrate facades and progress beyond ordinary sight to insight.

The eye of the poet visionary probes beyond dry facts and immediate circumstances to reach for liberating truth. Eyes are the means to look deeper into others and oneself. They are barometers of transformation and signals of salvation. In *El chantajista*, Lisardo refers to the eyes as gauges of the sincerity and uniqueness of his feelings for Lucila in a paradoxically deceitful yet truthful situation: "sí, uno, y tú, una, una aquí, delante, de verdad, y a estos ojos que te ven, de verdad, se los toca, sí de verdad." (yes, one, and you, one, one here, before me, real, and these eyes that see you for real, are touched; *Teatro completo* 300). For Soledad, in *La Bella Durmiente*, eyes are her means to take in the surroundings fully: "...las vistas que he devorado con los ojos" (... the sights I have devoured with my eyes; *Teatro completo* 78). Using their eyes, these poets aim for the most profound kind of contact and understanding.

In *Caín o una gloria científica*, Abel fixes his gaze upon Paula's eyes to pursue comprehension beyond what he receives from auditory sources: "El oído me dice: "bien," pero la vista... ¡Esos ojos, esos ojos...! ¿Qué ha pasado por esos ojos? Algo ha sido... y no hace mucho... Paula, dime la verdad... " (My ears tell me that it's all right, but my eyes... Your eyes, your eyes...! What has passed by those eyes? It's been something... and not long ago... Paula, tell me the truth...; *Teatro completo* 173). Through intense reminiscence of the eyes of her son, the Madre in *Los santos* suffers the pain of his assassination: "Y, entonces, estos ojos míos lo vieron, estos ojos, y lo están viendo ahora, y lo verán mañana, y ya no verán nada más mientras estén abiertos... estos ojos míos" (And then, these eyes of mine saw it, these eyes, and they are seeing it now, and they will see it tomorrow, and they will see nothing else as long as they are open... these eyes of mine; *Teatro completo* 258). In addition to serving as focal point of a shared agony, the eyes are the link between them that allows the Madre to bear the tragic vision of her son: "Cayó del láo que yo estaba, y la mirada como que me dijo adiós... que se despidió. Suerte que cayó de ese lado, que le vi los ojos..." He fell to the side where I was, and his look was as if he were telling me good-bye... that he was saying good-bye. It was luck that he fell to that side, that I saw his eyes...; *Teatro completo* 258).

In *Ella y sus fuentes*, the contrast between the real Julia Riscal and her mistaken image as heroine of liberty is emphasized through the references to her eyes. Merlín describes to his visitor how the eyes of the legendary Julia Riscal have become a part of the collective national memory (*Teatro completo* 53). Merlín sees the eyes of the woman of his research as a source from which springs a spirit of liberty and recites the poem that celebrates them. But having to confront the reality of the appearance of the real Julia and to acknowledge that Julia Riscal has, in fact, "un mirar de ángel" (the look of an angel; *Teatro completo* 53), nothing like the personage of "ojos negros, y una mirada ardiente" (dark eyes, and an ardent expression; *Teatro completo* 53) he has investigated, takes Merlín well beyond his sources.

Sometimes eyes serve as indicators of the receptivity of characters to transformation and as an indication of changing perception in an overall movement directed toward spiritual emancipation. In *Sobre seguro*, Angel notes the happiness in his mother's eyes after they burn the money and she signs the document that ensures their freedom: "¡Qué alegría tiene usted en los ojos!" (What happiness is in your eyes!;*Teatro completo* 162). In *La isla del tesoro*, when Marú is pursuing the truth about the existence of the notebook writer, she asks the hotel maid to concentrate on her face to discern if she looks like a bad person; *Teatro completo* 111).

At times, Salinas's stage directions indicate a sharp focus on the transformed expressions of characters that indicate their marked change in perception. In *Ella y sus fuentes*, after Julia's gradual delivery of proof, Merlín's expression and manner of looking changes drastically to reflect wonder and fear (*Teatro completo* 52). In *Los santos*, Orozco's physiognomy communicates his mysterious encounter with the statue of Soledad (*Teatro completo* 250). At the end of the play, after the miracle, the stage directions emphasize the looks of amazement and fear of the two men, Severio and Paulino, with their eyes glued to the door; and the expression of joy of the Madre, centered in the tableau of prisoners and saints, immobile, and looking toward the sky (*Teatro completo* 263).

In *Judit y el tirano*, references to eyes underline the power of what cannot be observed in a material sense. For Judit, the faceless guise of the tyrant increases his nightmarish appearance in her imagination (*Teatro completo* 366). Her acute suffering from this torturous situation makes her decide that she alone must be the one to kill the tyrant. Judit's self-selection is reinforced in a number of sequences that make reference to her eyes as reflectors of her annointment as deliverer. Early in the play, Valentín tells Judit that her face reveals her destiny: "Te veo en la mirada que eres tú, tú, la que lo tiene que matar" (I see in your eyes that it is you, you, who has to be the one to kill the tyrant; *Teatro completo* 367). The words of Valentín are reiterated later in the play to emphasize the fateful results. When Judit struggles to understand why she has saved the tyrant from the bullet of another, she remembers what Valentín had foretold: "Valentín me lo vio en los ojos, se convenció por algo que yo tenía en los ojos. 'Ahí te lo veo..., tú le matarías...'" (Valentín saw it in my eyes, he was convinced by something in my eyes. 'I see it there in you..., you would kill him...'; *Teatro completo* 382). In her closing lines, when she reacts to the killing of the Regente by a policemen with her gun, she reconfirms the tragic paradox of her role as liberator: "Ya me lo dijeron: 'Te lo veo en los ojos. Tú le matarás'..." (They already told me: 'I see it in your eyes. You will kill him'...; *Teatro completo* 410). This attention to the eyes of Judit underscores her special role in the salvation process.

Windows, like eyes, appear repeatedly as conduits to realms beyond ordinary circumstances. In her biography of Salinas, Newman describes Salinas's own attraction to windows and their potential for visual adventure: "People and places. Salinas needed to explore every possibility. Windows were important for their potential for new experience, for the uniqueness of each one's perspective. Arriving at a new lodging as he travelled from place to place, Salinas would rush straight to the window to assess the view. His letters are filled with references to the view from his windows (28)." Also, in his essay "Registro de Jorge Carrera Andrade," Salinas underlines a bidirectional function of the window for the poet. The window not only allows for things outside to enter the poet, but leads the poet to the outside world:

> La función primaria y humilde de la ventana es iluminar y ventilar, abrir el cerrado habitáculo a la luz y al aire. Misión que yo llamaría fuera adentro, de la ventana. Pero un día alguien descubre uno de esos perogrullescos prodigios del hombre, y es que la ventana tiene otro menester, de dentro afuera, este. Ver, desde un recinto cerrado, lo que hay, o lo que sucede en el vasto ámbito exterior. Enlazar al hombre clauso con el mundo abierto. La ventana cobra una significación altísima; actúa de puente entre lo interior y lo exterior y entre el hombre y el mundo. Sirve sobre sus modestos oficios de iluminadora y ventiladora, para ver, para mirar al mundo. Y ¿no es ese noble oficio exactamente similar al que cumplen en el cuerpo del hombre

los ojos? Así se explica que desde hace muchos siglos ruede por varios idiomas esa metáfora en que se llama a los ojos las ventanas del alma. (Salinas, "Registro de Jorge Carrera Andrade" en *Ensayos de la literatura hispánica...* 365)

The primary function of the window is to illuminate and to ventilate, to open the closed interior to the light and the air. A mission that I would call outside in, of the window. But one day someone discovers one of those platitudinous marvels of man, and it is that the window has another function, from inside out. To see, from a closed space, what is there, or what is happening in the vast exterior sphere. To connect closed man with the open world. The window takes on a very lofty meaning; it acts as a bridge between the inside and the outside and between man and the world. It serves above its modest illuminating and ventilating function, in order to see, to look at the world. And is not that noble function just like that which the eyes fulfill in the body of man? It is thus explained that for many centuries in many languages still exists the metaphor that calls the eyes the windows of the soul.

This perspective is apparent in a number of Salinas's poems as well. In "Lección de la ventana" (The Lesson of the Window; *Poesías completas* 749-52), for example, the poet discovers through the window an infinite wealth of knowledge, tradition, history, and enlightenment. Likewise, the role of the window as an enhancement to clear vision has been noted by Nagel in a study of Salinas's fictional work *Mundo cerrado* and her description of the protagonist's perspective: "The window, the transparent pane of glass that separates two worlds, is what allows his vision the clarity he needs to place both worlds into perspective" (80).

In his plays, Salinas's poet characters exploit well the bidirectionality of windows. While they absorb the world and see into themselves, they also comprehend the outside in their search for a redemptive sphere. Salinas represents three figures explicitly engaged in quest via windows for some form of liberation. Near the conclusion of *La fuente del arcángel*, the audience sees a culmination of the transformation of Claribel when she gives her hand through the window to the Arcángel figure (*Teatro completo* 241). In *Sobre seguro*, Don Nazario describes his futile attempt to communicate with Petra, who is fixated upon Angel and insistent upon communication with her missing son in a sphere which over-reaches the situation circumscribed by the insurance agents and her family: "Sigue quieta en su silla, mirando a la ventana" (She remains quietly in her chair, looking at the window; *Teatro completo* 151). Marú, of *La isla del tesoro*, connects most emphatically the view of windows and the process of spiritual emancipation. Marú's hotel room is the "Treasure Island" with a window that links to an extraordinary realm. Before her arrival at the room, the audience learns of the disappearance of the mysterious previous occupant through the high window of the room and of the chambermaid's discovery of his diary near the window. Marú's first words upon entering the play and the room suggest her out-of the-ordinary state of mind and her attraction to the absent poet figure: "Sí, me gusta la ventana.... Nos quedamos con esta ventana, digo, con esta habitación" (Yes, I like the window.... We'll keep this window, I mean, this room; *Teatro completo* 97). She stresses to her mother the affinity she has for windows (*Teatro completo* 97). Marú uses the window to seek a romanticized vision of self entwined with nature (*Teatro completo* 98), and later finds her kindred spirit in the words of the diary. What confirms her outlook is his description of windows in connection with seeing and pursuing an image of oneself:

> ¿Por qué mirarse siempre a los espejos, que nos devuelven la imagen material y externa de nuestro rostro? No sería mejor mirarse en los paisajes, por las ventanas, figurándonos que nos vemos a nosotros mismos, en algo más ancho, hermoso... (*Teatro completo* 108)

> Why always look at oneself in mirrors, which return to us the physical and external image of our faces? Wouldn't it be better to look at oneself in landscapes, through windows, shaping ourselves to see ourselves in something broader and more beautiful...

Like her counterpart, Marú believes that windows and what lies beyond them carry the seeker out of the confines of the vistas offered by commonplace mirrors with conventional utilitarian function. The final scene of the play has Marú looking toward the window, fully engaged in her emancipating quest.

In other plays, mirrors, like windows and eyes, break the boundaries of restrictive situations and allow entry into realms inaccessible by way of non-probing, surface observation. Moraleda has noted how for many of Salinas's characters the mirror may serve as a conduit toward an essential reality. She marks the intertextuality between Salinas's works that explore duality, doubling, and fragmentation, with those of Unamuno (*Teatro completo* 14-15). In *El parecido* and in *Judit y el tirano*, the references to mirror-gazing show small attempts to transcend superficial levels of communication. In the former, Julia, upon finding the artist pursuing her relentlessly, looks in the mirror to discover some truth about herself and to face herself with a perception of herself different from the idealization created by the artist (*Teatro completo* 37). In the latter, in his endeavor to verify with understanding the identity of Judit, the Regente directs her to stare at herself in a mirror as she listens to his enumeration of her features (*Teatro completo* 384). The mirror in *El director* provokes no unusual reaction from those who present themselves as they are, but it reveals to the typist the dishonest facade she shows to the Director and generates fright at the unfamiliar self she sees presented there. From Inocencio the mirror elicits marvel at the never-before-seen emanation of self-confidence he views.

A number of Salinas's poems contain similar references to the poet's confrontation of his image in a mirror. As early as in his first volume of poems, *Presagios*, the poet faces the coldness and inexactness of his image (#8), its lack of familiarity (#11), its ambiguities (#18), and its insufficiency (#38) (*Poesías completas* 60, 64, 72, 92). In the poems of *Todo más claro*, the mirror connects to the poet's reflections upon modern life, for example, in "Hombre en la orilla"(Man on the shore) and "Error de cálculo" (Error in calculation; *Poesías completas* 621-33, 680-85). The poem "Adrede" (On purpose), from the volume *Confianza*, contains reference to the poet seer's acceptance of his mirror image, though it may be painful (*Poesías completas* 761-62).

Mirrors figure importantly in the play *La Cabeza de Medusa*, Salinas's creative version of the myth of the deity with the petrifying gaze, famous for her power to turn to stone anything that eyes her directly. The play is centered upon an elaborate system of allusions to seeing through eyes and mirrors as means of penetrating the meaning of human happiness and existence. Many of the stage directions offer evidence of Salinas's adaptation of the myth of the goddess of the deadly stare. Mirrors are prominent in the set design of "La Cabeza de Medusa" hat boutique, which is the microcosm of owner Lucila's world and experience. Lucila, "la directora y el alma del establecimiento" (the director and soul of the establishment; *Teatro completo* 132), plays the symbolic role of goddess Medusa of fatal influence. Twice, Salinas mentions the penetrating stare of Lucila at Andrenio (*Teatro completo* 118, 119), and the stance that Andrenio will assume until the end of the play is not unlike that of one of Medusa's victims turned to stone: "...esta actitud de observación casi impasible" (...this posture of almost impassive observation; *Teatro completo* 123). At the end of the play, Andrenio dies after exposure to "La Cabeza de Medusa," after viewing Lucila and the happenings in her shop.

The three separate, though related scenes that he observes are charged with references to seeing and mirrors and mark a progression in the action of the play, which climaxes with his death. First, Andrenio witnesses the radiant, idealistic Gloria, who sees ahead only a bright and promising future for herself and her fiancé. Her obliviousness to the role of Andrenio is at the same time humorous and allusive to the myth of Medusa: "¡Bah, ese hombre no nos ve! Está mirando a las musarañas. Ni oye ni entiende" (Bah, that man doesn't see us! He's looking at the cobwebs. He doesn't hear or understand; *Teatro completo* 124). Second, Andrenio views the reserved, preoccupied Rosaura, who, after ten years of marriage, has lost her idealism. Life with her artist husband has not given her complete happiness, but she still reaches for moments of happiness, as evidenced by her coming to "La Cabeza de Medusa" to buy

a new hat, and by her definition of happiness as fragments of a large mirror:

> Mire usted, señorita Lucila, para mí la felicidad, con mayúscula, se me figura como un espejo muy grande, hermoso, claro, en que no podemos vernos enteros sino empaño. Lo otro, las felicidades, como pedazos del espejo grande, roto, de formas muy variadas, irregulares... No nos cabe la persona entera en ninguna, pero nos podemos ver a pedacitos, un poco en cada una... Y no todos los trozos están limpios, en algunos nos vemos desfigurados o velados. (*Teatro completo* 131)

> Look, Miss Lucila, for me, happiness, with a capital "H," is like a very big, beautiful, clear mirror, in which we cannot see ourselves whole, but blurred. The little happinesses, are like pieces of the big mirror, broken, in many varied, irregular forms... The whole person does not fit in any one of them, but we can see ourselves in little pieces, a little bit in each one... And not all the fragments are clean, and in some we see ourselves disfigured or blurred.

Rosaura's final words to Lucila describe the blindness of her love ten years before, and close the scene connoting the peril of staring at Medusa: "pero yo entonces no veía nada, no oía nada"; but then I did not see or hear anything; *Teatro completo* 132).

Third, Andrenio watches the scene between Lucila and Valentina, which makes clear the role of "La Cabeza de Medusa" in Lucila's life. Upon understanding Lucila's need to leave Lorenzo behind as she pursues her personal happiness, Valentina exclaims, "¡Sí, ya veo!" (Yes, now I see!; *Teatro completo* 135). Hearing her conversation with Lucila, Andrenio meets the full force of Gorgon's gaze. He echoes Valentina's words of recognition (*Teatro completo* 136), and closes his eyes to die seeing, that is, comprehending. Andrenio's observation of Lucila's world has brought him to a stop at this crossroads of human passions. Though overwhelmed by what he has seen, he has come to understand better

than before the struggles and confusions that can be found beneath surface appearances. It is noteworthy that Andrenio retains the deeper vision with the shutting of his eyes.

These bittersweet sensations of "ver-no ver," of apprehending love and freedom, Salinas expresses in his own romantic discourse with Katherine Reding Whitmore. Passages from two of his letters, one written during the midst of their affair, dated March 30, 1933, from Santander, and the other from Berkeley dated July 7, 1941, after Katherine's marriage to Brewer Whitmore, show the writer in love exploring these complex contradictions of the true meanings of seeing. After a day's work, Salinas writes about the mirror and his reflection in it:

> Personaje. Le veo muy bien. Tengo, en esta incoherencia de los cuartos de hotel, un espejo a mi derecha. Le veo, en el espejo. Un hombre alto, corpulento, con dos rayas, ya en la frente, con una cara un poco cansada. ¿Soy yo? No me gusta. No, no soy yo. Yo soy el que escribe, el que se inclina sobre la mesa, el que pone en el papel y en la pluma su mejor momento del día. Me veo, me reconozco, me gusto, mirándome en esta hoja de papel y no en la lámina del espejo. Porque en el espejo me veía con mis señas personales inevitables, ligado a mis condiciones. Pero la hoja de papel no me devuelve la imagen de un hombre cansado, etc., sino la de un hombre sin edad, que quiere, que está queriendo en plena juventud de su ser. Así me gusto. Yo en el papel soy yo. Liberado, escapado de mis condiciones con la ilusión de ser tan joven, tan fuerte como es mi amor. También tú me tiendes en el espejo, al quererme. El amor es siempre un espejo que tendemos al amado. Y es un espejo no de deformación, sino de depuración, de elevación. En cosa alguna nos vemos, nos miramos con tanto placer y alegría como en ese espejo. Yo hoy, Katherine, estoy contento de mi mismo en la imagen que tú tienes de mí, que tú me das de mí, y no en la que veo yo en torno mío. (*Cartas a KW* 207-08)

> Somebody. I see him very well. I have, in this incoherence of hotel

rooms, a mirror on my right. I see him, in the mirror. A tall man, stout, with two lines now on his forehead, with a somewhat tired face. Is it I? I don't like him. No, it is not I. I am the one who writes, the one bent over the table, the one who puts on paper and into the pen the best moment of his day. I see myself, I recognize myself, I like myself, looking at myself on this sheet of paper and not on the surface of the mirror. Because in the mirror I was seeing myself with all the inevitable personal signs, tied to my circumstances. But the sheet of paper does not return to me the image of a tired man, etc., but rather that of an ageless man, who loves, who is loving in the full youth of his being. I like myself like this. I on paper am myself. Freed and liberated from my circumstances and with the illusion of being young, as strong as my love. Also you extend yourself to me in the mirror, when you love me. Love is always a mirror that we extend to the beloved. And it is not a mirror of deformation, but of purification, of elevation. In something we see ourselves, we look at ourselves with such pleasure and happiness as in that mirror. I today, Katherine, I am happy with myself in the image you have of me, that you give me of myself, and not in that which I see here around me.

The real mirror does not offer the physical reflection Salinas wants to see, but does provoke his contemplation, soul-searching, and recognition of what it means to find redemption through love. After their affair, Salinas retains a profound perception of himself transformed through the vision of his beloved:

Verte en mi alma, en mi memoria, es ver lo más alto de mí mismo. Verte así, en mi interior, es ver la vida más completa y luminosa que la suerte me ha dado. Y por eso te seguiré viendo sin que me veas, ni me oigas, porque lo necesito para sentir y saber lo que fue la cima de mi existencia, un día, sin tiempo. (*Cartas a KW* 362-63)

To see you in my soul, in my memory, is to see the highest part of my

self. To see you so, inside of me, is to see the most complete and luminous life that luck has given me. And therefore I will continue seeing you without you seeing me, or hearing me, because I need it to feel and know what was the high point of my existence, a day, without time.

Genuine sight does not require eyes, windows, or mirrors in any conventional physical or temporal sense. Salinas continues to dramatize this vividly in the references to sightedness and blindness and those seeking love and freedom in his dramatic works.

SIGHTEDNESS AND BLINDNESS
References to sightedness and blindness in Salinas's plays constitute a solid part of the framework that portrays poet characters as protagonists of the self-society, freedom-confinement dialectic, as representatives of a minority seeking to deliver a fuller, more far-reaching vision of life to a majority that sees too restrictedly. Blindness is the inability to discern the significance of more that meets the eye. Sightedness is the capacity to grasp existence in all its plenitude. The discourse of sightedness and blindness steers toward a richer contemplation of existence and veers away from over-preoccupation with contemporaneous trivialities in the most obvious paths of sight. What the eye beholds in the material world constitutes incomplete seeing. Keen perception necessitates an inner eye that gropes for spiritual awareness and a joining of internal and external realms.

The one physically sightless character to appear in the dramatic works is Tío Liborio in "*La Estratoesfera.*" Though Tío Liborio plays a minor role, he articulates the longstanding view of the blind person endowed with extraordinary visionary powers deriving from a special compensation for the loss of the specific sensory faculty: "el que no ve sabe mucho" (he who does not see knows much; *Teatro completo* 200). This is the perspective taken repeatedly throughout the dramatic works when it occurs that actual, physical seeing is not the key to keen perception.

With characteristic Salinian fusion of tradition and originality, the dialogue and circumstances of "*La Estratoesfera*" echo the Spanish tradition of the blind man and his "lazarillo" with a creative twist. Felipa is the guide to her blind grandfather, but she is able to see only a dark and confining view of herself and her world. It is Felipa, led by the poet Alvaro, who finds a sphere beyond the disgrace of her past. Alvaro deems her "luz de la ceguera" (light of blindness; *Teatro completo* 203), and gives her a greater capacity to see. Felipa's receptivity to the poet allows her to experience the fulfillment of regaining her honor. This high point, followed quickly by the death of her grandfather, enables Felipa a comprehensive view of existence. Felipa's expression of the broad gamut of emotions contains explicit reference to the paradoxical nature of blindness: "Y de sopetón cegá me quedé, cegá del tó, sólo con faltarme aquel agüelo mío, que la gente le llamaba el ciego... No hay prenda como la vista, que él solía decir. ¡Pero mi vista, la tenía, no yo!" (And suddenly I was left blind, totally blind, just from the loss of that grandfather of mine, that people called the blindman... There is no gift like sight, he used to say. But he, not I, had my sight!; *Teatro completo* 210). The conclusion of the play suggests that a comprehensive view of existence cannot be rooted in pure egotism. It is a fusion of the gaze upon external circumstances and the internal. When Felipa calls for a shared seeing which includes guidance of perception by another, it is Alvaro the poet who answers her plea (*Teatro completo* 211).

Passages in many other dramatic works point explicitly to the lesser importance of conventional visual perception of the tangible. Claribel's response to the Arcángel figure's question if she recognizes him suggests her engagement in two kinds of seeing: "Te he visto y no te he visto" (I have seen you and I have not seen you; *Teatro completo* 240). In *La isla del tesoro*, Tula alludes to Marú's unusual way of seeing things and to the impenetrability of her daughter's mental activity (*Teatro completo* 97, 98). In *El precio*, Jáuregui assures the Doctor and Alicia that he has a perfectly clear conception of his creation although he has never "seen" her (*Teatro completo* 285). Jáuregui's lost sight of his creation as a result of his temporary amnesia is for him a terrifying breakdown of the powers of his creative capacities (*Teatro completo* 287). Prudencio, another character in search of a poet figure reminiscent of Melisa, underlines the pain of realizing too late that one has not taken real notice of what was right in front of the eyes. Hoping that the lost woman is his missing wife, he confesses to the doctor how he now perceives seeing and blindness. He explains how the inadequacy of his previous mode of seeing has killed the possibility of seeing in a creative manner and of adopting the perspective he earlier refused to share with his wife (*Teatro completo* 282). In *El director*, the Gerente's description to the Mecanógrafa of his closeness with the Director resembles the author-character relationship of Jáuregui and Melisa. In ordinary terms, they never see each other, and their intimacy transcends the levels of contact typical in the material world (*Teatro completo* 333-34). In *Ella y sus fuentes*, the physical presence of evidence proves more baffling and confusing to Merlín than the self-assured imaginings of his research. There are many references to his ability and inability to see when Julia presses him to recognize her (*Teatro completo* 49). Merlín reconciles the incredible truth of Julia's appearance and mission by insisting upon the tangibility of the fabricated history he is perpetuating and the illusory nature of Julia's appearance (*Teatro completo* 62).

In a number of the plays, the development of a romantic relationship occasions discourse favoring sight that transcends physicality. In *El chantajista*, Lucila envisions for Lisardo their first kiss, an experience into which conventional sensory perceptions do not enter: "Ni árbol, ni planta, ni fuente..., ni cerca, ni lejos, ni en la vista, ni en el oler, sin verde" (Nor tree, nor plant, nor fountain..., nor near, nor far, nor in sight, nor in smell, without green; *Teatro completo* 300). Their orchestration of the kiss perpetuates the shift of emphasis: to see better with the eyes closed (*Teatro completo* 302). In *La Bella Durmiente*, Alvaro's desire to see Soledad has him so engrossed and fixated on the path from which he expects her to arrive that her actual appearance takes him by surprise (*Teatro completo* 78). Soledad's preoccupation with opening and closing her eyes reflects her desire to experience an existence that surpasses the sordid materiality she seeks to escape. Paradoxically, her oppressive fame in the material world derives from her closed-eye repose as Sleeping Beauty, so she insists upon opening her eyes in order to receive clearly the marriage proposal of Alvaro. Yet she shuts her eyes to apprehend as profound truth the fantasy they are living (*Teatro completo* 83). At the end of the *Judit y el tirano*, as Judit awaits the return of the Regente after his speech, she addresses the new morning in very visual terms that emphasize the importance of insight: "No necesito abrir los ojos, vienes por otro camino…, día nuevo, por dentro de mí vienes…. No veré tu luz hasta que no se encuentre la mía… No la veré hasta que envuelta en ella venga la forma que espero" (I do not need to open my eyes, you come by way of another path…, new day, within me you come. … I will not see your light until mine is not found… I will not see it until, enveloped in you, comes the form that I await; *Teatro completo* 409). The opening of her eyes brings with the return of the awaited Regente the harsh reality of pain, death, and confinement in an existence contrary to what they have sought. Another example earlier in the play offers a look at the sensitivity of the perceptions of the Regente as his relationship with Judit develops. When the Regente wants to verify her marksmanship, he tells her in very concrete terms that he wants to see her shoot into the white tree (*Teatro completo* 382), but what he is searching to discover is her ultimate innocence. He is administering to her a spiritual test.

Throughout *El parecido*, the couple's discourse centered on the relativity of sightedness and blindness strongly suggests the importance of seeing beyond what merely meets the eye. Julia claims she was blind not to realize that the Incognito is the driver who had taken her to the wrong but right railroad station and away from the artist infatuated with her (*Teatro completo* 39). She becomes conscious of her and her husband's blindness after the Incógnito shows them the missing button (*Teatro completo* 35). Roberto describes briefly the extrasensory nature of seeing: "Pero tenemos la vista para otras cosas. Ya ves, ese chico del ascensor era mi miedo, hecho persona. Lo no visto, visto, o previsto" (But we have sight for other things. Now you see, that elevator boy was my fear, turned into a person. What is not seen, is seen, or foreseen; *Teatro completo* 36). When Julia closes her eyes to envision better her confession to

Roberto, he comprehends that this action is an ironic reversal of what it means to see and not to see in conventional terms (*Teatro completo* 36). After Julia confesses, Robert feels reborn, upholds the significance of what lies beyond the perception of the exterior (*Teatro completo* 39). The concluding conversation about the ashes further emphasizes the importance of seeing things beyond their physical definition. Never having noticed anyone other than Julia and Roberto in the restaurant, the waiter sees the contents of the ashtray just as ashes. Roberto, on the other hand, considers them evidence of the presence of the Incógnito who has inspired the couple to look more deeply into their relationship. Salinas's open-ended conclusion also presents the ashes as the metaphorical remains of the human condition, whose meaning transcends mere physical existence.

In *Caín o una gloria científica*, the discourse of sightedness and blindness emphasizes the pain of the human condition in terms of Abel's supersensory visionary powers. Early in the play, he describes the glaring blindness of the discovery burning within him (*Teatro completo* 177). Seeing no danger greater than the one he confronts, Abel gives examples of its horrible repercussions. The magnitude of the terrifying effects is measured in the millions whose faces Abel is unable to see. He describes them in very human terms: they have eye color, they come and go, they laugh and kiss, and are ignorant of impending destruction. Though he does not see the actual faces of his potential victims, his nightmarish vision is all too vivid, and even makes mention of the relative blindness of the sufferers: "Veo a los hombres, al pie de las máquinas, en la tierra, por las nubes, enloquecidos por la acción... Cegados están, si no perciben que tanto hacer desemboca en la muerte" (I see men at the feet of machines, on land, in the clouds, crazed by action. They are blind if they do not perceive that so much doing results in death; *Teatro completo* 185). Through Abel, Salinas defines blindness as the tragic innocence of those ignorant of their fate. The poet figure bears the difficult burden of sight and conscience as he struggles with self and circumstance.

Examination of the three key components of Salinas's construction of a discourse of seeing in the dramatic works—the system of references to poet-guiders and guided-viewers, to a poetic scoping via eyes, mirrors, and windows, and to sightedness and blindness—emphasizes the prominence and heroism of the poet characters in their roles as redemptive forces. Endowed with a special capacity to see, to comprehend a realm beyond immediate limitations, Salinas's poet characters hold a power to transcend restrictions of the material world, although in the plays with tragic outcome, they are unable to sustain their victories. The mature Salinas, witness to threatening modern-day circumstances, creates perceptive characters that give voice and action to his preoccupations. These characters reflect his hope for an end to the spiritual blindness that he sees killing humanity. A return to the play *El precio* and author Jáuregui's formulation of the relationship between the poet and reality summarizes well Salinas's outlook and stresses the keen eye of the poet for discerning possibilities for deliverance from the confines of the ordinary:

> Es que no hay nada que esté fuera de la poesía... Usted y yo, y esta muchacha, y... su enferma, todos estamos en la poesía... Y la tierra, y este cuarto, y las palabras que están sonando ahora... Sólo se ve de tarde, sólo algunos hay que lo vean... Ella lo veía... que estamos todos en ella... como en el aire, aunque no lo vemos... (*Teatro completo* 287)

> It is that there is nothing outside the realm of poetry. You and I, and this girl, and... your patient, we are all in poetry... And the land, and this room, and the words that are sounding now... Only it is seen late; there are only some who may see it... She saw it... that we are all in it... like in the air, although we do not see it...

Salinas urges that everything be perceived within the realm of poetry. For Salinas, it is the poet who best sees, understands, realizes, and actualizes this. In other words and in the context of his own life, close to when he first begins to write plays, he communicates this viewpoint to Katherine. In a letter dated Thanksgiving Day, November 26, 1936, from Wellesley, he writes in English:

> ...my theory is that we, modern people, are too inclined to overlook the magic power, the miracolous (sic) reality of many things, that we use as prosaic tools in our ordinary, ever-day (sic) life, just because custom and habit have caused us to loose (sic) our powers of comprehension and appreciation of these wonders. We take for granted too many things, we fail to realize that lots of things around us go far beyond many of the dreams and illusions of a human mind a century ago, that they are really *working dreams*.... sometimes I feel like starting, in this country of associations, companies, leagues, and so on, a "Brotherhood for the restauration of the sense of wonder." (*Cartas a KW* 289)

The poet possesses this special ability to see and serves as a corrective lens through which to seek and perhaps find an ideal world, a poetic, profound, spiritual, moral existence. The following treatment of Salinas's melding of modernity with tradition will explore the powerful echoes of Cervantes and Don Quixote in this vision.

7
Poet and Circumstance: The Poet's Bridge between Tradition and Modernity

...debe cumplir toda generación de hombre u obras, su papel: conservar y añadir.
    Salinas, *Ensayos de literatura hispánica* 340

... each generation of man or works must fulfill its role: to conserve and to add.

IN HIS STUDY OF medieval poet Jorge Manrique, Salinas calls tradition the natural habitat of the poet. Born poetically into tradition, the poet finds air to breathe and fulfills a creative destiny within its scope (*Jorge Manrique o Tradición y originalidad* 115). Tradition holds open a plurality of spiritual attitudes and is the fullest form of freedom available to an artist (*Jorge Manrique o Tradición y originalidad* 123). The contemporary artist finds before him more paths than ever to explore and untangle, and he must shoulder the responsibility of channeling his awareness of the tradition into choosing his own direction (*Jorge Manrique o Tradición y originalidad* 124). This way of inserting oneself into history effects a blend of tradition with originality.

For Salinas, tradition is a permanently living reality, an active force, and a springboard. Confronting modernity, Salinas the playwright in exile firmly embraces tradition. The poet-dramatist creates with the consciousness of being rooted in and working within the language and culture, seeking to inherit it in a personal manner. Connection to the past is not in opposition to originality and modernity. Tradition opens the way to being original and modern (Morón Arroyo 20). Morón Arroyo has contrasted Salinas's position with Paul De Man's view of the incompatibility of history and modernity (20). Sotelo Vázquez has associated Salinas's perspective with T.S. Eliot's conception of tradition as an enormous reserve of materials with which the poet can expand his horizons and with Gadamer's notion of the fusion of horizons (243-44). García Tejera notes that for Salinas, tradition has a direct and stimulating effect on progress and on artistic and literary renovation (63). Oriented toward the present and the future, Salinas does not embrace tradition to display static icons of the past; he bridges tradition and modernity for accessing contemporary existence and enhancing the social significance of his theater.

Attention to the playwright's special appropriation of Cervantine values, and his blending of Cervantine spiritual perspectives with other traditional sources will illuminate the leading poet's role in transcending the pressures of modern life. An interesting curiosity is that Salinas's doctoral dissertation, a work that to date has not been located, focused on illustrators of the *Quijote* across the centuries. His own modern portraits of characters and situations indicate that he too assumes the role of illustrator of the *Quijote* through his dramatic representations. Salinas's leading characters tellingly resemble Cervantes's knight and seem descendents of Don Quixote in a contemporary world. Following discussion of Salinas's outlook on the blending of tradition and modernity and his use of Cervantes and Don Quixote, an examination of three plays with different outcomes will demonstrate the poet's function as a guide for those seeking a higher life.

TRADITION, MODERNITY, AND CERVANTINE VALUES
The conditions of Salinas's exile make him more acutely aware of modern ills and lead in his plays to concern about loss of freedom and degeneration of communication. Tradition offers a means of exalting poet heroes

to oppose that destruction. Drawing frequently upon Cervantes, the *Quijote*, and Spanish national culture, Salinas also builds upon popular legend, myth, and biblical traditions to affirm the poet's goal of creating "a new reality within the old reality" (*Reality and the Poet* 3). This bridge building gives his theater contemporeanousness and universality, qualities identified by Claudio Guillén, who noted Salinas's cultivation of his Spanish roots and of the influences of Cervantes in particular:

> Salinas quería resaltar las visiones singulares del hombre conformadas por los grandes escritores españoles y su pertinencia actual para nuestros contemporáneos. Nuestra herencia literaria adquiere así calidad de actualidad y de universalidad. (Guillén, "Cervantes entre Dámaso Alonso y Pedro Salinas" 111)

> Salinas wanted to project man's singular visions shaped by the great Spanish writers and their current relevance for our contemporaries. Our literary legacy thus acquires a quality of currency and universality.

Salinas seeks to harmonize tradition with modernity and to see tradition as the poet's circumstance. Ciplijauskaité, emphasizing Salinas's personal role as a bridge and his defense of tradition, cites his study of Manrique and relates Salinas's goals as an educator to his artistic aims:

> Su defensa de la tradición subraya el deseo de tender un puente entre siglos y generaciones: 'El milagro de la tradición es atenuar las discordancias y conservar las diferencias. Su signo es el de la concordia. Así la del artista. La tradición total le proporciona crianza y acompañamiento, como el mundo al individuo.'

> His defense of tradition underlines the desire to extend a bridge between centuries and generations: 'The miracle of tradition is to attenuate discord and preserve differences. Its sign is that of concord. That is also the artist's. The whole tradition provides him rearing and

accompaniment, like the world to the individual.'

Other scholars commenting on tradition and modernity in Salinas's writings have pointed to his prefiguring of postmodernity (Brines, 131, 135; Siles 152ff.), his fascination with and fears of technology (Maurer, "Salinas y 'las cosas'..." 137ff.), the legacy of Cervantes (Fernández Méndez, "Pedro Salinas: Quijote moderno" 84-86, Guillén, "Cervantes entre Dámaso Alonso y Pedro Salinas" 109-20), and his similarities to and differences from T.S. Eliot (Young 76-95). Studies of his theater have noted its pervasive employment of intertextual elements (Moraleda, "El binomio..." 267-79), for example, his affinities with Cervantine perspectives (Orringer 74-86; Torres Nebrera, *Pedro Salinas Teatro* 89), with allegory and fantasy in the style of French writer Giraudoux and with Spanish national and religious themes (Marichal, "Tradición y modernidad..." 3), and with the myth of Pygmalion (Hartfield-Méndez).

Rooted in Cervantine tradition, the poet-playwright's connecting of tradition with contemporary existence echoes the Orteguian preoccupation with self and circumstance. Ortega y Gasset's oft-quoted characterization of human existence—"yo soy yo y mi circunstancia, y si no la salvo a ella, no me salvo yo (322)," (I am myself and my circumstance, and if I do not save it, I cannot save myself; *Meditations on Quixote* 45)—appears in his first book, *Meditaciones del Quijote*, written in 1914. Ortega describes the *Meditaciones* as a kind of salvation, either direct or indirect, of Spanish circumstances. Inspired by the Cervantine world, Ortega's meditations on Spain bring together self and situation and tradition and modernity. Don Quixote is a symbol of man as a heroic figure "who fights with his environment and tries to achieve the humanization of his surroundings in order to make a 'world' out of them, while material things press heavily upon him with their meaninglessness and absurdity, trying to suffocate the flame of his projects and aspirations" (Marías, "Prologue for American Readers to the Meditations" in Ortega y Gasset, *Meditations...* 10).

Salinas the playwright advocates this quixotic perspective for modernity. His four essays on Cervantes's novel —"Don Quijote en presente" (Don Quijote in the Present), "Lo que debemos a Don Quijote" (What We Owe Don Quijote), "La mejor carta de amores de la literatura española" (Spanish Literature's Best Love Letter), and "El polvo y los nombres" (Dust and Names)—identify the vision of Don Quixote that Salinas dramatizes in the characters and circumstances of his plays (*Ensayos de literatura hispánica*...75-142).

Salinas calls the *Quijote* the drama of the individual and society, "el gran drama de un individuo frente a la sociedad; el gran drama de este hombre solo, con todas las gentes de todas clases que le rodean" (the great drama of the individual facing society; the great drama of this man alone, with all the people of every class who surround him; "Lo que debemos a don Quijote," *Ensayos de literatura hispánica*...93). Don Quixote functions in the world as an integral being true to his inner spirit, one who never deserts his soul and who holds a perfect harmony between thought and deed. He is "el caballero de la unidad" (the knight of unity), "el caballero íntegro" (the integral, whole, upright knight; "Don Quijote en presente," *Ensayos de literatura hispánica*... 84, 86):

> Hace lo que cree, y por eso lo consuma con tal temple de heroísmo, porque lo que ejecuta con todo su cuerpo lo cree con toda su alma. ("Don Quijote en presente," *Ensayos de literatura hispánica*... 84)

> He practices what he believes, and therefore accomplishes it with such courage of heroism, because what he carries out with all his body he believes with all his soul.

In contrast, asserts Salinas, the typical individual in present day society is a fragmented being with an underdeveloped sense of morality who suffers from the distractions of modern life:

> La mano derecha, el sentido moral, se hace la distraída sobre los movimientos de la mano siniestra, la codicia adquisitiva; la cual se aprovecha copiosamente de la distracción para todos sus manejos. ("Don Quijote en presente," *Ensayos de literatura hispánica*... 83)

The right hand, the moral sense, gets carried away with the movements of the sinister hand, the acquisitive greed; which takes full advantage of the distraction for its manipulations.

Salinas even likens these figures to T.S. Eliot's hollow men, "Los hombres huecos" (83):

> hecha pedazos su unidad psíquica, desmembrada la integridad del ser, pero tan sonrientes, tan activos, en su automóvil, con sus máquinas, tan revolvedoras, tan ardilleros, que se les admira como a un nuevo dechado: el hombre dinámico; sobre su inopia espiritual se quiere construir, como sobre cimientos ideales, un orden social. ("Don Quijote en presente," *Ensayos de literatura hispánica...* 83)

> their psychic unity in pieces, the integrity of their being dismembered, but so smiling, so active, in their automobiles, with their machines, so roused, so skilled, admired like a new model: the dynamic man; upon his spiritual blindness he wants to construct for himself, as upon ideal foundations, a social order.

Salinas's principal characters look to diminish the deleterious and divisive distractions affecting them and their fellow beings. His heroes often asume the equivocal position of the knight errant who stands apart while at the same time exerting a crucial unifying force. They share the knight's moral grounding and perpetuate his conception of goodness and justice to combat defeatist, rationalistic negativity. Salinas endows his poet characters with a sense of possibility and with the capacity to feel and think beyond the usual and ordinary. His plays thus reflect a Cervantine perspective on the transcendence of everyday reality ("Lo que debemos a Don Quijote," *Ensayos de literatura hispánica...* 96). In the tradition of Cervantes, they dignify, humanize, and beautify existence, forging a special combination of the real, concrete, tangible, Spanish, and modern with the ideal, imaginary, illusory, universal, and timeless. In

Through the Shattering Glass Cervantes and the Self-Made World, Spadaccini and Talens write that "the mad Don Quijote defies the most sacred institutions and authorities of his society, while Cervantes, in telling the story of a madman, challenges the norms of narrow realism and offers an unlimited space for imagination" (146). Salinas carries forward this search for extraordinary reality by endowing his characters with the knight's ardent spirit of challenge to society's pressures. The poet saviors of his modern stage set their sights toward a *más allá* (a beyond), and engage in quests to transform others and their surroundings. Salinas recasts the model relationship between Don Quixote and Sancho. Sancho's progressive ability to live with his complex master signals a faith in the potential to overcome obstacles.

Keenly attuned to modern circumstance, Salinas plays creatively with tradition as he adopts with innovative twists Cervantes's vision of exemplary conviviality, tolerance, and mutual understanding. His poet characters strive to harmonize disparate worlds, sometimes succeeding happily and other times only making some headway through tragic sacrifice. His modern reformers, with strong resolve, signal what is out of joint, open perspectives toward change, and propel changes leading toward emancipation.

Salinas further enhances his presentation of the poet's mission by melding the Cervantine legacy with other traditional sources. While every endeavor to redefine milieu echoes broadly Cervantine preoccupations with quest and the interplay of reality and illusion, many of the settings allude explicitly to other literary antecedents and to mythical, legendary, and biblical sources. In a creative fusion that emphasizes the social function of poet figures as liberators and harmonizers, Salinas adapts themes, characters, and circumstances from *Don Juan* ("*La Estratoesfera*"), the myths of Eros (*La fuente del arcángel*), Medusa (*La Cabeza de Medusa*), Pygmalion (*La fuente del arcángel, El chantajista, El director, Judit y el tirano, El precio*), the legendary Sleeping Beauty (*La Bella Durmiente*), Treasure Island (*La isla del tesoro*), Mariana Pineda (*Ella y sus fuentes*), and biblical accounts of Cain and Abel (*Caín o una gloria científica*), Judith and Holofernes of the Apocrypha (*Judit y el tirano*), the

Archangel Michael (*La fuente del arcángel*), and other Christian saints (*Los santos*). Some of his appropriations are allegorical representations reflected in the play titles and carried throughout the works, for example, *Judit y el tirano* or *Caín o una gloria científica*. In other pieces, Salinas adapts some elements of plot, characterization, symbolic names, or key images from his Spanish heritage and beyond.

Three plays by Salinas will serve as prominent examples in the discussion of Salinas's bridging of tradition and modernity: "*La Estratoesfera,*" *Judit y el tirano*, and *Los santos*. The first two works feature leading characters who are poet figures—Alvaro of "*La Estratoesfera*" and Judit of *Judit y el tirano*. While in the former the outcome is happy and in the latter it is tragic, both protagonists launch a remaking of milieu in search of a romantic ideal. Alvaro supports and transforms Felipa in La Estratoesfera, a neighborhood bar of Madrid, to guide her toward a happy existence away from dishonor and sad solitude. Of all of Salinas's plays, "*La Estratoesfera*" bears the most explicit allusions to Don Quixote along with reflections of other sources. *Judit y el tirano*, grounded in the bibilical story of Judith and Holofernes, features a female defender and resonates with strong Cervantine echoes. Judit as tyrannicide offers a condemnation of tyranny in the modern world.

The third example, *Los santos*, is the one play by Salinas in which central roles are occupied by a group of heroes rather than a main protagonist defender. The poetic saviors in this work are saint statues that gradually come to life to link with their living counterparts in a miraculous redemption. Solita Salinas de Marichal has called *Los santos* "the play that perhaps most happily joins tradition and modernity" ("Tradición y modernidad…" 3). The vitality of the dialogue and popular language evokes the *entremeses* of Cervantes. The concluding miracle recalls the marvelous substitution of the virgen turnkey for the penitent in Berceo. The work itself is what she calls an "auto sacramental *a lo humano*" (a human-style eucharistic play; "Tradición y modernidad…" 3). Salinas is trying to offer in 1945 a message to all Spaniards to counteract the messages of revenge so prominent in the postwar years ("Tradición y modernidad…" 3). Salinas weaves religious tradition with strong Cervantine spirit to advocate peace, generosity, and genuine fraternity among humankind. His blend in this play of tradition and modernity erects a strong bridge of hope.

THE POET'S BRIDGE COMPLETED: *"LA ESTRATOESFERA"*

The casting of Don Quixote characters in Salinas's *"La Estratoesfera"* reveals inventively twisted roles. The explicitly named Don Quixote character, movie actor César Riscal, is in fact a Don Juan figure, the seducer of Felipa and chief cause of her suffering. It is the poet Don Alvaro who assumes the role of the knight. He confronts Felipa's wrongdoer and ultimately leads her out of her unfortunate situation. From the opening moments of the play, the poet's actions and words along with those of the other bar patrons show Salinas's interweaving of tradition into this Madrid tavern scene around 1930.

About forty years old, Don Alvaro is a younger, neatly groomed, bohemian Don Quixote with a friendly air. With his exaggerated, latinized utterances, Don Alvaro is as conspicuous in *"La Estratoesfera"* as is Cervantes's hero amidst the characters at the inn where he receives his knighthood. Alvaro makes Felipa his Dulcinea, and from their first encounter, addresses her with an abundance of references to classical literature. Persistently he transforms the prosaic through elevated language. The words that accompany his simple act of lending Felipa a pencil initiate the process: "Acepte momentáneamente este estilo, doncella pitagórica. ¡Es préstamo!" (Accept for a moment this stylus, Pythagorean damsel. It is a loan; *Teatro completo* 195). To him, this humble seller of lottery tickets and guide to her blind grandfather, is "doncella pitagórica" (Pythagorean damsel), "diva de la Fortuna" (diva of Fortune), "Flor de Lacio" (Fleur de lis), "joven aleatoria" (fortuitous young woman), "Lesbia," "Clásica," "Magna" (Great One), "Antígona de la Guindalera" (Antigone of the Guindalera neighborhood of Madrid), "inmortal" (immortal), "luz de la ceguera" (light of blindness), "Venus," "diosa de los caminos urbanos" (goddess of the urban ways), "progenie de Sófocles" (progeny of Sophocles), "predestinada" (predestined one), "criatura ecuménica" (ecumenical creature), "paloma sin mácula" (unblemished dove), "piélago de inocencia" (sea of innocence), "Ariadne del laberinto matritense" (Ariadne of the labyrinths of Madrid; *Teatro completo* 195-210). This verbal glorification, vehicle for some of Salinas's refined humor, recalls many of Don Quixote's outbursts of adulation for Dulcinea as well as other women of humble condition he encounters during his adventures. Their conversation, like the communication between Don Quixote and his interlocuters, intersects comically on very different levels. When Alvaro explains that his compliment to her has originated in imperial Rome, she understands "imperial" to mean the upper level seating area on the buses of the city.

Felipa is drawn into the sphere of the poet. She tells him that though she understands nothing he is saying, it all sounds very pretty (*Teatro completo* 197). The milieu redefinition and redemptive process develop with the impetus of the poet:

> ALVARO   Las gracias a esos dedos nacarinos que lo restituyen a estas manos indignas y mortales.
> FELIPA   Yo no entiendo de música, pero se me figura que usté se va a quedar con un billete entero de 34.256.
>   …
> FELIPA   ¡Pero qué fino habla usté! Será usté de esos que escriben tós los años pa el día de los Difuntos los versos del Tenorio…
> ALVARO   Estás maculando mi dignidad estética. ¡Yo, el Tenorio! Después de todo, tiene sus cosas… (*Teatro completo* 196)

> ALVARO   Thanks to those fingers of mother-of-pearl that return it to these undeserving, mortal hands.
> FELIPA   I don't understand anything about music, but I think you're going to keep a whole ticket of 34,256.
>   …
> FELIPA   How refined you speak! You must be one of those who write the verses of Tenorio every year for All Souls' Day…

ALVARO   You are besmirching my aesthetic dignity. I, the Tenorio! But after all, it has its points...

Reacting to Felipa's upset at the allusion to Tenorio and to the arrival of the Don Juan of her past, Alvaro moves beyond the demonstration of his verbal virtuosity to assume a moral stance. Threads of the novel of Cervantes continue to entwine in what transpires. César is described in the stage directions as a movie actor with the manner of an easygoing, confident gentleman dressed as a Don Quixote figure without armor and in costume corresponding to the dress in the palace of the Duke and Duchess of the second part of the novel. Actors posing as the Duke and Duchess and also a genteel Sancho accompany him. Alvaro confronts César in order to elevate Felipa. With a battle cry to announce his intention to combat the false knight, he waves his standard of poetry and assumes the role of authentic defender:

Un apócrifo... Se hace pasar por el Hidalgo Inmortal... No lo tolero. ¡Va usted a ver! La poesía muere, pero no se rinde. Seré yo su último mártir... (*Teatro completo* 201)

An apocryphal knight... He pretends to pass for the Immortal Gentleman... I will not tolerate it. You will see! Poetry dies, but it does not surrender. I will be its last martyr...

He rises to take up his charge, and with cup in hand exclaims "¡Viva Don Alonso Quijano! ¡Abajo la farsa! ¡San Quijote y cierra España!" (Long live Don Alonso Quijano! Down with the farse! Saint Quixote and to battle in Spain!; *Teatro completo* 201).

César surprises Alvaro momentarily when he stands to join in the toast and to respond with a measure of congenial humility. He thanks Alvaro for his kudos to the hero he acknowledges he is unworthy of playing (*Teatro completo* 201). Salinas weaves allusions to Spanish romantic literature into the Cervantine scheme. The haunting vision of Felipa before César in the tavern recalls the ghost lovers of the seducers' pasts in Espronceda's *El estudiante de Salamanca* and Zorrillas's *Don Juan Tenorio*. Language from the latter play appears in Felipa's reference to her lover's words "ángel de amor y la apartada orilla " (angel of love and the distant shore; *Teatro completo* 203). When Alvaro recites the next words of Don Juan to Doña Inés and confirms to Felipa that the seducer has kneeled before her, he proves that this is a dramatized seduction scene. In the ensuing events that have the poet Alvaro leading Felipa to her destiny, there is also obvious reference to the Rivas play *Don Alvaro o la fuerza del destino*. As Alvaro begins to put his art into action to transform Felipa's circumstance, he tells her, "¡Estaba escrito! La fuerza de los hados!" (It was written! The force of destiny...; *Teatro completo* 202).

Lines between reality and illusion blur. "Avellaneda de la pantalla"-Don Juan-César (Impostor of the screen; *Teatro completo* 202) had seduced Dulcinea-Doña Inés-Felipa in Toboso, her home town, and Don Quijote-Alvaro liberates her from the pain of the experience by creating a story for César to tell. First Alvaro directs Felipa to control her emotions. Alvaro's design of a counterpart to himself is the blueprint for the reconstruction of a broken-spirited Felipa. He has initiated the altering of her self-perception by naming her his complement: the Lesbia to his Propercio (*Teatro completo* 196), the Venus to his Apollo (*Teatro completo* 201). He amplifies his invention through a direct invitation to Felipa to stand as his creation. Calling her a progeny of Sophocles (*Teatro completo* 202), a tragic figure, he appeals to her to confide in him and to let him invent her:

> ¿No ves que te estoy haciendo personaje? Te estoy inventando... Déjame que te invente... ¿Nos entendemos, verdad? (*Teatro completo* 202)

> Don't you see that I am making you a character? I am inventing you... Let me invent you... We understand each other, don't we?

Her humorous reply indicates that though his words still make no sense, her bond with the poet himself is strengthening:

De tó eso que dice usté yo no entiendo papa... Habla como en los folletines... Pero... a usté... vamos, sí que paece que le entiendo... No sé como... (*Teatro completo* 202)

I don't understand a thing you are saying... You talk like they do in serial stories... But... you... somehow, yes it seems like I understand you... I don't know how.

When Alvaro returns to the table of actors to have a word with César, his request to address the "caballero andante" (knight errant; *Teatro completo* 204) here insinuates the ironic truth about César's wanton behavior. Alvaro continues to accent prominently his role as a poet actor. He appeals to César to be frank and to consider their common bond as brothers in the great fraternity of art. He applies the word and perspective of a writer, "inédita" (unedited; *Teatro completo* 204), to assure César that for the moment his own relationship with Felipa is uncertain. César confesses to being a Don Quixote who has played the role of modern cad. With his admission comes a small measure of regret and a hint of his existential pain in the contemporary scene. He complains to Alvaro of the artificiality of his life of screen acting. He has had moments of nostalgia for "that pure swallow of country water" amidst the "orgy of champagne" he lives (*Teatro completo* 205), and entertains the thought that ultimately Felipa might be happier than he.

Alvaro blends reality and illusion in his challenge to César to play the role of the traditional Don Quixote in what he calls a real life situation:

Dialogo con Don Quijote de la Mancha, ... Con el defensor de la honra ultrajada y la virtud escarnecida, con el amparo de los inocentes... Y compenetrado, como debe usted estar, con su personaje, calcúlese lo que en esta peripecia, tomada de la vida real, habría hecho el Caballero de la Triste Figura... (*Teatro completo* 205-06)

I am engaging in dialogue with Don Quixote de la Mancha, ... with

the defender of offended honor and mocked virtue, with the refuge of innocents... And identifying as you should be, with your character, calculate what the Knight of the Woeful Countenance would have done...

Luis, his companion playing Sancho, hears this as a call to marry Felipa, and Rita, the actress playing the Duchess, is entertained by the publicity possibilities of a marriage between the Iberian Valentino and the lowly lottery ticket seller, but César aims to separate fiction from base reality. Literature is one thing, he tells Alvaro, but the prose of this world is quite another *(Teatro completo* 206). For him, Don Quixote is a crazy man of times past. After all is said and done, César is a rational modern man who has a career and a future to consider. To improve his reputation, he will look to marry a chic, sophisticated, French-speaking woman of his station, and there is no room in his plans for the artistic ideal. What he can offer Felipa is access to a job in makeup, and hands Alvaro his card to pass to her.

Poet Alvaro, upholding the ideal of Don Quixote, is the one who works to save Felipa. Rational and modern, but in a very different sense from César, Alvaro mixes reality and fiction to orchestrate the redemption of Felipa. He tears up the card and directs César to deliver to Felipa an illusion to restore her sense of honor. Under the direction of Alvaro, César poses as his own twin brother, gives Felipa a photo of her lover, and tells her that he has died in America, where he had gone to seek his fortune with intentions to return to marry her. It appears that he has achieved his purpose when Felipa, holding on to portrait and the fantasy, tells Alvaro that she now feels transformed.

Alvaro raises Felipa out of her lowly situation into his spiritual domain. The glorification of the humble girl from Toboso arises out of his inventive doubling with César. His quixotic ideal is a truth and justice that transcends ordinary appearances. Alvaro becomes Don Quixote the liberator and makes the Don Quixote-Dulcinea link. Almost immediately the recomposition of Felipa is fractured by the death of her grandfather, and her mournful prayer tells her sense of crumbling and desolation:

> ...y al menuto, derrocá estás otra vez por el suelo y yo no eres na... más que Felipa, tu servidora. (*Teatro completo* 210)
>
> ...and in a minute, you are defeated again on the ground and you are nothing... more than Felipa, your humble servant.

Yet her monologue indicates that she has indeed become "other" and has entered the realm of the poet. Echoing the laments of Cervantes's maidens in distress, the words of Felipa sound eloquent and poetic, even with the popular elements of her *madrileño* dialect. Alvaro had anticipated their connection when earlier he described himself to César as a casual acquaintance of Felipa for the moment, but also as her fellow sufferer and possible close consort:

> ...compañero de mesa puramente casual en el establecimiento de vinos y cervezas "La Estratoesfera," y hermano suyo en este valle de lágrimas. Poco más que nada... Pero mañana... ¡quién sabe! (*Teatro completo* 204)
>
> ...purely accidental table companion in the wine and beer establishment The Stratosphere, and brother of hers in this vale of tears. Little more than nothing... But tomorrow... who knows!

Alvaro's forecast comes to be and projects them into the future to overcome together the travails of the immediate situation of Felipa. The play ends with a graphic representation of Felipa's ascension to an open and promising milieu with her poet redeemer. She obeys Alvaro's command, "Levanta, Felipa de la suerte" (Rise, Lucky Felipa the Lottery Seller) and they exit hand in hand. The final lines of the play reveal Alvaro's self-definition as the creator of Felipa's liberated status in open-ended time and space: Soy lo que te queda, tu futuro, Felipa, Felipa de la suerte..., tu futuro. (I am what is left to you, your future, Felipa, Lucky Felipa the Lottery Seller..., your future; *Teatro completo* 211).

Beyond the main scenes of this slice-of-life *sainete* that highlights the mission of poet Alvaro, Salinas further incorporates references to the Cervantine world to augment the social dimensions of the play. At the other tables in the bar, secondary characters such as Julián and his friends, full of malapropisms, puns, erroneous logic, and false Marxist pedantry, contribute to the lively, earth-bound ambience of the bar. Julián claims to be a working-class intellectual, though social inequities have deprived him of formal schooling. He speaks with his companions about justice and the rights of all. Their conversation about the novel by Cervantes juxtaposes past and present, entertains notions about the social function of art across time, and suggests indirectly the playwright's positive posture with respect to Cervantes. According to Julián, the *Quijote* belongs to a genre of bourgeois art from an age now extinct, but that Cervantes, by virtue of his birth, placed himself on the side of the proletariat of his time (*Teatro completo* 207). When one of the friends then asks if it is a social work, and if not, what purpose does it serve, Julián responds with ridiculous chronological confusion, locates the novel in the Middle Ages, and gives reverence to the original version that has found its way into film. Salinas thus playfully joins tradition with modernity in the banter of the characters and plays with the notion of the social purposes of the writer facing challenging times:

JULIAN	...¡Cómo quiés que haya arte social en la Edad Media! Son los siglos del fanático oscurantismo. Ahora, como español, a mí me paece un poco irreverente que la pongan en película.... si bien es cierto que así llega a las masas...
AMIGOTE 1º.	Pero se pierde la letra..., que por lo que dices debe de estar bien... en su género... (*Teatro completo* 207)
JULIAN	How can you believe that there is social art in the Middle Ages! They are the centuries of fanatical obscurantism. Now, as a Spaniard, it seems to me a little irreverent that they put it into film.... even

	though it's certain that in this way it will reach the masses...
FIRST BUDDY	But the word is lost..., that from what you say must be good... for its genre.

Salinas's congenial assortment of characters, with the quixotic Alvaro most prominent, forms a happy Cervantine recreation. The playwright Salinas in exile reaches into the heart of his Spanish past to portray an ideal realm reachable with the guidance of the poet. The legacy of Salinas's theater, infused with the spirit of Cervantes, is one that resonates into the future. The assertion of Juan Marichal in his and Solita Salinas de Marichal's interview with *El País Semanal* in January of 2003 about exile and the evolution of Spain clearly upholds the perspective of Salinas the dramatist:

Yo creo que España es todavía un país muy tradicional y muy moderno. Parece que la relación entre tradición y modernidad es patente. Pero me parece que aún hay mucho que hacer para que haya más justicia social y más solidaridad entre nosotros. (Cruz 85)

I believe that Spain is still a very traditional and a very modern country. It seems that the relationship between tradition and modernity is obvious. But it seems that still there is much to do so that there can be more social justice and solidarity among us.

The conclusion of *"La Estratoesfera"* celebrates the optimistic vision of Felipa and Alvaro crossing together toward a new sphere. They are standing on a bridge built on human solidarity and social justice promoted by the poet. The problematic outcome of *Judit y el tirano* emphasizes that the challenges of building such a bridge are enduring and the construction incomplete.

THE POET'S BRIDGE INTERRUPTED: *JUDIT Y EL TIRANO*
In *Judit y el tirano*, his modern rendition of the biblical story of Judith and

the general Holofernes, Salinas casts a female hero into Cervantine tradition. The poet Judit Velasco is a member of a group of artists who pretend to be apolitical dilettantes, considered by the police to be harmless eccentrics. The group's extravagant public face masks its activist plotting. In the spirit of Don Quixote, Judit's quest is both philosophical and deeply personal. She feels an urgent need to be the one to kill the monstrous tyrant and the hollow modernity of his regime. His government maintains that the individual human being means nothing and that all is done for the sake of the idea and the system. Akin to the knight offended by violators of the laws of chivalry and justice, Judit the artist activist is incensed by the tyrant's farsical and deceitful uses of art to subjugate and dehumanize his people. His surprise public appearances with the histrionics of his black cape, mask, and hollow voice torment her. The tyrant is a faceless phantom driving her crazy. His inhumanity and theatricality have transcended politics and entered her imagination to represent the incarnation of diabolical evil. She feels a driving need to confront the tangible reality of her enemy face-to-face and to decry the soulless existence he foists upon others. Otherwise she will not be convinced of his defeat.

Judit leads the group. Even after her failed attempt to rig the lots so that she will be chosen, her name is drawn to be the assassin. At the end of Act One, it appears that Judit is on a divine mission. Smiling, radiant, and looking forward, she positions herself ready to act. Like her namesake in the Apocrypha, Judit Velasco is a young, beautiful, and courageous woman who takes it upon herself to deliver her people from the oppression of the despot. She gains entry into the enemy's personal domain, wins his trust, ignites his passion for her, and eventually causes his death. In his tragic retelling, Salinas replaces the exalted, epic tone of the biblical story with a lyrical, warmly human, Cervantine accent. The play between reality and illusion, with emphasis on self and situation, tolerance and understanding, change and emancipation is ever present. As he blends tradition with modernity, Salinas depicts with refined irony the poet heroine's attempt to effect change in a political sphere. Advancing in secrecy, the quixotic Judit enters a surprising realm where reality, illusion, intentions, and results are confused.

Judit hides behind a curtain in the sitting room of the tyrant to wait for her opportunity to strike. What she observes and hears causes her to save rather than to end the life of her enemy. The tyrant appears a kind, well-mannered, cultured man. He and his personal servant share a genuinely affectionate relationship from which stiffness and severity are absent. He does not relish the responsibilities of his office. He dismisses the suspicions of the colonel that a nostalgic momento of his past, his music box of waltzes of Coppélia, holds a bomb. He finds it hard to believe the colonel's information about the plot of the intellectuals to assassinate him, especially Judit's role. Salinas's amiable jab at the eccentricities of modern artists is apparent in the tyrant's empathetic defense of the group, whose words and deeds, he claims, are misunderstood and disconcerting to those who do not know them (*Teatro completo* 377). Judit's disarming behavior illustrates immediately his asssertion that these artist types seem to be about to do one thing and then do something entirely different. Although she loads her gun, the ensuing crisis startles her into yielding to instinct. When two masked figures break through a window and attack the peaceful tyrant with knives, Judit impulsively fires two shots. Wounding one of the assailants and frightening them both away, she faints from the shock of her response.

When Judit searches the dictionary to find words to describe the unexplicable reality of her act, it is the tyrant who points out to her that the word "adelante" (forward) gives some shape to her action (384). He seeks to understand her and her motives. She struggles to make sense of his kindnesses, sensitivity, and astuteness. They meet under circumstances where the boundaries between sanity and lunacy are unclear:

REGENTE   Porque entonces yo estoy loco…
JUDIT   ¿Y por qué no va usted a estar loco…? Todos podemos estar locos…: usted…, yo… (*Teatro completo* 384)

TYRANT   Because then I am crazy…
JUDIT   And why would you not be crazy…? We all could be

crazy...: you..., I...

Confusion increases after the tyrant returns to her the fully loaded gun. He requests that she indulge him in one sentimental whim before regaining her freedom: to shoot a bullet in the manner of William Tell into his garden alder tree while he sits beneath it. After she gives up a second opportunity to fulfill her mission, Judit realizes that the emergence of the genuinely human face of her enemy before her has confounded her conception of his cruel facade and nullified her mission. Judit is now able to articulate the incongruity between her preconceived notion of the ruler and her actual experience of the man. She can justify how his humanity enabled his salvation:

> Vine a matar al tirano, al monstruo, a esa figura del espantapajo, que no nos deja vivir, que no me dejaba vivir. ¡Y ya está muerto! ¿No ves que ha nacido un hombre? Delante de mí nació... .... ¿Cómo te iba a matar? Si lo que vine a matar no era a un hijo de mujer... era lo inhumano, el antihombre, tu embuste. Tú, tú te has salvado contra él, tú. Y quiero que me oigas este *tú*, así con toda mi fuerza, porque este *tú* te distingue de todo, te señala, solo, único, *tú*. Es la marca de hombre, que te pongo en el alma... (Teatro completo 394)

> I came to kill the tyrant, the monster, that scarecrow of a figure that doesn't let us live, that did not let me live. And he is already dead! Don't you see that a man has been born? He was born in front of me... .... How was I going to kill you? If what I came to kill was not the child of a mother..., it was the inhuman part, the anti-man, your fraud. You, you have saved yourself from him, you. And I want this *you* to hear me, with all my power, because this *you* distinguishes you from everything; it signals you alone, unique, *you*. It is the mark of man, that I put on your soul...

Like the modern, hollow men to which Salinas alludes in his essay on the *Quijote*, the tyrant is an alienated, fragmented soul. He acknowledges the inner betrayal he has been experiencing since Judit has gained entry into his domain:

> Hace quince horas que me estoy traicionando a mí mismo... Hablando como lo que no soy, sintiendo como lo que no soy... como lo que no quiero ser..., como un hombre... (*Teatro completo* 393)

> For fifteen hours I have been betraying myself... Speaking like what I am not, feeling what I am not... like I don't want to be..., like a man...

Though the play does not supply direct demonstration of the negative side of the tyrant, Salinas incorporates distinct references to his sense of separation and places Judit the poet in crucial position to open the world to him and to help dismantle the false self or "embuste" (fraud) of his official role (397). Judit moves him beyond his existence circumscribed by loneliness and cruelty. Under her guidance, after spending every evening with her for a month, the Regente learns to go out among people and to participate in many things closed to him in his rank of tyrant. Yet during the course of their romantic liaison, Judit remains distressed by a continuing dissonance:

> No, Andrés, no. Dudo. Siento la lucha..., la división. La misma división de casi todos los días desde hace un mes... Tú, por la mañana, eres todavía... eso..., lo que odio..., el Regente. Son tus horas de despacho..., de trabajo oficial... Yo en casa me distraigo, leo, escribo... Pero no dejo de sentir que estás en ese otro mundo, que eres... el que queremos matar..., que sigues siéndolo. Estamos separados mucho más que por la distancia en esa hora. (*Teatro completo* 397)

> No, Andrés, no. I have doubts. I feel the struggle..., the division. The same division of almost every day for a month now... You, during the morning, are still... that thing..., what I hate..., the Ruler. They

are your office hours..., of official work... At home I distract myself, I read, I write... But I do not stop feeling that you are in that other world, that you are... the one we want to kill..., that you continue to be him. We are separated by much more than distance during that time.

Andrés strives to resolve the persisting struggle between the man and the tyrant, and he is determined to follow the lead of Judit to open that human dimension of himself he has thus far denied.

Judit's remedy for the tyrant reflects the spirit of Cervantine episodes of pretense and play-acting. For the tyrant to be cured, he and Judit must assume the life of a young and carefree couple out on the town. This charade directed by the poet can eradicate the malevolent ruler and save the man. Judit's explanation of her method underscores the truth, fantasy, and sympathetic irony of their performance. Her words also convey Salinas's definition of the social role of theater and suggest the significance of the poet's creative action in the modern context:

> La vida más verdadera hay que vivirla algunas veces como luz de comedia, con palabras de comedia... Porque su verdad es tan tremenda que, vista cara a cara nos aterraría... Hay que jugar con ella... hacer nuestra comedia... de verdades... que se disfrazan de juegos... Vestidas de su fría razón serían insufribles. Las salvamos fantaseándolas... Y así entrando en nuestro papel, entramos en la vida verdadera... La comedia de las verdades... para acabar con el embuste. (*Teatro completo* 399)

> We must live the truest life sometimes like the light of a play, with the words of a play... Because its truth is so frightful that, if seen face to face, it would terrify us... We must play with it... make our play... of truths... that disguise themselves as games... Dressed in their cold reason they would be insufferable. We save them by fantasizing them... And in this way by entering our roles, we enter true life... The play of truths... in order to end the fraud.

The ethical, political, romantic aspirations of the poet appear realized when Judit is convinced that the identity of the genuine man has filled the chasm in the soul of the tyrant. She envisions their future in a lyrical outpouring, and she addresses the light of a new day and a new man. Judit's definition of a new day transcends the concrete significance of the rising of the sun in the physical world. In the rhythmic, evocative passage, she internalizes the notions of "light" and "new day," then reconnects them with another aspect of the external world, the swelling approach of the waves of the sea, which in turn suggest an impending fulfullment with the arrival of the man she has helped emancipate. Her reference to the bird again points to a tangible reality, but with spiritual significance and dramatic foreshadowing. The chirping, normally indicative of the beginning of a new day, here carries to Judit a message that she cannot decipher, but her words about the bird's song suggestively warn of approaching trouble, and begin to cloud the light of her idealism:

Ya te siento… Ya estás ahí, día nuevo. ….. ¿Días nuevos, todos, sólo porque cada día hay un amanecer? No es así… Nuevos serán para el mar, y los árboles, y las montañas, que no aguardan más que la luz. Nosotros esperamos lo que nos trae la luz… Y la luz llega muchas veces con las manos vacías… No, esos días no son días nuevos… Lo que me vas a traer tú, luz—ya te siento en los párpados que te resisten—no me lo trajo nunca día alguno. Tú serás el nuevo entre todos, el más nuevo de la vida, y te siento crecer, cada vez más claro, onda tras onda, como el mar que se hinche y se acerca, hasta que llegue y me ponga delante la dicha que me trae, la que su marea está lentamente empujando hacia mí… No, no podía venir de noche… (…) Y el pájaro que no se cansa de cantar… Quizá cante cuando él llegue… Y puede que él entienda lo que dice el pájaro, como quería la muchacha… Pero ¿qué es esto?…. Es que viene, es que está aquí… (…) Así tenía que ser… La luz y tú. (*Teatro completo* 409)

Now I feel you… Now you are here, new day. ….. New days, all, just

because every day there is a dawn? It is not like that... They will be new for the sea, the trees, and the mountains, that wait only for the light. We wait for what the light brings us... And the light arrives many times with empty hands... No, those are not new days... What you will bring me, light—now I feel you on my eyelids that resist you—no day ever brought me. You will be the new one among all, the newest of my life, and I feel you growing, each time clearer, wave after wave, like the sea that swells and approaches, until it arrives and puts before me the joy it brings me, that which its tide is pushing slowly toward me... No, he couldn't come by night... (...) And the bird that does not tire of singing... Perhaps it will sing when he arrives... And perhaps he will understand what the bird is saying, like the girl wanted him to... But what is this? .... He is coming, he is here... (...) It had to be like this... The light and you.

The conclusion of the play follows the plot of the original Judith story because the heroine is instrumental in the death of the tyrant, but Salinas replaces the exalted praises of God, Judith, and the Israelite victory with a tragic dramatic irony and a grieving heroine. The assassination of the redeemed tyrant by his own secret police and Judit's weapon is the final proof of man's lack of worth within the tyranny. He is captured by his own underlings and a corrupt system, and his death appears to make no difference. Indications are that the order will continue, with another faceless creature acting as figurehead. While the work conveys the poet's abhorrance of tyranny and the urgency of seeking the positive force of each person, it shows the authority of a dictatorial system over the individuals embedded in it, including the tyrant himself.

The unfortunate outcome points to the contemporary scene that so disturbs Salinas. Salinas's bridging of tradition with modernity in this illustration of the poet's search for a more humane world underscores his hopes and fears about modern circumstance. Without specifying names or places, Salinas alludes to the inhuman behaviors and depersonalizing effects of modern tyrannical regimes, but what he emphasizes are the desired individual qualities to combat their ills. Though her attempt to topple the cruel tyranny is foiled because of the dominance of the political structure, Judit accomplishes her quixotic mission to uncover the exemplary humanity of the tyrant. While the tragic finale indicates a failure to sustain the ideal milieu sought by the poet, it upholds the validity of her vision, strongly grounded in Cervantes's conception of the mission of his hero. Salinas advocates strongly for the dreams of poet actors and for the quixotization of others they seek to involve in their quests.

THE POET'S BRIDGE OF HOPE: *LOS SANTOS*
In *Los santos*, a composite of impassioned characters rather than a single, leading poet hero, motivates a wondrous redemption. The play depicts the catalytic force of the *santos de palo* (statues of saints) and their progressive animation to the point of stepping in to replace five condemned prisoners. The prisoners inspire this miracle through an act of generosity toward a sixth person they encounter in their midst in the basement of a church in a town in New Castile. The stories of the five ill-fated sufferers underscore the ironically tragic play between self and circumstance that has brought them to death's door. Salinas weaves Christian symbolism together with Cervantine threads of illusion and reality, tolerance, transformation, and salvation.

The six individuals, Orozco, Severio, Paulino, Angustias, Pelona, and Palmito, differ greatly in age and come from diverse walks of life. Victims of the civil war, these strangers unite in the fleeting minutes before their anticipated death. Orozco emerges from hiding to offer cigarettes to the prisoners just herded into the church basement. Although the gesture at first frightens them, it initiates the spirit of fellowship and charity that grows among them. The grateful prisoners respond with their own act of benevolence to Orozco's kind overture. Pelona points out that the enemy does not know of Orozco's existence, and Severio offers to him his and Paulino's civilian clothing so that he will have a real chance to escape. In the conversations that follow, the six individuals connect in ways that make clear that their comradeship transcends their republican leanings.

Each prisoner awaiting death relates the history behind his or her present circumstance. Salinas highlights not only their compassion and understanding with regard to each other's anguish, but also their bond in innocence. The presentations of the prostitute, mother, and nun, three radically different women who join together to show the possibility of living, sharing, and saving each other along with the other prisoners, offer bright reflection of authentic Christian charity and the Cervantine posture of tolerance. Though the others do not approve of the life of prostitution Palmito has chosen, they accept her as a fellow sufferer. Lack of understanding among people has led to the horrible injustice they all experience. Angustias, after telling about the senseless murder of her son, sums up the situation to Palmito, and links their misfortune with that of her murdered son Juan:

> Por nada, hija... me lo mataron por nada... a todos nos matan por nada... por cosas que hablan, muy de prisa, y no se las entiende... Por nada. (*Teatro completo* 259)

> For nothing, child... they killed him for nothing... they are killing all of us for nothing... because of things they say, very quickly, and nothing is understood... for nothing.

Through the character of Pelona, Salinas further emphasizes the power of truly humanitarian motivations to break through meaningless political barriers. A nun, Pelona could easily save herself by proving her identity, but instead chooses authentic union with her fellows. This she explains to Orozco:

> Es verdad, no era de ellos, pero ya lo soy, ya estoy con vosotros. Todos padecemos la misma injusticia, entre todos nos repartimos... (...) ¿Tú no ves que si yo me salvara, si a mí me perdonaran, encima de la pena tendrían, pobrecillos, la envidia? Morirían envidiosos, envidiándome a mí, odiándome. Así moriremos queriéndonos, todos. Compadecidos los unos de los otros. Los que no se sintieron hermanos en vida... aun pueden morir como hermanos. (*Teatro*

completo 261-62)

> It is true, I was not one of them, but now I am, now I am with you. We all suffer the same injustice, we all share it among us... (...) Don't you see that if I were to save myself, if they were to pardon me, on top of their pain the poor things would harbor envy. They would die envious, envying me, hating me. This way we will all die loving each other. Sympathizing with each other. Those who didn't feel like brothers and sisters in life... can still die as brothers and sisters.

In addition to sacrificing herself in this manner, La Pelona inspires the other prisoners to save Orozco. Severio gives over his civilian clothing and wishes Orozco good luck just as the death squad is heard arriving.

Christian tradition grounds the correspondences Salinas has formulated between the five prisoners and particular saints. Although the stage directions and dialogue create some ambiguity about the number of statues, the Virgin of La Soledad, La Magdalena, San José, San Francisco, and San Mauricio are clear counterparts to the captives (Polansky, "How Many Saints..." 4). The mother who has lost her son represents La Soledad. La Palmito the prostitute resembles La Magdalena, known in the Christian tradition as a penitent sinner (Attwater 237). Severio the carpenter, "el hombre más honrado del pueblo" (the most honorable man of the town; *Teatro completo* 255), bears similarity to San José, foster father of Jesus, also a carpenter and an upright man. Paulino, the youngest and most naive of the prisoners who sees no evil in La Palmito, is reminiscent of San Francisco de Asís, a saint closely identified with those ostracized from society (Attwater 136-37). Finally, La Pelona the nun can be considered a reflection of San Mauricio. She had been granted refuge by relatives of a church sexton, and later was accused of aiding in the escape of two members of that family, brothers who were imprisoned as "rojos" (communists). Like San Mauricio, a Roman soldier who refused to prosecute fellow Christians on an opposing political side, Pelona knows no sides where true brotherhood is the issue (Attwater 35).

The transformation of the saint statues and the reactions of the characters again reveal Salinas's appropriation of a Cervantine-like blurring of reality and fiction. The captives deny the ability of the saints to walk, talk, and exist in conventional terms of human flesh and blood. Two of the characters communicate their doubts about the auditory powers of the statues. Yet La Madre and La Pelona invoke the humanity of the saints and appeal to their capacity to hear. The boundaries between art, imagination, everyday life, and concrete reality are hard to distinguish. Severio and Orozco liken the state of the town, the country, and the suffering people to a world of fiction and dream:

> SEVERIO ¿Es que no parece esto, todo esto, lo que está pasando en el pueblo y en España, invención? ¿No nos parecemos nosotros, aquí... y tú sales de entre esos santos, cosa de esas de las novelas? Pues es verdad... Tóa mi vida, ahí en mi trabajo, y de pronto, hace quince días parece que vivimos tós de invención.
>
> OROZCO Es verdad... esos santos, aquí y nosotros, todo revuelto, parece un sueño... (*Teatro completo* 254)
>
> SEVERIO Doesn't this, all this, what is happening in the town and in Spain seem invention? Don't we seem here... and you emerging from those saints, something out of those things from novels? Well it is true... all my life, here in my work, and suddenly, for two weeks now it seems as if we are all living a fiction.
>
> OROZCO It is true... those saints, here, and we, all mixed up, it seems a dream.

In the closing lines of the play, the awestruck Severio comprehends the extraordinary circumstance to be a marvelous invention. The redemption is imaginative truth and the fulfillment of a creative ideal: ¡Más invención, cada vez más invención! (More invention, more and more invention!; *Teatro completo* 263).

A vivid blend of tradition and modernity, *Los santos* is a play of tragic dimension and hopeful outcome. Without the single quixotic hero seen in other plays by Salinas, it displays an intense and uplifting deliverance from doom through a composite of quixotic heroes. Through his saints, both real prisoners and supernatural iconic forces, Salinas, in his own "precise time and space," continues in the manner of Cervantes to comment on "our presence in the world as problematic beings in an unending history, whose continuity depends on subjecting reality to imagination (Fuentes 15)."

Explaining Salinas's allusions to tradition in *Todo más claro* (1949), the volume of poetry that expresses most forcefully Salinas's anguish over the degeneration of modern life, Crispin offers a defensible rationale applicable to their appearance in the dramatic works as well:

> The use of so many cultural references in... *All Things Made Clearer* is in itself a reminder that, if they seem somehow out of place when dealing with present-day reality, it is because in the pursuit of strictly materialistic aims, man has lost touch with the great myths of the past, and with the spiritual aims and dreams they represented. Salinas thus could not have chosen a more appropriate medium to convey his lamenting commentary on the dangers of contemporary values to the proper spiritual evolution of man. (*Pedro Salinas* 128-29)

Salinas composed the poems of *All Things Made Clearer* between 1937 and 1947, the same years he was writing his plays. In this poetry and in his dramatic works, tradition serves as an anchor in the threating storm that modernity can be. In the plays, it is apparent that as Salinas dresses characters and circumstances in the garb of tradition, his innovative twists give not only somber commentary but at times also playful recreation.

In their pursuit of a realm of freedom and fulfillment highly preferable to existence under the constraints of the commonplace, Salinas's principal characters function as producers of and movers toward a redemptive milieu. His key characters go beyond their concrete surroundings in search of ideal spheres. Their melding of the concrete with the buoyant may be considered reflective of Salinas's poetic generation's revaluation of Spanish Baroque poet Luis de Góngora and of Salinas's own conception of metaphor. Salinas sees in Góngora's fusion of the tangible with the obscure, fantastical, and adventurous a new level of reality, an exalted way of viewing the world. Relatedly, Salinas defines metaphor as a creative act that takes two realities and absorbs them to produce a new third one. This idea, which he develops primarily in two essays, "Una metáfora en tres tiempos," and "Registro de Jorge Carrera Andrade," (*Ensayos de literatura hispánica*...168-82, 358-67), applies to the characters of his dramatic works who redefine milieu through blending the given with the ideal. These attempts to transform circumstances and other characters' perceptions illustrate Salinas's intertextual application of Cervantine and other literary, mythical, legendary, and biblical material to underscore the playwright's optimism and hope for the future.

Stressing tradition as the highest source of freedom open to a writer (*Jorge Manrique o Tradición y originalidad* 123), Salinas writes of Cervantes's work, "El *Quijote*, amigos míos, es una invitación a la libertad" (The *Quijote*, my friends, is an invitation to freedom; *Ensayos de la literatura hispánica*104). Salinas believes that Cervantes lauds the social mission of Don Quixote: "En el fondo de su alma, Cervantes está por Don Quijote. (In the depths of his soul, Cervantes is for Don Quixote; *Ensayos de la literatura hispánica* 104). But Salinas does not believe that Cervantes imposes this perspective on his readers. Salinas asserts that novelists, and also dramatists, although they should never try to push their audiences to hate or love certain characters, often do so. As an example, Salinas criticizes melodrama for slanting the public forcefully toward blatant, predetermined characterizations of good and bad. In contrast, Salinas marvels at the ability of Cervantes to extend to his readers a constant choice of options among the variegated cast of characters in his novel. Though Salinas detects the fundamental position of Cervantes, he believes that through masterful use of humor, Cervantes never tells his readers what to choose. Rather, as he introduces readers to the best and worst sides of his characters, he allows them to laugh or cry, to condemn or praise their wisdom or insanity.

Like Cervantes, the fundamental position of Salinas the poet-dramatist is clear. Like Cervantes, he upholds the quixotic vision of his poet characters. Nevertheless, his plays do not portray the depth of characterization seen in the novel of Cervantes. Although the plays are not melodramas with flat unidimensional characters and Salinas does extend to his audience an invitation to freedom by creating clashes with expectations and by portraying his key characters with sympathetic humor, ultimately the plays do not encourage readers to exercise a kind of choice and that would permit rejection of the world vision of his key figures. Through portrayal of his poets drawing others into their spheres, Salinas upholds their idealism as itself a stance of freedom to assume in order to reinvigorate milieu in spiritual, moral, and artistic terms.

It is telling that in ascribing contemporary significance to Don Quixote, Salinas employs the metaphor of the theater set to criticize the faulty, superficial vision of today and tomorrow held by many moderns. The legacy of Don Quixote links with the significance of the theater and its social function:

> Y he aquí la significación de Don Quijote, el actual. El mundo del mañana, esto es, el puerto de nuestra derrota, se lo imaginan algunos como decoración magna de teatro; ya está todo montado, cada máquina en su lugar, cada felicidad en su sitio. Acabará la guerra, se alzará el telón, y nos entraremos en ese ámbito de una Jauja electrificada. ¡Pobre espejismo! El mundo del mañana lo llevamos dentro, de nosotros ha de salir, y es labor nuestra, de hoy ya, y de mañana. (*Ensayos de la literatura hispánica* 85)

> And here is the meaning of Don Quixote, the current meaning. The world of tomorrow, is this, the port of our defeat, some imagine to be a huge theater set. Everything is already erected, every machine in its place, every happiness in its place. The war will end, the curtain will rise, and we will enter the sphere of an electrified paradise. Poor illusion! We carry within us the world of tomorrow; it must come out

of us, and it is our task, of today now, and of tomorrow.

Through his theater and heroic characters, Salinas offers the model for a better world defined not by static boundaries or imposing technology that divide and dissect humankind, but by dynamic thinking and feeling that promote the fellowship and unification of individuals. The poet, anchored in the live reality of tradition, transcends the barriers of time to touch the present and the future.

Conclusion
The Poet's Place

> The world is a possibility, but it is incomplete and perfectible.
> Salinas, *Reality and the Poet* 4

SALINAS THE LITERARY CRITIC describes the poet's perception of the world as a possibility, a place that can be perfected. This attitude toward reality clearly applies to Salinas's own stance as a poet and dramatist. For him, reality is "the life of the world that surrounds us and limits us, that gives to the individual the measure, at once tragic and magnificent, of his own creative possibilities" (*Reality and the Poet* 3). Study of the intersections of the life and works of Pedro Salinas has shown that through the medium of drama, Salinas the poet, correspondent, essayist, and exile from Spain expands his possibilities for creating new reality in the given world. Writing plays offers him an outlet for his nostalgia while also providing to a certain degree an antidote for his exile. Salinas derived enormous enjoyment from composing plays and special gratification from the one play he lived to see produced. He maintained hope that his exposure to audiences would grow.

In a letter to his daughter Solita and son-in-law Juan Marichal dated February 20, 1951, a few days following the premiere of *La fuente del arcángel*, Salinas communicated his satisfaction with this proof that his work now existed as theater brought to life in characters and action (*Cartas de viaje* 253). He wished to test the validity of his theater for a wider public. Contesting Dámaso Alonso's assessment that his was a theater for a minority audience, he noted that those attending were not simply a totally elite group, but rather a heterogeneous middle class public.

Dámaso Alonso's review of the play and his opinion of the promise of Salinas were nevertheless very positive. Alonso upheld the crucial role of the poet Salinas in effecting an extraordinary transformation of the everyday reality of an Andalusian town. The lyrical and spiritual development of characters and events would not be possible without the impetus of the poet. Moreover, Alonso praised the technical expertise of Salinas as a dramatist and the production's successful display of the playwright's intuitive sense of dramatic architecture ("Una generación poética" 201). Though the poet playwright's premiere was a bright moment, his potential was not to be fulfilled.

Salinas's early death, his exile, and the circumstances of Francoist Spain were clearly contributing factors to the limited staging of his work. And others less positive than Alonso about the theatrical sense of Salinas suggest that the literary merits of the plays overshadow the action (Ruiz Ramón, *Historia del teatro español Siglo XX* 284; Collado). Thus paradoxically, Salinas's plays have attained less popularity on stage because his intense preoccupation with verbal communication led to downplaying other essential dimensions of the theater. Dominating his plays is the dramatic dialogue, which although lauded in his essays as the preferred vehicle of social interaction, may overshadow other action and elements of scenic design. Manuel Collado, director of the centennial staging of *Judit y el tirano*, grants that Salinas's work has dramatic tension and potent dialogue, but he thinks it lacks *saber teatral* or theatrical know-how. Because so much of Salinas's theater depends on dialogue, Collado judges the faster moving one-act works with a single, coherent action to be the poet-playwright's best (Collado).

Salinas himself was confident about the literary merit of his plays, but during his exile he had expressed reservations about the quality of the Spanish theater of his time. In his essay "El romancismo y el siglo XX," Salinas had written about the resurgence of most literary genres in Spain, the promise of the novel, essay writing, and the supremacy of poetry in his time, but he had qualms about the promise of the theater and confessed he had "limited admiration for the theater of the past fifty years (318). In "La vida literaria en España," he had asserted that writing for the theater could be a way for a Spanish writer to gain exposure and overcome economic difficulties, but qualified this with criticism about the poor quality of works that attained financial success. He lamented that in the Spain of his time, the economic success of a theatrical work was customarily in exact inverse proportion to its literary and human value; and he jibed that unless a gifted writer had the ability to write sufficiently bad works, he would not escape economic difficulties by this route (298). Both Dougherty and Vilches de Frutos have traced this trend of the Spanish theater to become progressively profit-driven prior to the Spanish Civil War. A month before the production of *La fuente del arcángel*, anticipating its staging and that of *Judit y el tirano*, Salinas had assessed his own theater in this light to José Ferrater Mora: "Por supuesto, dada la alta calidad literaria de mi teatro, que no se rebaja a las tablas comerciales, todo será en *espectáculos de arte* sin cobrar una gorda" (Of course, given the high literary quality of my theater, that does not stoop to commercial stages, all will be in *art shows* without earning much; *Cartas de viaje* 251-52).

While mindful of the problematic times in which he lived and frustrated by the difficulties of getting his works produced, Salinas the poet dramatist remained forward thinking. Seeing obstacles to the staging of his works in Latin America some three and one half years before his death, in a letter to Guillén dated May 8, 1948, Salinas wrote,

> ...con la modestia que me cumple, habrá que decirse, poniendo un plazo más corto–también por modestia–hay que aguardar al público y al teatro de 1980. ¡Pero entonces ya estarán anticuadas! (PS/JG *Correspondencia* 444)

> ...with the modesty that befits me, it must be said, setting a shorter time frame—also out of modesty—it's necessary to wait for the audience and theater of 1980. But already then they will antiquated!

Salinas was mistaken. He did not have to wait until the 1980's to see one of his plays on stage. Before the 1980's a limited public did see his work, and publication of editions of his plays continues to introduce them to readers. Though his works have not shown such theatrical value by emerging posthumously like Valle-Inclán's, whose works have been widely staged in Spain and beyond, Salinas's plays nevertheless possess both an enduring literary quality and a significant social dimension that resonate well beyond his time.

Salinas's theater explores the "here and there" of exile experience. He puzzles out the interconnections of imagination and memory. He develops his vision of the activist role of the poet hero who "lives at the very center of the world" (*Reality and the Poet* 164). The voices of his poet figures offer very personal yet universal guidance for persisting and liberating ourselves within our circumstances. They champion holding close the near and dear and making special the ordinary reality we occupy. Inhabiting the spheres of technology, science, business, politics, art, and religion, in small towns or city neighborhoods of Spain or fictional locales, Salinas's guiding characters confront situations contemporary with his time, yet meaningful today and into the future.

In the first year of his exile, in his first essay in *Reality and the Poet in Spanish Poetry*, Salinas describes his nostalgia for the simplicity of the epic poet's reproduction of reality in the *Poem of the Cid*:

> But we shall always look back at it, at least I do, with nostalgia as for a paradise lost, for a virgin world where reality and poetry lived in peace and effortless conformity within the soul of man, or rather, perhaps, where war had not yet been declared between reality and poetry, a war which came later and which will never cease in the spirit of poets, in their attitude toward the world. Let us leave then, exiles that we are, this earthly and poetic paradise, this paradise of unity. (*Reality and the Poet* 29)

The time of the epic is supposed a time when poetic speaking is ordinary discourse. For later times, the unity of reality and poetry has become an ideal. All poets, then, are exiles from this ideal world of unity. With a persistent optimism, in the condition of exile he feels so strongly and shares with others, Salinas sees the heroic role of the poet in the effort to recapture—to re-produce— some measure of this unity. In his fourteen published plays, he dramatizes well the attempt of the poet to forge a blend of poetry and reality. Strong confirmation of this enterprise appears even in notes he drafted for proposed theatrical works.

Salinas's unpublished papers underscore his unfulfilled potential as a dramatist of the poet's role in a reorientation process. These writings are catalogued in the Houghton Library Collection of Harvard University in the microfilms labeled bms. Span 100 (995) "Temas para teatro" (themes for theater). Four folders bearing this label contain Salinas's typed or handwritten notes for roughly thirty theatrical works he did not live to complete. A few of the sketches are one or two pages long and contain a list of characters and brief dialogues. Two of these carry titles—*Ultimo toro o el retraso* (*The Last Bull* or *The Delay*) and *La llamada telefónica* (*The Telephone Call*) and others are scenes without titles. Most of the plans are paragraph-length plot summaries. Some some bear multiple titles and contain plot variations. In total there are about two dozen of these sketches with variations: *La cola* (*The Line*), *Salvada* (*Saved*) or *Salvación* (*Salvation*), *La posible* (*The Possible One*), *La secuestrada* (*The Kidnapped One*), *Ladrones de frac* (*Thieves in Tails*), *Camino de perfección* (*The Way of Perfection*) or *El héroe* (*The Hero*), *El hombre que vendió su pasado* (*The Man Who Sold His Past*), *El hombre dividido* (*The Divided Man*), *El anuncio* (*The Advertisement*), *El emigrante* (*The Emigrant*), *Esencia* (*Essence*), *La venta* (*The Sale*), *La informadora* (*The Informer*), *El generoso* (*The Generous One*), *La novela* (*The Novel*) or *La obra en suspenso* (*The Work in Suspense*), *La máquina* (*The Machine*), *¿Quién será el muerto?* (*Who Will Be the Dead One?*), and *El hijo* (*The Son*), *La tienda del inocente* (*The Shop of the Innocent One*), *Suceso* (*Event*). *El número trece* (*Number Thirteen*), *Los suicidas* (*The Suicides*), *Pasado* (*Past*).

In addition to the scene fragments and paragraph-length sketches, Salinas left brief notes of one or two lines with ideas for situations or plays. With vague similarities to the notebook of *La isla del tesoro*, he wrote of an auction scene with people in search of an object, for example a piano, that would serve as evocative center of the work. His ideas for a work with characters that included mannequins, clerks, owners, passersby, and a set with large shop window in the center of a stage with the three-part design including the interior of the shop, the display window, and the street, filter in part into *La Cabeza de Medusa*. Two jottings suggest particularly strong social and political dimension and possibly strike personal cords for Salinas the poet-dramatist in exile. One describes an individual whose false testimony leads to others' condemnation. In the other, Salinas makes reference to the arrival of refugees who live amidst a peaceful population. Conflict between the former, harmonious life and the newcomers brings tragedy. All in all, the proposed works show the presence of Salinas's confinement-to-freedom fabula and poet-like characters guiding a redemptive process.

The story lines of two of the sketches, *Salvada* and *La novela* are strong examples of Salinas's persistent thematic. In *Salvada*, a woman approximately forty years old meets a man in a station and shares the sad failure of her gray and empty life. Another man who turns out to be a poet or novelist approaches and sits beside her. The woman envies how he can paint things as they are desired and not as they are. She has the idea to tell him an imaginary tale of her life, one filled with adventure. The poet enthusiastically listens and says he will write it. She is thereby saved. The first man who has overheard everything tells the poet that it's a lie, to which the poet responds, "Who knows?"

The notes for *La novela*, with elements reminiscent of Salinas's completed works *El precio* and *Ella y sus fuentes*, define clearly the role of the writer as a redeemer. An old man pays a visit to a writer to clarify details of the events in the writer's work. The novelist shares with the old man the events he is writing, and as the man hears the events of his own life unfolding, he now anguishes that everything he experiences will depend on the writer's creation. Fearing a tragic end, he kills the writer, and then discovers on the table the final chapter, in which he was saved by the writer.

Other story seeds also reveal visions of hope and the poetization of the restrictions of material reality in the contemporary world. In *La cola*, people are waiting in line for help with the fulfillment of their dreams. A secretary emerges to ask some of those waiting what they desire. The seekers are granted their requests, but do not like what they had desired, and they return the next day to begin again. In *Esencia*, three gasoline pumps resemble human figures in a modernly grotesque way. Three cars arrive for fill-ups. One pump leads to happiness, another to disaster, and one to somewhere in between. The lovers take from the first pump and the gangsters from the second.

In *La posible*, a couple celebrating their twentieth anniversary acknowledges their success in attaining fame and fortune, but they are not happy. The maid speaks to them of their youth and when she first came to serve them. In the second scene the vision of the maid with a young woman and her enraptured fiancé suggests the passing of twenty years and uncovers the existence of letters that reveal the couple's decision to abort a child who would stand in the way of their success. Leaving her wedding dress in the middle of the room, the young woman disappears magically. The couple is left to contemplate what could have been.

The plot for *La secuestrada* suggests some of the circumstances Salinas develops in his play *Sobre seguro* about the insurance money and the mysterious disappearance of the son Angel, about narrow-viewed materialism and the modern world. It involves a dreamy, young woman who disappears from her home and communicates mysteriously by phone with her family. She asks her father for the same sum of money he had been paid years before for testifying against a young man who had been condemned to death. Later she drops in to claim that angels have forced her to make restitution for the death money and that having seen another better world, she will never be content in this one.

In distinct settings from the everyday world and with happy outcomes that underscore the significance of determination and action, two plot lines contain elements resembling those in Salinas's plays *El director* and *Ella y sus fuentes* as well as *Prohibido suicidarse en primavera* (*Suicide Prohibited in Springtime*) or *Los árboles mueren de pie* (*Trees Die*

Standing) by Alejandro Casona. *Ladrones de frac,* set in a luxury hotel, features three thieves, each of whom enters a different room. The first victim is a scientist who has stolen an invention and thinks that the thief is a spy from the workplace from which it was taken. The deal is that the thief will not rob the scientist if he agrees to return what he stole. In the second room is a woman who has stolen the husband of another. The thief takes her jewels and threatens to leave with them unless the woman agrees not to destroy the happiness of another. In the third room a woman is going to take her life. The thief will not rob her if she renounces her plan and accepts life. The three thieves are seen in the last scene as guardian angels who reunite in the hallway, show each other with pleasure their empty hands, and vanish through a window.

The notes for *Camino de perfección* describe a vagrant who enters a library through a window and makes himself at home in a chair. He and a maid witness a romantic scene between the widow of a national hero and the teacher of her children. There are plans to make a statue to honor the memory of the hero. The widow confesses that her late husband was a coarse and unscrupulous individual, but she is determined to preserve his memory and save his name. Her suitor the teacher admires her sacrifice. The vagrant now tells the maid to let the woman know she has a visitor. Sitting in the shadows, the vagrant, who is the husband returned, asks insinuating questions about the return of the husband and his reentry into her life. She wants only his memory, where alone his fame and her love for him can survive. He leaves, and in anguish she hears the shot that seals his redemption. *El héroe* appears to be another version of *Camino de perfección* with less emphasis on the love component and more emphasis on the hero's desire to reconstruct the past and his inability to live with the burden of glory or notoriety.

A search for deliverance from disconnection and sense of separation in the modern human soul are themes evident in the notes for *El hombre que vendió su pasado* and *El hombre dividido*. *El hombre que vendió su pasado* sketches the situation of an experienced, forty year-old man who sells himself to a young, shy millionaire. This means he is left with no memory because the young man now has acquired it. When a woman of his past returns, she is unable to recognize him. Instead, she marries the young man who is familiar to her and thus proves that life without memory has no basis. *El hombre dividido* traces the idea of a man with many aptitudes and appetites. Tortured by his fragmented self, he makes a pact with the devil and becomes four men: a loyal husband, a lover, a poor poet, and a doctor. All of these beings are unhappy and frustrated. One night the poet and doctor quarrel and kill each other. The wife and the lover of the divided self are frightened by the two deaths. Salinas notes that either the women will disappear or one will sacrifice her relationship in order to restore their man to unity.

With circumstances related to the salvation of a young girl and a varied cast of characters including Spanish types such as a gypsy, a bullfighter, a blind man, a policemen, a pimpish dandy, and a female go-between, the sketch for *Ultimo toro o el retraso* suggests the style and Spanishness of "*La Estratoesfera.*" *Los suicidas* contains elements of *El director* and *La Bella Durmiente*. Two couples come to a hotel to commit suicide, one out of poverty, the other because they fear their love will not last through the years. Salinas's notes indicate that a solution will be sought so that all are saved by seeing themselves in each other.

Elements of two of the proposed works surfaced in *Los santos*, with its portrayal of the contemplation of personal circumstance in the face of calamity and the encountering of unity in suffering. In *¿Quién será el muerto?*, several vacationers in a country home learn suddenly that the milk they have drunk the day before has the possibility of infecting some of them but not others. Wondering who will be affected and die or if all will be saved, they anguish with the threat of death hovering over their ambitions, loves, and passions. *El hijo* describes the situation of a woman still suffering from the death of her son nineteen years earlier. She is profoundly jealous of a high school friend with a son the age of her late son. This young man falls in love with the grieving woman's daughter, who becomes pregnant and aborts the baby. Her mother wonders about the daughter's action, in effect a revisiting of the loss of her own child. War breaks out, the young man is killed, and the three women are joined in their misery.

La máquina bears striking likeness to Salinas's novel *La bomba increíble* and points to Salinas's preoccupation with the threat of war and the atomic bomb. Notes indicate the initial setting to be in a museum where a guard discovers a mysterious machine and calls the director. The machine emits an incessant ticking sound that baffles all who try to determine its function and operation. A man obsessed with resolving its secret goes mad and attacks the machine with a hammer, but it keeps ticking. His wife helps him sleep and calls two men to throw the machine into the sea. The clock-like sound increases and drives the desperate woman to flee. Salinas's notes indicate that the machine could relate to a war secret, that the investigator lives on a cliff near the sea, and that in his house a meeting of wise men takes place.

In these undeveloped works as well as in the completed plays, the voice of the poet communicates strong resolve to seek and make a better world. Salinas's plays can be seen as a step toward the generation after him of "socially aware" poets of the generation of 1936. Ilie defines characteristics of this group: they move away from pure aestheticism, subjective feeling, intellectual exclusivism (Ilie, "The Poetics of Social Awareness..." 112). Describing the connections of these socially conscious poets to their circumstance, Ilie writes,

> There exists, then, a community of emotions that displaces private feeling and becomes one aspect of the sensibility of social awareness. In an afflicted society, each man is affected emotionally by the character of the larger affliction. Although private emotions will vary according to each individual, every man has a similar plight, and in this area their psychological response will show little variation. What emerges, consequently, is a correspondence of feelings that brings all men together into an emotional unity that is lacking in the political realm. ("The Poetics of Social Awareness..." 114).

Salinas's plays do not portray this totality of emotional unity, though his poet protagonists exert a leading force toward solidarity with their kindred characters. Salinas feels the universal plight and through his characters endeavors to express it, but his vision is highly personalized. Ilie also writes that the heroism of the socially aware poet is not a reckless and romantic position, but rather, it is considered, weighed, and formed in a quasi-existentialist framework (117). Salinas's poet heroes are romantic yet very reflective as they determine their courses of action. Salinas's poet heroes clearly respond to the everyday world around them, but they are not ideological or political in the ways that Ilie defines the engagé poet:

> The poet is obligated to report not only what can be seen by every member of the body politic, but also what cannot be seen, namely, his private feelings, about the situation. This involved a double duty, for he is morally bound both to his private emotional world, a realm which artists normally protect from society, and to the social environment which has trapped him. Once the poet recognizes these obligations, it becomes virtually impossible for him to remain obedient to an unjust state. He must speak out... (117)

Through his poet heroes, Salinas highlights the importance of individual response and communicates a criticism of faulty hierarchies, but also looks back through tradition to create a crucial conversation between tradition and the present with an eye toward the future. Salinas's plays thus stand at the crossroads between the modern and postmodern worlds. In architectural terms, the postmodern movement "generated a signature of colliding fragments, skewed grids, and warped planes. On occasion, the pained dislocations have a fateful propriety" (Kostof 759). Salinas's poet heroes uphold the creative sparks and juxtapositions of these dislocations, but navigate obstacles to seek an ultimate harmony. Salinas's constructions might be said to bear interesting marks resembling the works of architect Frank Lloyd Wright, who sought balance in modernity and erected structures infused with a spiritual depth he encountered in eternal qualities of the natural world:

> The tensions of industrial society were not his, nor was his faith

hitched to the miraculous epiphanies of a machine age. High technology had its place, and so did traditional materials and methods. So Wright continued to speak obscurely of an organic architecture, one that combined modern means with the forms of nature and their growth. He spoke of shelter not only as a quality of space but of spirit. (Kostof 712)

This brings us full circle to appreciate Salinas the poet and architect of his dramatic works and offer a final comment on his challenge to the Platonic conception of the role of the poet. Socrates asserts to his interlocutors:

> But, I take it, if he [the poet] had genuine knowledge of the things he imitates, he would far rather devote himself to real things than to the imitation of them, and would endeavor to leave after him many noble deeds and works as memorials of himself, and would be more eager to be the theme of praise than the praiser. (Plato, *Republic* X 599b, Shorey trans.)

In fertile interplay with what Plato writes, Salinas goes part of the way to meet the philosopher's challenge. Can poets enhance the modern world and its human relationships? This would seem as quixotic as a knight in the seventeenth century. Salinas did not build houses or tangible structures, but he did craft dramatic works. It is ironic that Salinas the poet presents the case for poet as savior through the drama. Through this genre he shows poets in action and aims for them to be the theme of praise and for their interactions to impact upon members of the audience. But how effective is this drama, especially given the limited staging of Salinas's works? Is it possible that this dramatization of the poet can point spectators or readers toward new realities? Like Cervantes, Salinas sees value in accentuating the quixotic character who makes one reassess priorities and possibilities. Salinas's plays carry an enduring message. They place hope in humankind and uphold a heroism of the poet for audience members to reflect upon privately and to carry into public life.

Bibliography

Abellán, José Luis, editor. *El exilio de 1939*. Madrid: Taurus, 1976-1978.

Alonso, Dámaso. "Una generación poética (1920-1936)." Finisterre, 1, marzo, 1948. Recogido en *Poetas españoles contemporáneos*. Madrid: Gredos, 1958. 167-92, 193-206.

———. "Con Pedro Salinas." Clavileño, núm. 11, septiembre-octubre 1951. (Recogido en *Poetas españoles contemporáneos*. Madrid: Gredos, 1958).

———. "España en las cartas de Pedro Salinas." *Insula* 74(15 febrero 1952), 1, 5.

Allen, Rupert C. *Symbolic Experience: A Study of Poems by Pedro Salinas*. University, Alabama: U of Alabama Press, 1982.

Andújar, Manuel. "Constancia de dos exilios españoles en nuestra literatura." *República de las Letras* 7 (January 1984): 24-26.

———. "Los exiliados transterrados y las Américas." *El exilio de las Españas de 1939 en las Américas: ¿Adónde fue la canción?* José María Naharro-Calderón. Barcelona: Anthropos, 1991. 127-32.

Anónimo. "Estreno en España de la obra *Los santos* de Pedro Salinas." *El País* (27 julio 1980): 29.

The Apocrypha of the Old Testament. Revised Standard Version (Translation from the Greek and Latin tongues being the version set forth A.D. 1611: Revised A.D. 1894; A.D. 1957. Toronto, New York, Edinburgh: Thomas Nelson and Sons, 1957. 65-81.

Aristotle. *Poetics*. Trans. I. Bywater. In *The Complete Works of Aristotle*. The Revised Oxford Translation. Volume II. Ed. Jonathan Barnes. Princeton: Princeton UP, 1984.

Attwater, Donald. *The Penguin Dictionary of Saints*. Baltimore: Penguin Books, 1965.

Ayala, Francisco. "Para quién escribimos nosotros." *Cuadernnos Americanos* VIII, 40(1949): 36-58.

Ayuso, José Paulino. "La ironía en el teatro de Pedro Salinas." *Letras de la España Contemporánea; Homenaje a José Luis Varela*. Alcalá de Henares: Centro de Estudios, 1998. 269-79.

Baader, Horst. *Pedro Salinas Studien zu seinem dichterischen und kritischen Werk*.

Diss. Kolner romantische Arbeiten, 1956.

Bell, Alan S. "Pedro Salinas en América: Su correspondencia con Eleanor Turnbull." *Insula* 38, 307(junio 1972): 1, 12-13.

Bellver, Catherine. "Antidotes for Exile: Rafael Alberti's Struggle against a Persistent Malady." *Monographic Review/Revista Monográfica* 2 (1986): 68-83.

Bennett, Tony. *Formalism and Marxism*, London: Methuen 1979.

Berenguer, Angel. "Veinticinco años de exilio en el teatro contemporáneo." *Insula* 371 (octubre 1977): 1, 10.

Berroa, Rei. "Discurso poético y exilio interior: la poesía española en los inicios del franquismo." *Cincinnati Romance Review* 4 (1985): 1-21.

Blecua, José Manuel. "Una charla con Pedro Salinas." *Insula* 7, 70(12 octubre 1952): 2, 3, 6.

Borrás, A. A. "Twentieth Century Spanish Drama: In Defense of Liberty." 55-76. In Borrás, Angelo Augusto (ed.) *The Theatre and Hispanic Life: Essays in Honour of Neale H. Taylor*. Waterloo: Wilfrid Laurier UP, 1982.

Bou, Enric. "'Descubrimiento' o 'encuentro': Pedro Salinas en las Américas." *La Torre* 8, 32(octubre-diciembre 1994): 437-56.

———. "Ligeros de equipaje: Exilio y viaje en la España peregrina (1936-1969). *Revista Hispánica Moderna* 52, 1(1999): 96-109.

Bou, Enric and Gascón-Vera, Elena, editors. *Signo y memoria: Ensayos sobre Pedro Salinas*. Madrid: Editorial Pliegos, 1993.

Bou, Enric and Soria Olmedo, Andrés. "Pedro Salinas Cartografía de una vida." In *Pedro Salinas 1891-1951*. Comisión Organizadora del I Centenario del Nacimiento de Pedro Salinas. Madrid: Consorcio para la Organización de Madrid Capital Europea de la Cultura, 1992, 21-160.

Brines, Francisco. "Pedro Salinas, precursor de los movimientos alternativos." *Revista de Occidente* 126(Noviembre 1991): 121-36.

Cabrera, Vicente. *Tres poetas a la luz de la metáfora*. Salinas, Aleixandre y Guillén. Madrid: Gredos, 1975.

Campos, Jorge. "Balance del exilio republicano." *Insula* 363, 32(febrero 1977): 11.

Cano, J. L. "*La fuente del arcángel* de Pedro Salinas." *Insula* VII:75 (1952): 12.

———. "El teatro de Pedro Salinas." In *La poesía de la Generación del 27*. Madrid: Guadarrama, 1973, 59-62.

Cate-Arries, Francie. "Poetics and Philosophy: José Ortega y Gasset and the Generation of 1898." *Hispania* 71:3(September 1988): 503-11.

Cazorla, Hazel. "Art Mobilized for War: Two Spanish Civil War Plays by Rafael Alberti and Pedro Salinas." *Estudios en Homenaje a Enrique Ruiz-Fornells* (1990): 92-98.

Chatman, Seymour. *Story and Discourse Narrative Structure in Fiction and Film*, Ithaca and London: Cornell University Press, 1978.
Ciplijauskaité, Biruté. Pedro Salinas: Conciencia y Responsabilidad. *Sin Nombre* 2,1(1971): 34-48.
———. "Los puentes de Pedro Salinas." *Sin nombre* 9, 1(1978): 18-28.
———. "Oasis en el destierro." *Insula* 356-357 (julio-agosto1976): 7.
———. *De signos y significaciones. Juegos con la Vanguardia: poetas del 27*. Barcelona: Anthropos, 1999.
Cirre, José Francisco. *El mundo lírico de Pedro Salinas*. Granada: Don Quijote, 1982.
Cervantes Saavedra, Miguel de. *El ingenioso hidalgo Don Quijote de la Mancha*. Ed. preparada por Justo García Soriano y Justo García Morales. Madrid: Aguilar, 1968.
Coates, Paul. *The Double and the Other. Identity as Ideology in Post-Romantic Fiction*. London: Macmillan Press, 1988.
Collado, Manuel. Phone interview. Madrid, July 20, 1995.
Costa Viva, Olga. *Pedro Salinas frente a la realidad*. Madrid: Alfaguara, 1969.
Cowes, Hugo W. *Relación yo-tú y trascendencia en la obra dramática de Pedro Salinas*. Buenos Aires: Universidad de Buenos Aires, Facultad de Filosofía y Letras, 1965.
———. Realidad y superrealidad en 'Los santos' de Pedro Salinas." *Cuadernos Americanos* 188(1973): 262-77.
Crispin, John. *Pedro Salinas*. New York: Twayne, 1974.
———. *La estética de las generaciones de 1925*. Valencia: Pre-textos. Nashville: Vanderbilt University, 2002.
Cruz, Juan. "Juan Marichal y Solita Salinas Tierra de fortuna." *El País Semanal* 1372 (12 enero 2003), 82-87.
Darmangeat, Pierre. *Antonio Machado, Pedro Salinas, Jorge Guillén*. Prólogo de José Manuel Blecua. Trad. y nota introductoria: Jacinto-Luis Guereña. Madrid: Gredos, 1969.
Debicki, Andrew P., Ed. *Pedro Salinas*. Madrid: Taurus, 1976.
———. "The Play of Difference in the Early Poetry of Pedro Salinas." *Modern Language Notes* 100:2(March 1985): 265-80.
———. *Estudios sobre la poesía española contemporánea*. Madrid: Gredos, 1968.
———. "La obra crítica de Pedro Salinas: de la modernidad a la postmodernidad." *Signo y memoria: Ensayos sobre Pedro Salinas*. Eds. Enric Bou and Elena Gascón-Vera. Madrid: Editorial Pliegos, 1993. 109-19.
Dehennin, Elsa. *Passion d'absolu et tension expressive dans l'oeuvre poétique de Pedro Salinas*. Gent: Rijksunivte Gent, 1957.

Del Río, Angel, et. al. *Pedro Salinas; vida y obra. Bibliografía, antología*. New York: Hispanic Institute, 1942.
Del Río, Angel. "El poeta Pedro Salinas: vida y obra," *Estudios sobre la literatura contemporánea española*. Madrid: Gredos, 1969.
Devlin, John. "Reality and the Poet, Pedro Salinas." *Renascence. Essays on Values in Literature* 24, 2 (Winter 1972), 102-09.
Di Pinto, Mario. La professione critica de Pedro Salinas. *Filologia Romanza* 1, 4(October-December 1954), 89-94.
Diez de Revenga, "De la poética al autoanálisis." *Signo y memoria: Ensayos sobre Pedro Salinas*. Eds. Enric Bou and Elena Gascón-Vera. Madrid: Editorial Pliegos, 1993. 121-33.
Dougherty, Dru and Vilches de Frutos, María Francisca. *La escena madrileña entre 1918 y 1926: Análisis y documentación*. Madrid: Fundamentos, 1990.
———, editors. *El teatro en España entre la tradición y la vanguardia 1918-1939*. Madrid: Tabapress, 1992.
Durán, Manuel. "La influencia del exilio en la obra de Pedro Salinas y Jorge Guillén." *Insula* 41(enero-febrero 1986): 1, 18.
———. "La calzada de los poetas: un paseo lírico por la ciudad de México." *El exilio de las Españas de El exilio de las Españas de 1939 en las Américas: ¿Adónde fue la canción?* José María Naharro-Calderón. Barcelona: Anthropos, 1991. 213-25.
Elam, Kier. *The Semiotics of Theatre and Drama*. London and New York: Methuen, 1980.
Escartín Gual, Montserrat. "El sentimiento amoroso en la obra de Pedro Salinas." *DAI* 50/02c(1988): 173.
———. "El uso de los tópicos literarios en la obra de Pedro Salinas." *Signo y memoria: Ensayos sobre Pedro Salinas*. Eds. Enric Bou and Elena Gascón-Vera. Madrid: Editorial Pliegos, 1993. 135-57.
Feal Deibe, Carlos. *La poesía de Pedro Salinas*. Madrid: Gredos, 1965, 1971.
———. *Poesía y narrativa de Pedro Salinas*. Madrid: Gredos, 2000.
———. "El contemplado de Pedro Salinas: La voz a Puerto Rico debida." *La Torre: Revista de la Universidad de Puerto Rico* 5, 20(October-December 1991): 461-73.
Feldbaum, Judith. "El trasmundo de la obra poética de Pedro Salinas." *Revista Hispánica Moderna* 22(1956): 12-34.
Ferguson, Margaret W. "The Exile's Defense: Dubellay's La Deffence et Illustration de la Langue Françoise." *PMLA* 93(1978): 275-89
Fergusson, Francis. *The Idea of a Theater. A Study of Ten Plays. The Art of Drama in*

Changing Perspective. Princeton: PrincetonUP, 1949.
Fernández Almagro, M. "Teatro por Pedro Salinas." *ABC* (31 julio 1962): 7.
Fernández de Lewis, Piri. "Salinas y Puerto Rico: contemplación desde el mar." *La Torre* 8, 32(octubre-diciembre 1994): 519-38.
Fernández Méndez, E. "Pedro Salinas: Quijote moderno." *Asomante* 2(abril-junio 1952): 84-86.
———. "Pedro Salinas. Teatro." *La Torre* 1,1(1953): 188-89.
Gaos, Vicente. *Antología del grupo poético del 1927*. Salamanca: Anaya, 1973.
García Tejera, María del Carmen. *La teoría literaria de Pedro Salinas*. Cádiz: Seminario de Teoría de la Literatura, 1988.
Gila, Antonio. "El chantajista y el teatro de Salinas." *Duquesne Hispanic Review* 6(1968): 13.
Gilman, Stephen. "America and Don Pedro Salinas." *Hispania* 35, 2(1952):147-48.
González, Angel. "El exilio en España y desde España." *El exilio de las Españas de 1939 en las Américas: ¿Adónde fue la canción?* José María Naharro-Calderón. Barcelona: Anthropos, 1991. 195-209.
González Muela. Joaquín. "Poesía y amistad: Jorge Guillén y Pedro Salinas." In Andrew P. Debicki, ed. *Pedro Salinas*. Madrid: Taurus, 1976.
Guillén, Claudio. "Cervantes entre Dámaso Alonso y Pedro Salinas." *Ecos de la Generación del 98 en la del 27*. Madrid: Ediciones Caballo Griego para la poesía, 1998. 109-20.
———. "On the Literature of Exile and Counter-Exile." *Books Abroad*, 50, 2(Spring 1976): 272.
———. "Pedro Salinas y las palabras." *La Torre: Revista de la Universidad de Puerto Rico* 3:10(Apr.-June1989): 337-56.
———. "Salinas en verso, Salinas en prosa." *Revista de Occidente* 126(noviembre 1991): 73-89.
Gullón, Ricardo. "Pedro Salinas, novelista." *Insula* VXX 3(1951): 3.
———. "Los prosistas de la generación de 1925." *Insula* 126(mayo 1957):1,8.
———. "Salinas el intelectual." *Insula*, 7:74(15 febrero 1952): 9.
Hartfield-Méndez, Vialla. "El dilema de Pigmalión: El uso del personaje autónomo en Pedro Salinas." *ALEC* 17 (1992): 395-408.
———. The Privileged Moment: Perceptions of Woman and Infinity in Pedro Salinas Art." *DAI*51/3 (1990): 876A.
———. *Woman and the Infinite. Epiphanic Moments in Pedro Salinas's Art*. Lewisburg: Bucknell University Press. London: Associated University Presses, 1996.
Hatzfield, Helmut. "The Language of the Poet." *Studies in Philology* 43(1946):93-

119.

Havard, Robert. "Guillén, Salinas, and Ortega: Circumstance and Perspective." *Bulletin of Hispanic Studies* 60(1983): 305-18.

Hawkes, Terrence. *Structuralism and Semiotics*. Berkeley: UC Press, 1977.

Helman, Edith F. "The Innocent and the Guilty." *Hispania* XXXV 2(1952):151-52.

———. "Verdad y fantasia en el 'teatro' de Pedro Salinas." *Buenos Aires Literaria* 13(1953): 69-78.

Holmes, Oliver W. *Human Reality and the Social World: Ortega's Philosophy of History*. Amherst: UMassachusetts Press, 1975.

Ilie, Paul. *Literature and Inner Exile: Authoritarian Spain, 1939-1975*. Baltimore, Johns Hopkins UP, 1980.

———. "The Poetics of Social Awareness in the Generation of 1936." *Spanish Writers of 1936. Crisis and Commitment in the Poetry of the Thirties and Forties.* Eds. Jaime Ferrán and Daniel P. Testa. London: Tamesis, 1973. 109-23.

Keppler, C.F. *The Literature of the Second Self*. Tucson, Arizona: The University of Arizona Press, 1972.

Kostof, Spiro. *A History of Architecture: Settings and Rituals. Second Edition.* Oxford: Oxford UP, 1995.

LaBelle, Jenijoy. *Herself Beheld. The Literature of the Looking Glass*. Ithaca: Cornell UP: 1988.

Lama, Víctor de. *Poesía de la Generación del 27 Antología crítica comentada*. Madrid, Edaf, 1997.

Langer, Suzanne K. *Feeling and Form*. New York: Scribner's, 1953.

Lida, Clara E. *Inmigración y exilio. Reflexiones sobre el caso español*. México: Siglo xxi Editores, 1997.

Lloréns, Vicente. *Aspectos sociales de la literatura española*, Madrid: Castalia, 1974.

———. "El desterrado y su lengua. Sobre un poema de Pedro Salinas." *Asomante* 1(marzo 1954):46.

———. *Memorias de una emigración. Santo Domingo 1939-1945*. Barcelona: Ariel, 1975.

———. "El retorno del desterrado." *Literatura, historia, política*. Madrid: Revista de Occidente, 1967. 9-30.

Magnini, Shirley. "Three Voices of Exile." *Monographic Review/Revista Monográfica* 2 (1986): 208-14.

Marichal, Juan. *Tres voces de Pedro Salinas*. Madrid: Taller de Ediciones Josefina Betancor, 1976.

———. "Pedro Salinas y la ampliación del ensayo." *Homenatge a Pedro Salinas*. Barcelona: Universitat de Barcelona, 1992. 15-22.

Martínez Moreno, Isabel. "La intuición del espacio edénico en el teatro de Pedro Salinas." *Revista de Literatura* 52:104(1990):457-86.

Materna, Linda S. "The Dialogue of Pedro Salinas' *La fuente del arcángel*: A Dialectic of Poetry and Realism." *Hispanic Review* 54,3(1986):297-312.

———. "Ideology and Vivification of Art in Pedro Salinas' *Los santos* and Rafael Alberti's *Noche de guerra en el Museo del Prado*." *Hispanófila* 34,100(1990): 15-28.

———. "Poetry and Realism in Modern Spanish Theater: Pedro Salinas and Other Dramatists of the Generation of 1927." *DAI* 41, 12(1981): 5120-5121.

Maurín, Mario. "Temas y variaciones en el teatro de Pedro Salinas." *Insula* 104 (1954): 1,3.

Maurer, Christopher. "Salinas y 'las cosas': tradición y vanguardia." *Revista de Occidente* 126(Noviembre 1991): 137-50.

———. "Sobre 'joven literatura' y política: cartas de Pedro Salinas y de Federico García Lorca (1930-1935)." *Estelas, laberintos, nuevas sendas: Unamuno, Valle-Inclán, García Lorca, la Guerra Civil*. Ed. Angel G. Loureiro. Barcelona: Anthropos, 1988. 297-319.

———; Kristal, Efraín; Salinas de Marichal, Solita; Ríos Font, Wadda. "Homenaje a Pedro Salinas." *Boletín de la Fundación Federico García Lorca* 2: 3(June 1988):9-61.

Mermall, Thomas. *The Rhetoric of Humanism: Spanish Culture after Ortega y Gasset*. New York: Bilingual Press, 1976.

Miras, Domingo. "Exilio: En torno a Salinas." *Primer Acto: Cuadernos de Investigación Teatral* 234(1990): 123-29.

Miró, Emilio. *Antología de poetisas del 27*. Madrid: Castalia, 1999.

Monleón, José, "Teatro español y teatro latinoamericano." *Estreno* 17(primavera 1992): 6-11.

Moraleda, Pilar. "El binomio tradición y originalidad en el teatro de Pedro Salinas." In *Perspectivas sobre la cultura hispánica: XV aniversario de luna colaboración universitaria*. Cordoba: Servicio de Publicaciones, Universidad de Córdoba, 1997, 267-79.

———."Pedro Salinas: el dramaturgo y las fases de la realidad." *Signo y memoria: Ensayos sobre Pedro Salinas*. Eds. Enric Bou and Elena Gascón-Vera. Madrid: Pliegos, 1993. 161-74.

———. "Un pueblo andaluz llamado Alcorada." *Axerquía* 11(1984): 271-91.

———. "Rasgos unamunianos en el teatro de Pedro Salinas." *Alfinge* 1(1983): 113-20.

———. *El teatro de Pedro Salinas*. Madrid: Pegaso, 1985.

———. "La vocación dramática de Pedro Salinas." *Insula* 540(1991): 22-23.
Morello Frosch, Marta. "Teatro y crítica de Pedro Salinas." *Revista Hispánica Moderna* XXVI:1-2(1960): 116-17.
Morón Arroyo, Ciriaco. "Pedro Salinas y su generación." *Pedro Salinas Estudios sobre su praxis y teoría de la escritura*. Eds. Ciriaco Morón Arroyo y Manuel Revuelta Sañudo. Santander: Sociedad Menéndez y Pelayo, 1992. 11-39.
Morris. C. B. "*Visión* and *mirada* in the Poetry of Salinas, Guillén and D. Alonso. *Bulletin of Hispanic Studies*, 37(1960): 103-12.
Nagel, Susan. *The Influence of the Novels of Jean Giraudoux on the Hispanic Vanguard Novels of the 1920s-1930s*. Lewisburg: Bucknell University Press. London and Toronto: Associated University Presses, 1991.
Naharro-Calderón, José María. *El exilio de las Españas de 1939 en las Américas: ¿Adónde fue la canción?* Barcelona: Anthropos, 1991.
Newberry, Wilma. "Pirandellism in the Plays of Pedro Salinas," *Symposium* 25(1971): 59-69.
Newman, Jean Cross. *Pedro Salinas and His Circumstance*. San Juan: Inter American University Press, 1983.
———. "El renacimiento de un poeta: Pedro Salinas en Puerto Rico." *La Torre* 8, 32(octubre-diciembre 1994): 615-26.
Oliva, César. *El teatro desde 1936*. Madrid: Alhambra, 1989.
Orringer, Stephanie. *Pedro Salinas' Theater of Self-Authentication*. New York: P. Lang, 1995.
Ortega y Gasset, José. *Meditations on Quixote*. Norton translation by Evelyn Rugg and Diego Marín. Introduction by Julián Marías. New York: W. W. Norton and Company, 1961.
———. *Obras completas*. Tomo I (1902-1916). Segunda Edición. Madrid: Revista de Occidente, 1950.
Paco, Mariano de. "Judit y el tirano: del mito bíblico a la realidad vivida." *La Torre* 8, 32 (octubre-diciembre 1994), 497-505.
Palley, Julián. *La luz no usada: la poesía de Pedro Salinas*. México: Studium, 1966.
Peacock, Ronald. *The Poet in the Theater*. New York: Hill and Wang, 1960.
Pérez Firmat, Gustavo. "Pedro Salinas' 'Mundo cerrado' and Hispanic Vanguard Fiction." *La Chispa '81: Selected Proceedings, February 26-28, 1981*. Ed. Gilbert Paolini. New Orleans: TulaneU, 1981. 261-67.
Pérez Minik, Domingo. *Teatro europeo contemporáneo*. Madrid: Guadarrama, 1961.
Pérez Romero, Carmen. *Etica y estética en las obras dramáticas de Pedro Salinas y T. S. Eliot*. Cáceres: Universidad de Extremadura, 1995.
Pérez-Stanfield, Pilar. "Un exilio sin exilio en el teatro español vanguardista

actual: situación y problemática." *Monographic Review/Revista Monográfica* 2 (1986): 126-39.
Plato. *The Republic*. Trans. Paul Shorey. Loeb Classical Library. Cambridge: Harvard UP, 1937.
Polansky, Susan G. *'Aprecio y defensa del lenguaje' in the Dramatic Works of Pedro Salinas*. DAI 45, 4(1984): 1128A.
———. "Communication and the 'Poet Heroes': The Essence of the Dramatic Works of Pedro Salinas." *Hispania* 70:3(September 1987): 437-46.
———. "How Many Saints are in Salinas's *Los santos?*" *Estreno* 9(1983): 4.
———. "Lorca and Salinas in New York: Mannequins and the Modern Landscape." *Hispania* 84:3(September 2001): 451-61.
———. "Mail and Blackmail: Pedro Salinas's Cartas de amor a Margarita and El Chantajista." *Hispania* 78(March 1995): 43-52.
———. "La personalidad extraordinaria de la bomba increíble en *La bomba increíble* de Pedro Salinas." *Hispanic Journal* 9:2(Spring 1988): 113-18.
Pope, Randolph. "La autobiografía del exilio: el ser previamente preocupado de Rafael Alberti y María Teresa León. *El exilio de las Españas de 1939 en las Américas: ¿Adónde fue la canción?* José María Naharro-Calderón. Barcelona: Anthropos, 1991. 369-78.
Pozuelo Yvancos, José María. "Pedro Salinas, crítico literario." *Lingüística Española Actual* 14, 1(1992): 107-25.
Ramoneda, Arturo. *Antología poética de la generación del 27*. Madrid: Castalia, 1990.
Ritivoi, Andreea Deciu. *Yesterday's Self Nostalgia and the Immigrant Identity*. Lanham, Boulder, New York, Oxford: Rowman and Littlefield Publishers, Inc., 2002.
Rivera, Susana. "España y el exilio en los poetas hispanoamericanos." *El exilio de las Españas de 1939 en las Américas: ¿Adónde fue la canción?* José María Naharro-Calderón. Barcelona: Anthropos, 1991. 227-38.
Rodríguez Monegal, Emir. "La crítica literaria en el siglo XX: El ejemplo de Pedro Salinas." *Número* 1(Marzo-abril 1949):29-42.
———. "La obra en prosa de Pedro Salinas." *Número* IX:18(1952) 66-92 (reprinted in Debicki, ed. *Pedro Salinas*, Madrid: Taurus, 1976, 229-48).
Rodríguez Richart, José. "Sobre el teatro de Pedro Salinas." *Boletín de la Biblioteca Menéndez y Pelayo* XXVI(1960): 397-427.
Rotger Salas, Sofía. *La crítica liberal: Pedro Salinas*. Barcelona: Promociones y Publicacioines Universitarias, S. A., 1994.
Rubio, Javier. "Etapa americana del gobierno de la república española en el exilio." *El exilio de las Españas de 1939 en las Américas: ¿Adónde fue la canción?*

José María Naharro-Calderón. Barcelona: Anthropos, 1991. 87-110.

Ruiz, Juan. *Libro de buen amor*. Edición crítica de Joan Corominas. Madrid: Gredos, 1967.

Ruiz Ramón, Francisco. "Contexto y cronología del teatro de Pedro Salinas." *Pedro Salinas Estudios sobre su praxis y teoría de la escritura*. Eds. Ciriaco Morón Arroyo y Manuel Revuelta Sañudo. Santander: Sociedad Menéndez y Pelayo, 1992. 173-98.

———. *Historia del teatro espanol,2. Siglo XX*. Madrid: Alianza, 1971, 1986.

———. "Salinas lector del teatro clásico español." *La Torre* 8, 32(octubre-diciembre 1994): 627-644.

———. "Para la cronología del teatro de Pedro Salinas." *Insula* 540(1991): 20-22.

———. "Salinas, dramaturgo: ¿Compromiso o evasión?" In *Estudios sobre literatura y arte dedicados al profesor Emilio Orozco Díaz*. Publicaciones de la Universidad de Granada, 1979, 189-201.

———. "Trágica ironía: Los santos fusilados." *Estreno* 7,2(1981): 12.

Salinas, Pedro. "Aprecio y defensa del lenguaje." Discurso pronunciado en ocasion de la cuadragésima colación de grados de la Universidad de Puerto Rico, celebrada el día 24 de mayo de 1944. Río Piedras: Junta Editora de la Universidad de Puerto Rico, 1944.

———. *La bomba increíble; fabulación*. Madrid: Aguilar, 1988.

———. *Cartas a Katherine Whitmore. (1932-1947). El epistolario secreto del gran poeta de amor*. Segunda edición. Edición y prólogo de Enric Bou. Barcelona: Tusquets, 2002.

———. *Cartas de amor a Margarita (1912-1915)*. Edición preparada por Solita Salinas de Marichal. Madrid: Alianza: 1984.

———. *Cartas de viaje [1912-1915]*. Edición, prólogo y notas de Enric Bou. Valencia: Pre-Textos, 1996.

———. *El defensor (ensayos)*. Bogotá: Universidad Nacional, 1948.

———. *El defensor*. Introducción de Juan Marichal. Madrid: Alianza Editorial, 1983, 2002.

———. *El desnudo impecable y otras narraciones*. México: Texontle, 1951.

———. *Ensayos completos*, I, II, and III, Madrid: Taurus, 1981.

———. *Ensayos de la literatura hispánica. Del Cantar de Mío Cid a García Lorca*. Edición y Prólogo de Juan Marichal. Madrid: Aguilar, 1961.

———. *Jorge Manrique; o tradición y originalidad*. Buenos Aires: Editorial Sudamericana, 1962.

———. *Literatura española siglo XX*, Madrid: Alianza, 1970.

———. *Mundo real y mundo poético y dos entrevistas olvidadas 1930-1933*. Edición,

prólogo y notas de Christopher Maurer. Valencia: Pre-textos, 1996.
―――. *Narrativa completa*. Ed. preparada por Soledad Salinas de Marichal. Barcelona: Barral Editores, 1976.
―――. *La poesía de Rubén Darío*. México: Séneca, 1946.
―――. *La poesía de Rubén Darío*. Buenos Aires: Losada, 1948.
―――. *Poesías completas*. Ed. preparada por Soledad Salinas de Marichal. Prólogo de Jorge Guillén. Barcelona: Seix Barral, 1971.
―――. *Reality and the Poet in Spanish Poetry*, translated by Edith Fishtine Helman, with an Introduction by Jorge Guillén, translated by Elias L. Rivers, Baltimore: Johns Hopkins UP, 1940, 1966.
―――. *La responsabilidad del escritor*. Barcelona: Seix Barral, 1961.
―――. *Los santos*. Cuadernos americanos. (México) 13 3(1954):265-91.
―――. *Los santos*. Estreno 7,2(1981): 12.
―――. *Teatro Completo*. Ed. Juan Marichal. Madrid: Aguilar, 1957.
―――. *Teatro Completo*. Edición crítica e introducción de Pilar Moraleda García. Sevilla: Alfar, 1992.
―――. *Víspera del gozo*. Madrid: Alianza, 1974.
Salinas de Marichal, Solita. "Cronología biográfica." *Poesías completas*. Pedro Salinas. Prólogo Jorge Guillén. Barcelona: Seix Barral, 1981. 37-46.
―――. *España en la poesía hispanoamericana (1892-1975)*. Madrid: Fundación Juan March/ Cátedra, 1987.
―――. "Introducción a *Los santos* de Pedro Salinas." *Estreno* VII:2(1981): 10-11, 20.
―――. "Tradición y modernidad en el teatro de Pedro Salinas." *El País* (2 agosto 1980): 3 (Suplemento "Artes").
Scanlan, David. *Reading Drama*. Mountain View, CA: Mayfield Publishing Co., 1988.
Scarano, Laura R. "La función del arte en el fin de siglo hispánico y su derivación en la obra de Pedro Salinas." *Hispanic Journal* 12,1(Spring 1991): 97-108.
Siles, Jaime. "La poesía primera de Salinas y la postmodernidad." *Revista de Occidente* 126(Noviembre 1991):151-57.
Silver, Phillip. "La estética de Ortega y la generación de 1927." *NRFH* 20(1971): 361-80.
Smiley, Sam. *Playwriting The Structure of Action*. Englewood Cliffs, NJ: Prentice Hall, 1971.
Soria Olmedo, Andrés. *Pedro Salinas/Jorge Guillén: Correspondencia (1923-1951)*. Barcelona: Tusquets, 1992.
Soufas, C. Christopher. *Conflict of Light and Wind The Spanish Generation of 1927*

and the Ideology of Poetic Form. Middletown, CT: Wesleyan University Press, 1989.

Spadaccini, Nicholas and Jenaro Talens. *Through the Shattering Glass Cervantes and the Self-Made World*. Minneapolis and London: University of Minnesota Press, 1993.

Sotelo Vázquez, Adolfo. "Pedro Salinas entre el joven Eliot y el joven Unamuno." *Cuadernos Hispanoamericanos: Revista Mensual de Cultura* 514-515(abril-mayo): 239-45.

Stixrude, David. *The Early Poetry of Pedro Salinas*. Princeton: PrincetonUP, 1975.

Torre, Guillermo de. "Evocación de Pedro Salinas." *Asomante* 1(enero-marzo 1954): 12-18.

Torres Nebrera, Gregorio. "En el teatro." *ABC* (27 noviembre 1991):53.

———. *Pedro Salinas Teatro*. Madrid: Narcea,1979.

———. "Teoría del teatro de Pedro Salinas." *Insula* 370(1977): 10.

Trelles, Carmen Dolores. "Pedro Salinas, poeta del amor y la mirada. *El Nuevo Día, Revista Domingo*, 29 de noviembre de 1992, 1-2, 5-9.

Ugarte, Michael. "Luis Cernuda and the Poetics of Exile." *Monographic Review/Revista Monográfica* 2 (1986): 84-100.

———. *Shifting Ground, Spanish Civil War Literature*. Durham, Duke UP, 1989.

Unamuno, Miguel de. "Sobre la lectura e interpretación del 'Quijote,'" *OC*, ed. Manuel García Blanco. Tomo III. Madrid: Afrodisio Aguado, 1938.

Van Laan, Thomas F. *The Idiom of Drama*. Ithaca and London: Cornell UP, 1970.

Vila Selma, José. *Pedro Salinas*. Madrid: EPESA, 1972.

Vivanco, Luis Felipe. *Introducción a la poesía española contemporánea*. Madid: Guadarrama, 1957.

Weinstein, Arnold. *Fictions of the Self*. Princeton: Princeton UP, 1981.

Williams, David. "The Exile as Uncreator." *Mosaic* 8, 3-4(1975): 1-14.

Young, Howard. "Pedro Salinas y T.S. Eliot: Dos posturas ante la modernidad." *Pedro Salinas Estudios sobre su praxis y teoría de la escritura*. Eds. Ciriaco Morón Arroyo y Manuel Revuelta Sañudo. Santander: Sociedad Menéndez y Pelayo, 1992. 76-85.

Zardoya, Concha. "La 'otra' realidad de Pedro Salinas." *Poesía española del siglo XX, II*. Madrid: Gredos, 1974.

Zubizarreta, Alma de. *Pedro Salinas; El diálogo creador*. Prólogo de Guillén. Madrid: Gredos, 1969.

Zueras Torrens, Francisco. *La gran aportación cultural del exilio español (1939): poesía, narrativa, ensayo, pintura, arquitectura, música, teatro, cine*. Córdoba: Excma. Diputación Provincial de Córdoba, 1990.

Zuleta, Emilia de. *Cinco poetas españoles*. (*Salinas, Guillén, Lorca, Alberti, Cernuda*)

Madrid: Gredos, 1971.
———. "Pedro Salinas en su poesía y en su teatro." *La Biblioteca*. (Buenos Aires) IX, Segunda Epoca, 5(1960): 136-50.

Printed in the United States
35787LVS00004B/189